P9-CLC-810

THE TEACHER AND THE TAUGHT

Education in Theory and Practice from Plato to James B. Conant

Edited by

RONALD GROSS

A Delta Book

A Delta Book
Published by Dell Publishing Co., Inc.
750 Third Avenue, New York 17, New York

Library of Congress Catalog Card Number: 63-11236
Manufactured in the United States of America

Tenth Printing

Acknowledgments

The selections in this book are reproduced by permission of the authors, their publishers, or the sponsoring organization:

MORTIMER J. ADLER and MILTON MAYER, pages 14–34 from *The Revolution in Education,* © 1958 by The University of Chicago, Chicago, Illinois.

ARTHUR BESTOR, pages 55–75 from *Education in the Age of Science,* © 1959 by Basic Books, Inc., New York City. Reprinted by permission from *Daedalus* (the Journal of the American Academy of Arts and Sciences), Winter 1959, pp. 75–90.

JEROME S. BRUNER, pages 33–54 from *The Process of Education,* © 1960 by the President and Fellows of Harvard College, Cambridge, Massachusetts.

JOHN AMOS COMENIUS, excerpts from *The Great Didactic* reprinted from *Great Issues in Education,* Volume One, copyright 1956 by The Great Books Foundation, a nonprofit organization in Chicago, Illinois.

JAMES BRYANT CONANT, pages 77–87 from *Education and Liberty,* Harvard University Press, Cambridge, Mass., copyright 1953, by the President and Fellows of Harvard College.

GEORGE S. COUNTS, *Dare the School Build a New Social Order?,* copyright © 1932 by George S. Counts. Published by The John Day Company, Inc., New York City.

JOHN DEWEY, Chapter one from *Experience and Education,* copyright 1938, by Kappa Delta Pi, An Honors Society in Education. Published by The Macmillan Company, New York City.

JACQUES MARITAIN, pages 2–25 from *Education at the Crossroads,* © 1943, by Yale University Press, New Haven, Connecticut.

MARGARET MEAD, pages 23–27, 164–170, from *Harvard Business Review,* November-December 1958, copyright 1958, by the President and Fellows of Harvard College.

QUINTILIAN, excerpts from *Institutes of Oratory,* translated by H. E. Butler, The Loeb Classical Library, Harvard University Press, Cambridge, Mass.

BERTRAND RUSSELL, pages 28–42 from *Education and the Modern World,* copyright 1932, by Bertrand Russell. Published by George Allen & Unwin, Ltd., London, England.

ARNOLD TOYNBEE, "Conclusions" from *Education in the Perspective of History,* copyright © 1960, by Edward D. Myers. Published by Harper & Row Publishers, Inc., New York City.

J. LLOYD TRUMP and DORSEY BAYNHAM, excerpts from *Focus on Change; Guide to Better Schools,* copyright © 1961, by Rand McNally & Company, Chicago, Illinois.

ALFRED NORTH WHITEHEAD, "The Rhythm of Education" from *The Aims of Education,* copyright 1929, by The Macmillan Company, renewed in 1957, by Evelyn Whitehead. Published by The Macmillan Company, New York City, and Ernest Benn Limited, London, England.

Contents

Introduction

Our schools today are suffering the standard agonies of American success: critical attacks, self-doubt, loss of a sense of purpose.

As a nation we have finally realized that our educational system is the foundation stone of our national well-being and the key to our prospects as a people. The popularity of phrases like "human resources," "supply of trained manpower," and "talent search" signify that we fully appreciate Alfred North Whitehead's prophecy: "In the conditions of modern life the rule is absolute, the race which does not value trained intelligence is doomed."

But some genuine agonies accompany this appreciation of education. If the schools are so important to our survival, many critics argue, they should be much better than they are. Some of the critics think that education is too important to be left to the educators. Among the educators themselves, moreover, severe self-doubts have arisen as to their readiness and ability to fill their positions of responsibility.

Finally, and most important, Americans feel a genuine loss of the sense of purpose in their educational system today. Two conflicting viewpoints have brought confusion to our conception of the goals of the schools. On the one hand, the new importance attached to education is based on a distinctly utilitarian, nationalistic interpretation of the role of the schools in society. Progressive education, with its dream of taking the lead in reforming and revitalizing society, is dead. The schools are increasingly bent to the national purpose; education in its new role ranks as one of the nation's vital "industries," devoted to "producing" the trained manpower we need to improve our position in a dangerous and competitive world. Even on the personal level, figures showing how much a degree is worth in lifetime earnings have made a college education seem like an investment in capital goods.

That is one way of looking at our schools and colleges: as instruments of national advancement. Most Americans recognize that such a harnessing of education to the nation's interests is not only inevitable, it is necessary. However, a contradictory view of the purpose of education maintains its hold on our allegiance. This is the classical ideal of liberal education. The pursuit of knowledge for its own sweet sake and the development of the individual over and above what is required by his vocational and civic role, are still compelling educational aims today. These two viewpoints, frequently colliding within the same person, cause much of the current confusion about the goals of the schools.

There is one other way in which the new respect for education is causing anguish among educators and laymen interested in the schools. Now that it is considered an "industry," education is expected to increase its productive efficiency. Educators find themselves under great pressure to use new tools such as television and teaching machines to reach more students and to make the best teachers available to all. But the "conventional wisdom" of education, formulated before the days of mass communications and teaching machines, balks at the prospect of a school system that would be based as much on technology as on the hallowed personal relationship between student and teacher.

Education's sudden rise to the realm of national policy has not solved our schools' problems. Rather, it has posed those problems in their most basic and bewildering forms. During the next decades our ideas about education will have to be sharper than ever before, bolder and more intelligent. Only if we get down to the basic issues can we reach a consensus on priorities for the future.

To understand education, we must understand much more than the schools. We must answer questions more basic than burgeoning enrollments, or teachers' salaries, or the reading problem. Underlying any honest discussion of the technical problems of schools and teachers and curriculums are such questions as: What is man's nature? Can it be improved? What values should guide us in molding children through education? Are people essentially similar, or are they truly different in intelligence and character? If they are truly different how should a democratic educational system deal with this problem? Is scientific knowledge the only reliable source of truth for modern man?

The great educational questions are inseparable from the great questions about politics, about ethics, about life itself. It is no coincidence that the "Great Debate" over the schools that began in this country in the 1950s was matched by an intensive reexamination of national goals, personal character, and ultimate values.

These basic questions have challenged thinkers since men began to examine the processes of learning. They puzzled Aristotle when he first posed them twenty-three centuries ago:

> Consideration must be given to the question, what constitutes education and what is the proper way to be educated. At present there are differences of opinion as to the proper tasks to be set; for all peoples do not agree as to the things that the young ought to learn, either with a view to virtue or with a view to the best life, nor is it clear whether their studies should be regulated more with regard to intellect or with regard to character. And confusing questions arise out of the education that actually prevails, and it is not at all clear whether the pupils should practice pursuits that are practically useful, or morally edifying, or higher accomplishments—for all these views have won the support of some judges.

Many of these questions can never be answered once and for all. Each generation, each nation, even each community must work out answers to its own problems, in terms of its own values and commitments. Useful answers must combine a firm grasp of ultimate values with a sharp perception of the particular problem at hand.

Indeed, the essays in this book have this one remarkable characteristic in common. They fuse the theoretical and the concrete. The collection begins with a famous philosophical parable of the educational process, and concludes with an educator's recent blueprint of the school of tomorrow. But although Plato's vision is utopian, his meaning is precise; his point does not dissolve in a fog of rhetoric. And when J. Lloyd Trump argues that our schools are in need of thorough reform, he does not stop with catch phrases or the usual injunctions about meeting the needs of the individual student and stimulating the learner to think for himself. He outlines clearly and persuasively a plan for bringing about these general ends through a specific reorganization of the instructional program. Similarly, Arnold Toynbee brings his discussion of education through the ages to a focus in discussing the current status of teachers in America; Jacques Maritain documents the practical pitfalls as well as the philosophical defects of progressive education; Bertrand Russell weighs the theoretical advantages of a completely "negative" education against its actual dangers. Each writer has a comprehensive *theory* of education, but he knows that theory can find expression and validity only insofar as it helps to solve practical problems in the schools.

The balance of theory and practice, the fusion of principle and application—these are the achievements of the best educational writing. It is a rare balance, a hard-won fusion. Most writers on education succumb to Scylla or Charybdis: either they deal mainly in bloodless abstractions, or they bog down in the technical details of school practice.

The basic questions, while they can never be answered once and for all, are still the most useful questions that we can ask about any educational enterprise. They illuminate the facts of our situation as no other questions can, and they expose the general principles, conscious or unconscious, which underlie any pattern of educational practice. Moreover, they are worth asking in their own right because they lead us to basic questions about our lives and values. Look closely at any school and at the ideas that animate it, and you will discover the forces which drive the men and women whose children it serves. John Dewey said it best:

> There is no better way to realize what philosophy is about when it is living, not antiquarian, than to ask ourselves what criteria and aims and ideals should control our educational policies and undertakings. Such a question, if it is systematically followed out, will bring to light things that are morally and intellectually fundamental in the direction of human affairs. . . .

Despite their diverse interests and backgrounds, the writers represented here strikingly converge on the basic issues in education. The best way to see this is to examine their treatment of a specific issue. Perhaps the most fundamental and enduring educational question is: Should education consist of development from within the individual, or of formation from without? This question in one form or another frames nearly every discussion of educational theory. We know it today as the controversy between progressivism and the traditional view of education; an earlier time grappled with it in the conflict between Rousseau's belief in man's original goodness and Calvin's doctrine of his ultimate depravity. As is typical of basic educational questions, this issue of impulse versus discipline is a fundamental one in the conduct of human life as a whole.

Now, let us look briefly at how some of these writers engage this basic educational issue: Should education consist of development from within or formation from without? Plato, whose works contain in embryo the seeds of all the major philosophies of education, has a trenchant point to make about this controversy in the first selection. He takes to task "certain professors of education . . . [who] say that they can put a knowledge into the soul which was not there before, like sight into blind eyes."

Quintilian begins his famous treatise on pedagogy with the warning that "the student who is devoid of talent will derive no more profit from this work than barren soil from a treatise on agriculture." Comenius, the seventeenth-century Czech pioneer of modern educational technique, develops Quintilian's agricultural metaphor even further. He compares the child's mind with a developing plant, which cannot be hurried or compelled to grow. Rousseau carries this theme to its climax. He maintains that there should be no predetermined curriculum imposed on the student: the educational program should follow the child's developing interests and impulses. And Pestalozzi, the pioneer of schooling for the poor, agrees that the student's self-activity must be the motive force behind all true education.

Spencer reverses the tide of reform, insisting that the central educational question is not the nature of the student, but the relative value of different kinds of knowledge. For Spencer the chief guide for educational planning is not the student's developing mind, but the kind of knowledge he must master in order to survive.

Among the contemporary authors, John Dewey belies the stereotyped view of his position; he criticizes progressive schools which "proceed as if any form of direction and guidance by adults were an invasion of individual freedom." Going considerably further, another progressive educator, George Counts, argues that indoctrination, which is clearly a process of imposing preconceived notions on the student, is a proper job for the schools. Bertrand Russell, on the other hand, offers a contemporary reevaluation of the "negative theory of education" proposed by Rousseau.

Equally provocative citations about most of the other basic educational dilemmas could be excerpted from these essays, illuminating each from a variety of angles, offering a background for informed discussion, and providing a basis for wiser choices in the practice of teaching. For, taken together, the essays in this volume provide an introduction to the problems and prospects of contemporary education. Insofar as education has determined what we are, and will increasingly determine what we become, these essays also constitute an invitation to reconsider some of the basic postulates of modern Western culture.

Each of these essays was chosen first because of its intrinsic excellence, secondly because of its definition of a distinctive and important view on education, and finally because of its relevance to the educational concerns of Americans in the mid-twentieth century. One-third of the selections date from the centuries preceding ours; the rest were written in the twentieth century, and about half of those in the past decade or so. Obviously this is no fair chronological representation, nor was such the intention. The book is keyed to the dominant concerns of our educational time and place; the modern selections need the classics to give them resonance and perspective.

Several men who could have produced better books than this one have generously helped to make this one better. They are Professor William Brickman of New York University, Edward J. Meade, Jr., of the Fund for the Advancement of Education, and Professor Julian Roberts of the Yeshiva University Graduate School of Education. For patient and imaginative editorial advice I am indebted to Judith Murphy and Daniel Green. The book would not exist at all were it not for Jane Kronholtz and Alvin C. Eurich. Its remaining defects are, of course, my own responsibility.

If one could dedicate a book of other men's writings, this one would be inscribed for my wife, Beatrice Gross.

RONALD GROSS

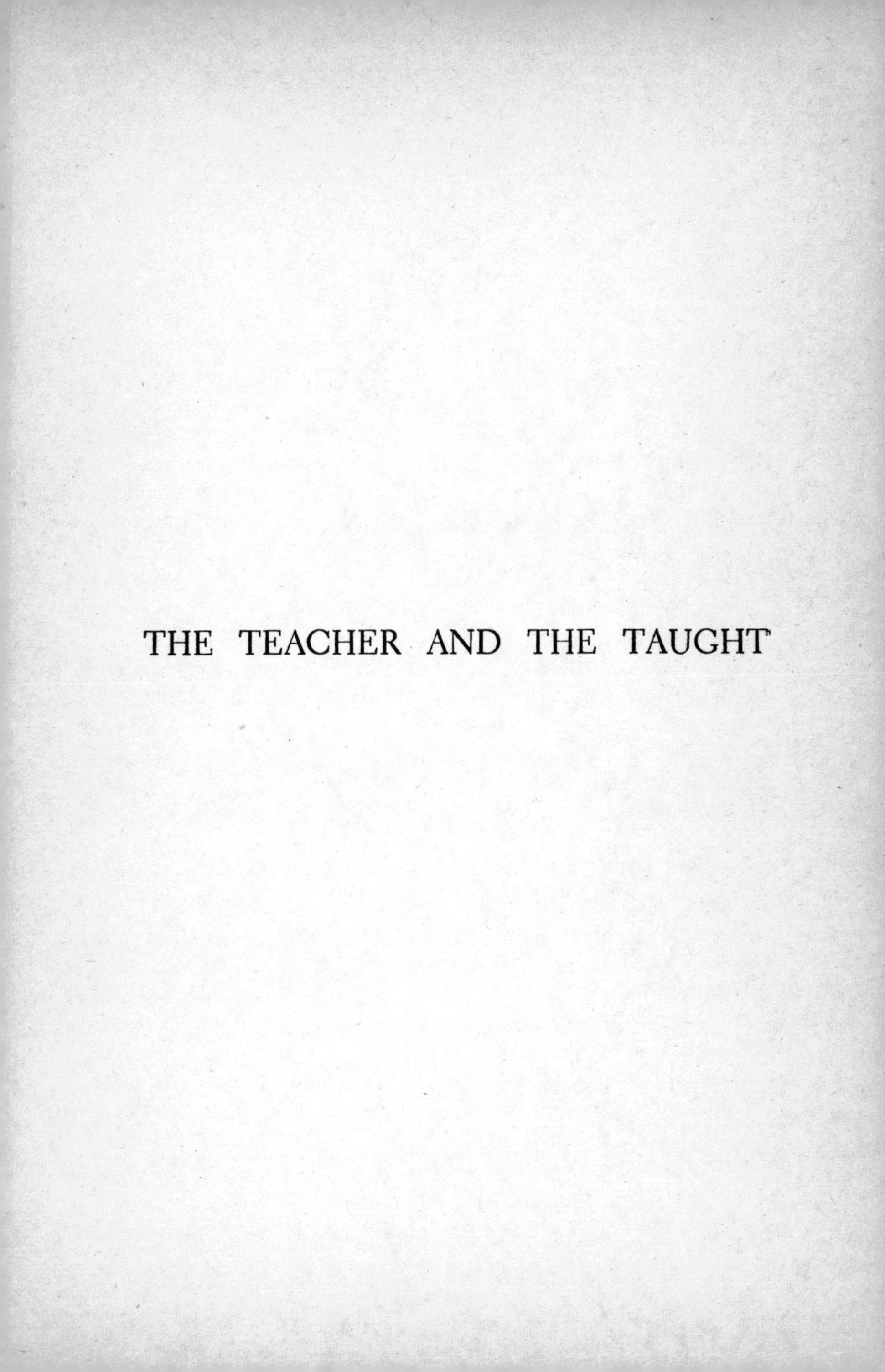

THE TEACHER AND THE TAUGHT

The Ascent to Wisdom

Plato

(*circa* 427 B.C.–*circa* 347 B.C.)

"If you wish to know what is meant by public education, read Plato's *Republic*. Those who merely judge books from their titles take this for a treatise on Politics, but it is the finest treatise on Education ever written." Thus Rousseau claimed for education the work which is the fountainhead of Western social thought.

Plato's system of schooling can be pieced together from a number of his works, but the result is grandly inconsistent. His enduring fascination lies in his unparalleled grasp of the critical importance of the educational enterprise. He never wavered in his faith that the character of any State depends, in the last analysis, on the quality of its people and their rulers. Therefore he always saw education as the central public concern of any well-ordered government, as well as a natural preoccupation of each man throughout his life.

Nowhere is Plato's vision of education expressed more powerfully than in the great parable of the cave, from *The Republic*. One of the prisoners in an underground cave, who has never seen anything more substantial than shadows, is unchained and brought out into the blazing sunlight. At first he wants to withdraw from the painful brightness, but eventually he comes to realize that the vision of things as they really are is the only life for a man. Now he resists returning to the cave and its world of illusion. But, just as he had an undeniable right to find the truth, so he has an inescapable duty to go back and help others see through their illusions.

This unforgettable and endlessly suggestive parable is a basic source of the classical philosophy of education. Plato portrays the process of learning as an individual's radical encounter with a truth that exists independently of himself. The process is, moreover, no mere preparation for a person's role in society. It is a lonely, harrowing experience through which each man frees his mind from the prejudices of those around him and accepts his responsibility for helping others achieve the same goal.

Obviously, such a conception of education goes far beyond the potentialities of what we usually think of as formal schooling. For Plato, one of the effects of true education is to make a man profoundly dissatisfied with what he has previously been taught. While schools may be necessary to provide the rudiments and tools of learning, it is futile and dangerous to ask them to bring immature pupils to an awareness of the highest truths. Formal schooling should culminate, not in a finished body of knowledge, but in the mastery of a method for the lifelong pursuit of wisdom.

Having had an aristocrat's education, Plato became, at the age of twenty, a pupil and friend of Socrates. After his master's execution by the Athenians he traveled widely in Greece, Egypt, and Italy. Returning to Athens in 387 B.C. Plato founded the Academy, a school of advanced studies in mathematics and philosophy, teaching there until his death.

Plato's dialogues are subtle and complex works of art. Their influence on subsequent thought has been enormous. As Whitehead has said, the European philosophical tradition consists of a series of footnotes to Plato. The following selection is Benjamin Jowett's translation of the opening of Book VII of *The Republic*, slightly amended.

And now, I said, let me show in a parable what education means in human life. Behold! human beings living in an underground den, which has a mouth open towards the light and reaching all along the den; here they have been from their childhood, and have their legs and necks chained so that they cannot move, and can only see before them, being prevented by the chains from turning round their heads. Above and behind them a fire is blazing at a distance, and between the fire and the prisoners there is a raised way; and you will see, if you look, a low wall built along the way, like the screen which marionette players have in front of them, over which they show the puppets.

I see.

And do you see, I said, men passing along the wall carrying all sorts of vessels, and statues and figures of animals made of wood and stone and various materials, which appear over the wall? Some of them are talking, others silent.

You have shown me a strange image, and they are strange prisoners.

Like ourselves, I replied; and they see only their own shadows, or the shadows of one another, which the fire throws on the opposite wall of the cave?

True, he said; how could they see anything but the shadows if they were never allowed to move their heads?

And of the objects which are being carried in like manner they would only see the shadows?

Yes, he said.

And if they were able to converse with one another, would they not suppose that they were naming what was actually before them?

Very true.

And suppose further that the prison had an echo which came from the other side, would they not be sure to fancy when one of the passers-by spoke that the voice which they heard came from the passing shadow?

No question, he replied.

To them, I said, the truth would be literally nothing but the shadows of the images.

That is certain.

And now look again, and see what will naturally follow if the prisoners are released and disabused of their error. At first, when any of them is liberated and compelled suddenly to stand up and turn his neck round and walk and look towards the light, he will suffer sharp pains; the glare will distress him, and he will be unable to see the realities of which in his former state he had seen the shadows; and then conceive someone saying to him, that what he saw before was an illusion, but that now, when he is approaching nearer to being and his eye is turned towards more real existence, he has a clearer vision—what will be his reply? And you may further imagine that his instructor is pointing to the objects as they pass and requiring him to name them—will he not be perplexed? Will he not fancy that the shadows which he formerly saw are truer than the objects which are now shown to him?

Far truer.

And if he is compelled to look straight at the light, will he not have a pain in his eyes which will make him turn away to take refuge in the objects of vision which he can see, and which he will conceive to be in reality clearer than the things which are now being shown to him?

True, he said.

And suppose once more, that he is reluctantly dragged up a steep and rugged ascent, and held fast until he is forced into the presence of the sun himself, is he not likely to be pained and irritated? When he approaches the light his eyes will be dazzled, and he will not be able to see anything at all of what are now called realities.

Not all in a moment, he said.

He will require to grow accustomed to the sight of the upper world. And first he will see the shadows best, next the reflections of men and other objects in the water, and then the objects themselves; then he will gaze upon the light of the moon and the stars and the spangled heaven; and he will see the sky and the stars by night better than the sun or the light of the sun by day?

Certainly.

Last of all he will be able to see the sun, and not mere reflections of him in the water, but he will see him in his own proper place, and not in another; and he will contemplate him as he is.

Certainly.

He will then proceed to argue that this is he who gives the season and the years, and is the guardian of all that is in the visible world, and in a certain way the cause of all things which he and his fellows have been accustomed to behold?

Clearly, he said, he would first see the sun and then reason about him.

And when he remembered his old habitation, and the wisdom of the den and his fellow prisoners, do you not suppose that he would felicitate himself on the change, and pity them?

Certainly, he would.

And if they were in the habit of conferring honors among themselves on those who were quickest to observe the passing shadows and to remark which of them went before, and which followed after, and which were together; and who were therefore best able to draw conclusions as to the future, do you think that he would care for such honors and glories, or envy the possessors of them? Would he not say with Homer,

"Better to be the poor servant of a poor master,"

and to endure anything, rather than think as they do and live after their manner?

Yes, he said, I think that he would rather suffer anything than entertain these false notions and live in this miserable manner.

Imagine once more, I said, such a one coming suddenly out of the sun to be replaced in his old situation; would he not be certain to have his eyes full of darkness?

To be sure, he said.

And if there were a contest, and he had to compete in measuring the shadows with the prisoners who had never moved out of the den, while his sight was still weak, and before his eyes had become steady (and the time which would be needed to acquire this new habit of sight might be very considerable), would he not be ridiculous? Men would say of him that up he went and down he came without his eyes; and that it was better not even to think of ascending; and if any one tried to loose another and lead him up to the light, let them only catch the offender, and they would put him to death.

No question, he said.

This entire allegory, I said, you may now append, dear Glaucon, to the previous argument; the prison house is the world of sight, the light of the fire is the sun, and you will not misapprehend me if you interpret the journey upwards to be the ascent of the soul into the intellectual world according to my poor belief, which, at your desire, I have expressed—whether rightly or wrongly God knows. But, whether true or false, my opinion is that in the world of knowledge the idea of good appears last of all, and is seen only with an effort; and, when seen, is also inferred to be the universal author of all things beautiful and right, parent of light and of the lord of light in this visible world, and the immediate source of reason and truth in the intellectual; and that this is the power upon which he who would act rationally either in public or private life must have his eye fixed.

I agree, he said, as far as I am able to understand you.

Moreover, I said, you must not wonder that those who attain to this beatific vision are unwilling to descend to human affairs; for their souls are ever hastening into the upper world where they desire to dwell; which desire of theirs is very natural, if our allegory may be trusted.

Yes, very natural.

And is there anything surprising in one who passes from divine contemplations to the evil state of man, misbehaving himself in a ridiculous manner; if, while his eyes are blinking and before he has become accustomed to the surrounding darkness, he is compelled to fight in courts of law, or in other places, about the images or the shadows of images of justice, and is endeavoring to meet the conceptions of those who have never yet seen absolute justice?

Anything but surprising, he replied.

Any one who has common sense will remember that the bewilderments of the eyes are of two kinds, and arise from two causes, either from coming out of the light or from going into the light, which is true of the mind's eye, quite as much as of the bodily eye; and he who remembers this when he sees any one whose vision is perplexed and weak, will not be too ready to laugh; he will first ask whether that soul of man has come out of the brighter life, and is unable to see because unaccustomed to the dark, or having turned from darkness to the day is dazzled by excess of light. And he will count the one happy in his condition and state of being, and he will pity the other; or, if he have a mind to laugh at the soul which comes from below into the light, there will be more reason in this than in the laugh which greets him who returns from above out of the light into the den.

That, he said, is a very just distinction.

But then, if I am right, certain professors of education must be wrong when they say that they can put a knowledge into the soul which was not there before, like sight into blind eyes.

They undoubtedly say this, he replied.

Whereas, our argument shows that the power and capacity of learning exists in the soul already; and that just as the eye was unable to turn from darkness to light without the whole body, so too the instrument of knowledge can only by the movement of the whole soul be turned from the world of becoming into that of being, and learn by degrees to endure the sight of being, and of the brightest and best of being, or in other words, of the good.

Very true.

And must there not be some art which will effect conversion in the easiest and quickest manner; not implanting the faculty of sight, for that exists already, but has been turned in the wrong direction, and is looking away from the truth?

Yes, he said, such an art may be presumed.

And whereas the other so-called virtues of the soul seem to be akin to bodily qualities, for even when they are not originally innate they can be implanted later by habit and exercise, the virtue of wisdom more than anything else contains a divine element which always remains, and by this conversion is rendered useful and profitable; or, on the other hand, hurtful and useless. Did you never observe the narrow intelligence flashing from the keen eye of a clever rogue—how eager he is, how clearly his paltry soul sees the way to his end; he is the reverse of blind, but his keen eyesight is forced into the service of evil, and he is mischievous in proportion to his cleverness?

Very true, he said.

But what if there had been a circumcision of such natures in the days of their youth; and they had been severed from those sensual pleasures, such as eating and drinking, which, like leaden weights, were attached to them at their birth, and which drag them down and turn the vision of their souls upon the things that are below—if, I say, they had been released from these impediments and turned in the opposite direction, the very same faculty in them would have seen the truth as keenly as they see what their eyes are turned to now.

Very likely.

Yes, I said; and there is another thing which is likely, or rather a necessary inference from what has preceded, that neither the uneducated and uninformed of the truth, nor yet those who never make an end of their education, will be able ministers of State; not the former, because they have no single aim of duty which is the rule of all their actions, private as well as public; nor the latter, because they will not act at all except upon compulsion, fancying that they are already dwelling apart in the islands of the blest.

Very true, he replied.

Then, I said, the business of us who are the founders of the State will be to compel the best minds to attain that knowledge which we have already shown to be the greatest of all—they must continue to ascend until they arrive at the good; but when they have ascended and seen enough we must not allow them to do as they do now.

What do you mean?

I mean that they remain in the upper world: but this must not be allowed; they must be made to descend again among the prisoners in the den, and partake of their labors and honors, whether they are worth having or not.

But is not this unjust? he said; ought we to give them a worse life, when they might have a better?

You have again forgotten, my friend, I said, the intention of the legislator, who did not aim at making any one class in the State happy above the rest; the happiness was to be in the whole State, and he held the citizens together by persuasion and necessity, making them benefactors of the State, and therefore benefactors of one another; to this end he created them, not to please themselves, but to be his instruments in binding up the State.

True, he said, I had forgotten.

Observe, Glaucon, that there will be no injustice in compelling our philosophers to have a care and providence of others; we shall explain to them that in other States, men of their class are not obliged to share in the toils of politics: and this is reasonable, for they grow up at their own sweet will, and the government would rather not have them. Being self-taught, they cannot be expected to show any gratitude for a culture which they have never received. But we have brought you into the world to be rulers of the hive, kings of yourselves and of the other citizens, and have educated you far better and more perfectly than they have been educated, and you are better able to share in the double duty. Wherefore each of you, when his turn comes, must go down to the general underground abode, and get the habit of seeing in the dark. When you have acquired the habit, you will see ten thousand times better than the inhabitants of the den, and you will know what the several images are, and what they represent, because you have seen the beautiful and just and good in their truth. . . .

Quintilian

(*circa* A.D. 35–*circa* A.D. 95)

Under the Roman Emperor Vespasian, Marcus Fabius Quintilianus was appointed the first publicly paid teacher of rhetoric. Such status was highly appropriate, for Quintilian was the archetypal "professional" in education. Just as Plato represents the educational visionary, Quintilian exemplifies the practical teacher who devotes himself not to revolutionizing the aims of education, but to developing more effective pedagogical methods. Whereas Plato had planned the education of the philosopher who ruled reluctantly because it was his duty, Quintilian designed a basically vocational course of training for the orator—his word for the man who found his fulfillment in political action.

The *Institutes of Rhetoric* is the most thorough, systematic, and comprehensive treatise on education to come down to us from antiquity. It had an overwhelming influence on the Renaissance educators who laid the foundations of modern pedagogical practice. Erasmus apologized for discussing the aims and methods of teaching, "seeing that Quintilian has said in effect the last word on the matter."

Quintilian's scheme of education, extending from infant care to the most advanced training in civic leadership, is an ideal projection, not a description of the declining Roman schools of his day. But his chief educational emphasis is practical, and his enduring fascination for teachers and parents stems from the wealth of detailed advice he offers. Like Plato, Quintilian maintains a paradoxical balance between the two views of education as development from within and as imposition from without. He stresses the importance of training through conditioning from the earliest age—like Plato, he realizes that what is learned in school is only a minor part of a person's total education. But he also points out that formal schooling, through neglect or mismanagement, frequently stifles early promise and inhibits intellectual growth. The fact that Quintilian was an experienced teacher is apparent in his portrayal of the process of teaching as a difficult, subtle, and rewarding craft.

Quintilian justified his exclusive concern with the training of the orator by pointing to the decadence of philosophy in his time. "Philosophy may be counterfeited, but eloquence never," he asserted, reflecting an epoch in which distinction was to be sought only in public life. But if we believe that education should have broader aims than producing "a good man, skilled in speaking," if we locate its central concern in the development of the individual rather than in the training of the statesman, then Quintilian's plan of schooling will seem limited and formalistic. The classics cannot live long as the mere ornaments and tools of the orator, they can only be reborn through each individual's "philosophic" engagement with their basic human questions.

The Renaissance schoolmasters adopted chiefly the negative aspects of Quintilian's legacy. The result was a stultifying emphasis on purely verbal training in ancient literature. Modern educators have embraced his more positive contribution: a pioneering analysis of the techniques by which the practicing teacher can best reach the mind of the individual student.

Like many authors in the "Silver Age" of Roman letters, Quintilian was born in Spain. He studied rhetoric in the capital, and later opened a school of his own in which his pupils included Tacitus and the younger Pliny. The following selections are from H. E. Butler's translation of the *Institutio Oratoria*, Books I and II.

There is one point which I must emphasize before I begin, which is this. Without natural gifts technical rules are useless. Consequently the student who is devoid of talent will derive no more profit from this work than barren soil from a treatise on agriculture. There are, it is true, other natural aids, such as the possession of a good voice and robust lungs, sound health, powers of endurance and grace, and if these are possessed only to a moderate extent, they may be improved by methodical training. In some cases, however, these gifts are lacking to such an extent that their absence is fatal to all such advantages as talent and study can confer, while, similarly, they are of no profit in themselves unless cultivated by skilful teaching, persistent study and continuous and extensive practice in writing, reading and speaking.

I would, therefore, have a father conceive the highest hopes of his son from the moment of his birth. If he does so, he will be more careful about the groundwork of his education. For there is absolutely no foundation for the complaint that but few men have the power to take in the knowledge that is imparted to them, and that the majority are so slow of understanding that education is a waste of time and labor. On the contrary, you will find that most are quick to reason and ready to learn. Reasoning comes as naturally to man as flying to birds, speed to horses and ferocity to beasts of prey: our minds are endowed by nature with such activity and sagacity that the soul is believed to proceed from heaven. Those who are dull and unteachable are as abnormal as prodigious births and monstrosities, and are but few in number. A proof of what I say is to be found in the fact that boys commonly show promise of many accomplishments, and when such promise dies away as they grow up, this is plainly due not to the failure of natural gifts, but to lack of the requisite care. But, it will be urged, there are degrees of talent. Undoubtedly, I reply, and there will be a corresponding variation in actual accomplishment: but that there are any who gain nothing from education, I absolutely deny. The man who shares this conviction, must, as soon as he becomes a father, devote the utmost care to fostering the promise shown by the son whom he destines to become an orator.

Above all see that the child's nurse speaks correctly. The ideal, according to Chrysippus, would be that she should be a philosopher: failing that he desired that the best should be chosen, as far as possible. No doubt the most important point is that they should be of good character: but they should speak correctly as well. It is the nurse that the child first hears, and her words that he will first attempt to imitate. And we are by nature most tenacious of childish impressions, just as the flavor first absorbed by vessels when new persists, and the color imparted by dyes to the primitive whiteness of wool is indelible. Further it is the worst impressions that are most durable. . . .

I am not so blind to differences of age as to think that the very young should be forced on prematurely or given real work to do. Above all things we must take care that the child, who is not yet old enough to love his studies, does not come to hate them and dread the bitterness which he has once tasted, even when the years of infancy are left behind. His studies must be made an amusement: he must be questioned and praised and taught to rejoice when he has done well; sometimes too, when he refuses instruction, it should be given to some other to excite his envy; at times also he must be engaged in competition and should be allowed to believe himself successful more often than not, while he should be encouraged to do his best by such rewards as may appeal to his tender years. . . .

At any rate I am not satisfied with the course (which I note is usually adopted) of teaching small children the names and order of the letters before their shapes. Such a practice makes them slow to recognize the letters, since they do not pay attention to their actual shape, preferring to be guided by what they have already learned by rote. It is for this reason that teachers, when they think they have sufficiently familiarized their young pupils with the letters written in their usual order, reverse that order or rearrange it in every kind of combination, until they learn to know the letters from their appearance and not from the order in which they occur. It will be best therefore for children to begin by learning their appearance and names just as they do with men. The method, however, to which we have objected in teaching the alphabet, is unobjectionable when applied to syllables. I quite approve on the other hand of a practice which has been devised to stimulate children to learn by giving them ivory letters to play with, as I do of anything else that may be discovered to delight the very young, the sight, handling and naming of which is a pleasure.

As soon as the child has begun to know the shapes of the various letters, it will be no bad thing to have them cut as accurately as possible upon a board, so that the pen may be guided along the grooves. Thus mistakes such as occur with wax tablets will be rendered impossible; for the pen will be confined between the edges of the letters and will be prevented from going astray. Further by increasing the frequency and speed with which they follow these fixed outlines we shall give steadiness to the fingers, and there will be no need to guide the child's hand with our own. The art of writing well and quickly is not unimportant for our purpose, though it is generally disregarded by persons of quality. Writing is of the utmost importance in the study which we have under consideration and by its means alone can true and deeply rooted proficiency be obtained. But a sluggish pen delays our thoughts, while an unformed and illiterate hand cannot be deciphered, a circumstance which necessitates another wearisome task, namely the dictation of what we have written to a copyist. We shall therefore at all times and in all places, and above all when we are writing private letters to our friends, find a gratification in the thought that we have not neglected even this accomplishment.

As regards syllables, no short cut is possible: they must all be learnt, and there is no good in putting off learning the most difficult; this is the general practice, but the sole result is bad spelling. Further we must beware of placing a blind confidence in a child's memory. It is better to repeat syllables and impress them on the memory and, when he is reading, not to press him to read continuously or with greater speed, unless indeed the clear and obvious sequence of letters can suggest itself without its being necessary for the child to stop to think. The syllables once learnt, let him begin to construct words with them and sentences with the words. You will hardly believe how much reading is delayed by undue haste. If the child attempts more than his powers allow, the inevitable result is hesitation, interruption, and repetition, and the mistakes which he makes merely lead him to lose confidence in what he already knows. Reading must therefore first be sure, then connected, while it must be kept slow for a considerable time, until practice brings speed unaccompanied by error. . . . And as we are still discussing minor details, I would urge that the lines, which he is set to copy, should not express thoughts of no significance, but convey some sound moral lesson. He will remember such aphorisms even when he is an old man, and the impression made upon his unformed mind will contribute to the formation of his character. He may also be entertained by learning the sayings of famous men and above all selections from the poets, poetry being more attractive to children. . . .

But the time has come for the boy to grow up little by little, to leave the nursery and tackle his studies in good earnest. This, therefore, is the place to discuss the question as to whether it is better to have him educated privately at home or hand him over to some large school and those whom I may call public instructors. The latter course has, I know, won the approval of most eminent authorities and of those who have formed the national character of the most famous states. It would, however, be folly to shut our eyes to the fact that there are some who disagree with this preference for public education owing to a certain prejudice in favor of private tuition. These persons seem to be guided in the main by two principles. In the interests of morality they would avoid the society of a number of human beings at an age that is specially liable to acquire serious faults: I only wish I could deny the truth of the view that such education has often been the cause of the most discreditable actions. Secondly, they hold that whoever is to be the boy's teacher, he will devote his time more generously to one pupil than if he has to divide it among several. The first reason certainly deserves serious consideration. If it were proved that schools, while advantageous to study, are prejudicial to morality, I should give my vote for virtuous living in preference to even supreme excellence of speaking. But in my opinion the two are inseparable. I hold that no one can be a true orator unless he is also a good man and, even if he could be, I would not have it so. I will therefore deal with this point first. It is held that schools corrupt the morals. It is true that this is sometimes the case. But morals may be corrupted at home as well. . . .

There is nothing to prevent the principle of "one teacher, one boy" being combined with school education. And even if such a combination should prove impossible, I should still prefer the broad daylight of a respectable school to the solitude and obscurity of a private education. For all the best teachers pride themselves on having a large number of pupils and think themselves worthy of a bigger audience. On the other hand, in the case of inferior teachers a consciousness of their own defects not seldom reconciles them to being attached to a single pupil and playing the part—for it amounts to little more—of a mere *paedagogus*.* . . .

Let me now explain my own views. It is above all things necessary

* A slave who accompanied children to and from school and had charge of them at home.

that our future orator, who will have to live in the utmost publicity and in the broad daylight of public life, should become accustomed from his early childhood to move in society without fear and habituated to a life far removed from that of the pale student, the solitary and recluse. His mind requires constant stimulus and excitement, whereas retirement such as has just been mentioned induces languor and the mind becomes mildewed like things that are left in the dark, or else flies to the opposite extreme and becomes puffed up with empty conceit; for he who has no standard of comparison by which to judge his own powers will necessarily rate them too high. . . . I say nothing of friendships which endure unbroken to old age having acquired the binding force of a sacred duty: for initiation in the same studies has all the sanctity of initiation in the same mysteries of religion. And where shall he acquire that instinct which we call common feeling, if he secludes himself from that intercourse which is natural not merely to mankind but even to dumb animals? Further, at home he can learn only what is taught to himself, while at school he will learn what is taught others as well. He will hear many merits praised and many faults corrected every day: he will derive equal profit from hearing the indolence of a comrade rebuked or his industry commended. Such praise will incite him to emulation, he will think it a disgrace to be outdone by his contemporaries and a distinction to surpass his seniors. All such incentives provide a valuable stimulus, and though ambition may be a fault in itself, it is often the mother of virtues. . . . It is a good thing therefore that a boy should have companions whom he will desire first to imitate and then to surpass: thus he will be led to aspire to higher achievement. I would add that the instructors themselves cannot develop the same intelligence and energy before a single listener as they can when inspired by the presence of a numerous audience.

For eloquence depends in the main on the state of the mind, which must be moved, conceive images and adapt itself to suit the nature of the subject which is the theme of speech. Further, the loftier and the more elevated the mind, the more powerful will be the forces which move it: consequently, praise gives it growth and effort increase, and the thought that it is doing something great fills it with joy. The duty of stooping to expend that power of speaking which has been acquired at the cost of such effort upon an audience of one gives rise to a silent feeling of disdain, and the teacher is ashamed to raise his voice above the ordinary conversational level. Imagine the air of a declaimer, or the voice of an orator, his gait, his delivery, the movements of his body, the emotions of his mind, and, to go no further, the fatigue of his exertions, all for the sake of one listener! Would he not seem little less than a lunatic? No, there would be no such thing as eloquence, if we spoke only with one person at a time.

The skillful teacher will make it his first care, as soon as a boy is entrusted to him, to ascertain his ability and character. The surest indication in a child is his power of memory. The characteristics of a good memory are twofold: it must be quick to take in and faithful to retain impressions of what it receives. The indication of next importance is the power of imitation: for this is a sign that the child is teachable: but he must imitate merely what he is taught, and must not, for example, mimic someone's gait or bearing or defects. For I have no hope that a child will turn out well who loves imitation merely for the purpose of raising a laugh. He who is really gifted will also above all else be good. For the rest, I regard slowness of intellect as preferable to actual badness. But a good boy will be quite unlike the dullard and the sloth. My ideal pupil will absorb instruction with ease and will even ask some questions; but he will follow rather than anticipate his teacher. Precocious intellects rarely produce sound fruit. By the precocious I mean those who perform small tasks with ease and, thus emboldened, proceed to display all their little accomplishments without being asked: but their accomplishments are only of the most obvious kind: they string words together and trot them out boldly and undeterred by the slightest sense of modesty. Their actual achievement is small, but what they can do they perform with ease. They have no real power and what they have is but of shallow growth: it is as when we cast seed on the surface of the soil: it springs up too rapidly, the blade apes the loaded ear, and yellows ere harvest time, but bears no grain. Such tricks please us when we contrast them with the performer's age, but progress soon stops and our admiration withers away.

Such indications once noted, the teacher must next consider what treatment is to be applied to the mind of his pupil. There are some boys who are slack, unless pressed on; others again are impatient of control: some are amenable to fear, while others are paralyzed by it: in some cases the mind requires continued application to form it, in others this result is best obtained by rapid concentration. Give me the boy who is spurred on by praise, delighted by success, and ready to weep over failure. Such a one must be encouraged by appeals to his ambition; rebuke will bite him to the quick; honor will be a spur, and there is no fear of his proving indolent.

Still, all our pupils will require some relaxation, not merely because there is nothing in this world that can stand continued strain, and even unthinking and inanimate objects are unable to maintain their strength, unless given intervals of rest, but because study depends on the good will of the student, a quality that cannot be secured by compulsion. Consequently, if restored and refreshed by a holiday they will bring greater energy to their learning and approach their work with greater spirit of a kind that will not submit to be driven. I approve of play in the young; it is a sign of a lively disposition; nor will you ever lead me to believe that a boy who is gloomy and in a continual state of depression is ever likely to show alertness of mind in his work, lacking as he does the impulse most natural to boys of his age. Such relaxation must not however be unlimited: otherwise the refusal to give a holiday will make boys hate their work, while excessive indulgence will accustom them to idleness. There are moreover certain games which have an educational value for boys, as for instance when they compete in posing each other with all kinds of questions which they ask turn and turn about. Games too reveal character in the most natural way, at least that is so if the teacher will bear in mind that there is no child so young as to be unable to learn to distinguish between right and wrong, and that the character is best molded, when it is still guiltless of deceit and most susceptible to instruction: for once a bad habit has become engrained, it is easier to break than to bend. There must be no delay, then, in warning a boy that his actions must be unselfish, honest, self-controlled, and we must never forget the words of Virgil: "So strong is custom formed in early years."

I disapprove of flogging, although it is the regular custom and meets with the acquiescence of Chrysippus, because in the first place it is a disgraceful form of punishment and fit only for slaves, and is in any case an insult, as you will realize if you imagine its infliction at a later age. Secondly, if a boy is so insensible to instruction that reproof is useless, he will, like the worst type of slave, merely become hardened to blows. Finally, there will be absolutely no need of such punishment if the master is a thorough disciplinarian. As it is, we try to make amends for the negligence of the boy's *paedagogus*, not by forcing him to do what is right, but by punishing him for not doing what is right. And though you may compel a child with blows, what are you to do with him when he is a young man no longer amenable to such threats and confronted with tasks of far greater difficulty? Moreover, when children are beaten, pain or fear frequently have results of which it is not pleasant to speak and which are likely subsequently to be a source of shame, a shame which unnerves and depresses the mind and leads the child to shun and loathe the light. Further, if inadequate care is taken in the choices of respectable governors and instructors, I blush to mention the shameful abuse which scoundrels sometimes make of their right to administer corporal punishment or the opportunity not infrequently offered to others by the fear thus caused in the victims. I will not linger on this subject; it is more than enough if I have made my meaning clear. I will content myself with saying that children are helpless and easily victimized, and that therefore no one should be given unlimited power over them. I will now proceed to describe the subjects in which the boy must be trained, if he is to become an orator, and to indicate the age at which each should be commenced.

. . . .

We need have no fear at any rate that boys will find their work too exhausting: there is no age more capable of enduring fatigue. The fact may be surprising, but it can be proved by experiment. For the mind is all the easier to teach before it is set. This may be clearly proved by the fact that within two years after a child has begun to form words correctly, he can speak practically all without any pressure from outside. On the other hand, how many years it takes for our newly imported slaves to become familiar with the Latin language. Try to teach an adult to read and you will soon appreciate the force of the saying applied to those who do everything connected with their art with the utmost skill, "He started young!" Moreover, boys stand the strain of work better than young men. Just as small children suffer less damage from their frequent falls, from their crawling on hands and knees and, a little later, from their incessant play and their running about from morn till eve, because they are so light in weight and have so little to carry, even so their minds are less susceptible of fatigue, because their activity calls for less effort, and application to study demands no exertion of their own, since they are merely so much plastic material to be molded by the teacher. And further, owing to the general pliability of childhood, they follow their instructors with greater simplicity and without attempting to measure their own progress: for as yet they do not even appreciate the nature of their work. Finally, as I have often noticed, the senses are less affected by mere hard work than they are by hard thinking.

. . . .

As soon therefore as a boy has made sufficient progress in his studies to be able to follow what I have styled the first stage of instruction in rhetoric, he should be placed under a rhetorician. Our first task must be to enquire whether the teacher is of good character. The reason which leads me to deal with this subject in this portion of my work is not that I regard character as a matter of indifference where other teachers are concerned (I have already shown how important I think it in the preceding book), but that the age to which the pupil has now attained makes the mention of this point especially necessary. For as a rule boys are on the verge of manhood when transferred to the teacher of rhetoric and continue with him even when they are young men: consequently, we must spare no effort to secure that the purity of the teacher's character should preserve those of tenderer years from corruption, while its authority should keep the bolder spirits from breaking out into license. Nor is it sufficient that he should merely set an example of the highest personal self-control; he must also be able to govern the behavior of his pupils by the strictness of his discipline.

Let him therefore adopt a parental attitude to his pupils, and regard himself as the representative of those who have committed their children to his charge. Let him be free from vice himself and refuse to tolerate it in others. Let him be strict but not austere, genial but not too familiar: for austerity will make him unpopular, while familiarity breeds contempt. Let his discourse continually turn on what is good and honorable; the more he admonishes, the less he will have to punish. He must control his temper without however shutting his eyes to faults requiring correction: his instruction must be free from affectation, his industry great, his demands on his class continuous, but not extravagant. He must be ready to answer questions and to put them unasked to those who sit silent. In praising the recitations of his pupils he must neither be grudging nor over-generous: the former quality will give them a distaste for work, while the latter will produce a complacent self-satisfaction. In correcting faults he must avoid sarcasm and above all abuse: for teachers whose rebukes seem to imply positive dislike discourage industry. He should declaim daily himself and, what is more, without stint, that his class may take his utterances home with them. For however many models for imitation he may give them from the authors they are reading, it will still be found that fuller nourishment is provided by the living voice, as we call it, more especially when it proceeds from the teacher himself, who, if his pupils are rightly instructed, should be the object of their affection and respect. And it is scarcely possible to say how much more readily we imitate those whom we like. . . .

It is worth while too to warn the teacher that undue severity in correcting faults is liable at times to discourage a boy's mind from effort. He loses hope and gives way to vexation, then last of all comes to hate his work and fearing everything attempts nothing. This phenomenon is familiar to farmers, who hold that the pruning hook should not be applied while the leaves are yet young, for they seem to "shrink from the steel" and to be unable as yet to endure a scar. The instructor therefore should be as kindly as possible at this stage; remedies, which are harsh by nature, must be applied with a gentle hand: some portions of the work must be praised, others tolerated and others altered: the reason for the alterations should however be given, and in some cases the master will illumine an obscure passage by inserting something of his own. Occasionally again the teacher will find it useful to dictate whole themes himself that the boy may imitate them and for the time being love them as if they were his own. But if a boy's composition is so careless as not to admit of correction, I have found it useful to give a fresh exposition of the theme and to tell him to write it again, pointing out that he was capable of doing better: for there is nothing like hope for making study a pleasure. Different ages however demand different methods: the task set and the standard of correction must be proportioned to the pupil's strength. When boys ventured on something that was too daring or exuberant, I used to say to them that I approved of it for the moment, but that the time would come when I should no longer tolerate such a style. The result was that the consciousness of ability filled them with pleasure, without blinding their judgment. . . .

It is generally and not unreasonably regarded as the sign of a good teacher that he should be able to differentiate between the abilities of his respective pupils and to know their natural bent. The gifts of nature are infinite in their variety, and mind differs from mind almost as much as body from body. . . . One boy will be better adapted for the study of history, another for poetry, another for law, while some perhaps had better be packed off to the country. The teacher of rhetoric will distinguish such special aptitudes, just as our gymnast will turn one pupil into a runner, another into a boxer or wrestler or an expert at some other of the athletic accomplishments for which prizes are awarded at the sacred games. But on the other hand, he who is destined for the bar must study not one department merely, but must perfect himself in all the accomplishments which his profession demands, even though some of them may seem too hard for him when he approaches them as a learner. For if natural talent alone were sufficient, education might be dispensed with. . . .

Though I have spoken in some detail of the duties of the teacher, I shall for the moment confine my advice to the learners to one solitary admonition, that they should love their masters not less than their studies, and should regard them as the parents not indeed of their bodies but of their minds. Such attachments are of invaluable assistance to study. For under their influence they find it a pleasure to listen to their teachers, believe what they say and long to be like them, come cheerfully and gladly to school, are not angry when corrected, rejoice when praised, and seek to win their master's affection by the devotion with which they pursue their studies. For as it is the duty of the master to teach, so it is the duty of the pupil to show himself teachable. The two obligations are mutually indispensable. And just as it takes two parents to produce a human being, and as the seed is scattered in vain if the ground is hard and there is no furrow to receive it and bring it to growth, even so eloquence can never come to maturity, unless teacher and taught are in perfect sympathy.

"To Teach All Things to All Men"

John Amos Comenius
(1592–1670)

Modern education begins with John Amos Comenius, a seventeenth-century Czech religious leader. Like Plato, who was of course primarily a philosopher, and Quintilian, who was essentially a rhetorician, Comenius was an educator only secondarily. He had two greater passions than education: mystical Christianity and the philosophical search for a universal system of knowledge.

As Alexander Meiklejohn has shown, Comenius' main interests served him well in his educational theory and practice. From his profound religious faith in the unity of mankind he drew the inspiration for his educational aim: schooling for everyone. From his search for the basic principles of knowledge he developed his methodology: teaching must begin with fundamental concepts which are to be constantly reconsidered and elaborated throughout the student's education. Both unities found their origin in God, for He made all men equally worthy of education, and He sustained the truths of nature.

Plato was most interested in educating philosophers; Quintilian, men of political action; the Medieval and Renaissance thinkers who preceded Comenius, rulers. Comenius set out to educate *men*. His stated objective was to find a way to teach "all things to all men." Until someone had stated the task of the educator as a universal mission, there was insufficient inspiration to devise ways of bringing education to everyone.

Comenius was a practicing teacher who criticized the schools of his time as "places where ten or more years are spent in learning what might be acquired in one." He devoted much of his life to preparing improved materials for use in actual instruction, especially in the teaching of languages. Comenius' portrayal of the learning process as analogous with growth in nature has seemed unscientific to most later thinkers. But for this man who sought to put education on an "immovable rock" of science, education was always more than science. The unity of nature and man expressed in his analogies embodies an attitude of reverence toward the developing mind of the student which is still the key to true education.

The life of Comenius lends both authority and poignancy to his educational writings. He was born into the pietist Moravian Brethren, followers of John Huss. This sect was singularly devoted to education—it founded the University of Prague and established elementary and secondary schools throughout northern Europe. Comenius took charge of a congregation and school at Fulneck in 1616. His career was first disrupted by the Thirty Years' War, when he had to flee to Poland. During the rest of his life he was frequently a political exile, but his growing reputation won him many refuges. In 1641 he traveled to England to present his plan for a great new institution of learning. His idea was greeted with the enthusiasm and support which eighteen years later led to the formation of the Royal Society. But Irish revolution was impending in England, Parliament failed to act on his plan, and Comenius returned disappointed to the Continent. He later traveled to Sweden to reform that country's schools, but the government assigned him to writing textbooks. After several years Comenius moved on to Hungary where the opportunity to start another school beckoned. He ended his life in Amsterdam, as the last chief Bishop of the Moravian Brethren. Comenius was, in the words of Otto Benesch, "the most sensible, the most human, the most Christian-minded thinker of (his) time."

Comenius' writings are many and diverse. *The Labyrinth of the World and the Paradise of the Heart* is a devotional classic similar to *The Pilgrim's Progress*. The *Orbis Pictus* is a pioneering pictorial textbook which was used for centuries; its title page proclaims that it contains "the pictures and names of all the principal occupations of man." This selection is from Comenius' *The Great Didactic,* translated by M. W. Keatinge.

Didactic signifies the art of teaching. For more than a hundred years much complaint has been made of the unmethodical way in which schools have been conducted, but it is only within the last thirty years that any serious attempt has been made to find a remedy for this state of things. Several men of ability, taking pity on the labor of the schools, have lately endeavored to seek out the principles of some such Art, but with unequal skill and unequal success.

Some wished to give assistance towards learning some language or other with greater ease. Others found ways of imparting this or that science or art with greater speed. Others suggested improvements of various kinds; but almost all proceeded by means of unconnected precepts, gleaned from a superficial experience.

We venture to promise a *Great Didactic,* that is to say, the whole art of teaching all things to all men, and indeed of teaching them with certainty, pleasantly, that is to say, without annoyance or aversion on the part of teacher or pupil; and further, of teaching them thoroughly, in such a manner as to lead to true knowledge, to gentle morals, and to the deepest piety. . . .

Man Must Be Formed by Education

While the seeds of knowledge, of virtue, and of piety are naturally implanted in us, the actual knowledge, virtue, and piety are not so given. These must be acquired by prayer, by education, and by action.

Examples show that those who in their infancy have been seized by wild animals, and have been brought up among them, have not risen above the level of brutes in intellect, and would not have been able to make more use of their tongues, their hands, and their feet than beasts can, had they not once more come into the society of men. About the year 1540, in a village called Hassia, situated in the middle of a forest, a boy three years of age was lost, through the carelessness of his parents. Some years afterwards the country people saw a strange animal running about with the wolves, of a different shape, four-footed, but with a man's face. Rumor of this spread through the district, and the governor asked the peasants to try to catch it alive and bring it to him. This they did, and finally the creature was conveyed to the Landgrave at Cassel.

When it was taken into the castle it tore itself away, fled, and hid beneath a bench, where it glared fiercely at its pursuers and howled horribly. The prince had him educated and kept him continually in men's society, and under this influence his savage habits grew gentler by degrees; he began to raise himself up on his hind legs and walk like a biped, and at last to speak intelligently and behave like a man. Then he related to the best of his ability how he had been seized and nurtured by the wolves and had been accustomed to go hunting with them. So true is Plato's remark: "Man is the gentlest and most divine being, if he have been made so by true education: but if he have been subjected to none or a false one, he is the most intractable thing in the world." He gave no bad definition who said that man was a teachable animal.

That education is necessary will be further evident if we consider the different degrees of ability. No one doubts that those who are stupid need instruction, that they may shake off their natural dullness. But in reality those who are clever need it far more, since an active mind, if not occupied with useful things, will busy itself with what is useless, curious, and pernicious; and, just as the more fertile a field is, the richer the crop of thorns and of thistles that it can produce, so an excellent intelligence becomes filled with fanciful notions, if it be not sown with the seeds of wisdom and of virtue; and as a millstone grinds itself away with noise and grating, and often cracks and breaks, if wheat, the raw material of flour, be not supplied to it, so an active mind, if void of serious things, entangles itself utterly with vain, curious, and noxious thoughts, and becomes the cause of its own destruction.

Thus, all who are born to man's estate have need of instruction, since it is necessary that, being men, they should not be wild beasts, savage brutes, or inert logs. And since all have been born with the same end in view, namely that they should be men, it follows that *all* boys and girls, both noble and ignoble, rich and poor, in all cities and towns, villages and hamlets, should be sent to school.

Man Is Most Easily Formed in Youth

From what has been said it is evident that the circumstances of men and of trees are similar. As a fruit tree (an apple, a pear, a fig, or a vine) is able to grow from its own stock and of its own accord, while a wild tree will not bring forth sweet fruits until it be planted, watered, and pruned by a skilled gardener, so does a man grow of his own accord into a human semblance, but is unable to develop into a rational, wise, virtuous, and pious creature, unless virtue and piety are first engrafted in him.

It is the nature of everything that comes into being, that while tender it is easily bent and formed, but that, when it has grown hard, it is not easy to alter. Wax, when soft, can be easily fashioned and shaped; when hard, it cracks readily.

It is evident that this holds good with man himself. His brain, which we compare to wax, because it receives the images of external objects that present themselves to its organs of sense, is, in the years of childhood, quite wet and soft, and fit for receiving all images that come to it. Just as wax, taking every form, allows itself to be modeled and remodeled in any desired way, so the brain, receiving the images of all things, takes into itself whatever is contained in the whole universe. Later on, as we find by experience, it grows hard and dry by degrees, so that things are less readily impressed or engraved upon it. Hence Cicero's remark, "Boys pick up countless things with rapidity." In the same way it is only in the years of boyhood, when the muscles are still capable of being trained, that the hands and the other members can be trained to produce skilled work. If a man is to become a good writer, painter, tailor, smith, cabinetmaker, or musician, he must apply himself to the art from his early youth, when the imagination is active and the fingers flexible: otherwise he will never produce anything. If piety is to take root in any man's heart, it must be engrafted while he is still young; if we wish anyone to be virtuous, we must train him in early youth; if we wish him to make great progress in the pursuit of wisdom, we must direct his faculties towards it in infancy, when desire burns, when thought is swift, and when memory is tenacious. "An old man who has still to learn his lessons is a shameful and ridiculous object; training and preparation are for the young, action for the old" (Seneca).

This is further evident if we consider the following examples.

A jar, even though broken, preserves the odor with which it was imbued when new. When a tree is young its branches spread out all round it, and remain in this position for hundreds of years, until it is cut down. Wool is so tenacious of the color with which it is first dyed, that it cannot be bleached. The wooden hoop of a wheel, which has been bent into a curve, will break into a thousand pieces rather than return to straightness. And similarly, in a man, first impressions cling so fast that nothing but a miracle can remove them. It is therefore most prudent that men be shaped to the standard of wisdom in early youth.

Do not imagine that we demand from all men an exact or deep knowledge of all the arts and sciences. This would neither be useful of itself, nor, on account of the shortness of life, can it be attained by any man. For we see that each science is so vast and so complicated (as are physics, arithmetic, geometry, astronomy, or even agriculture and arboriculture) that it would occupy the lifetime of even the strongest intellects if they wished to master it thoroughly by investigation and experiment. It is the principles, the causes, and the uses of all the most important things in existence that we wish all men to learn; all, that is to say, who are sent into the world to be actors as well as spectators. For we must take strong and vigorous measures that no man, in his journey through life, may encounter anything so unknown to him that he cannot pass sound judgment upon it and turn it to its proper use without serious error.

If it be urged that some men have such weak intellects that it is not possible for them to acquire knowledge, I answer that it is scarcely possible to find a mirror so dulled that it will not reflect images of some kind, or for a tablet to have such a rough surface that nothing can be inscribed on it. A sieve, if you continually pour water through it, grows cleaner, although it cannot retain the liquid; and, in the same way, the dull and the weak-minded, though they may make no advance in letters, become softer in disposition and learn to obey the civil magistrates and the ministers of the Church.

If it be objected that with many students not the capacity to learn but the inclination is lacking, and to compel these against their will is as unpleasant as it is useless, I answer: In these cases the external distraction must first be removed; nature will then assert itself with its original vigor, and the desire for knowledge will once more be apparent. But how many of those who undertake to educate the young appreciate the necessity of first teaching them how to acquire knowledge? The turner shapes a block of wood with his ax before he turns it; the blacksmith heats iron before he hammers it; the clothweaver, before he spins his wool, first cleans, washes, cards, and fulls it; the shoemaker, before he sews the shoe, prepares, shapes, and smooths the leather; but who, I ask, ever thinks it necessary that the teacher, in the same way, should make his pupils eager for information? Teachers almost invariably take their pupils as they find them; they turn them, beat them, card them, comb them, drill them into certain forms, and expect them to become a finished and polished product; and if the result does not come up to their expectations (and I ask you how could it?) they are indignant, angry, and furious. And yet we are surprised that some men shrink and recoil from such a system. Far more is it matter for surprise that anyone can endure it at all.

Nature Is our Guide

Let us commence to seek out, in God's name, the principles on which, as on an immovable rock, the method of teaching and learning can be grounded.

We find on investigation that the principle which really holds together the fabric of this world of ours, down to its smallest detail, is none other than order; that is to say, the proper division of what comes before and what comes after, of the superior and the subordinate, of the large and small, of the similar and dissimilar, according to place, time, number, size, and weight, so that each may fulfill its function well.

The act of teaching, therefore, demands nothing more than the skillful arrangement of time, of the subjects taught, and the method. It is quite clear that this order can be borrowed from no other source than the operations of nature. If we wish to find a remedy for the defects of nature, it is in nature herself that we must look for it, since it is certain that art can do nothing unless it imitate nature. Very aptly does Cicero say: "If we take nature as our guide, she will never lead us astray." Taking nature as our guide we will proceed to seek out the principles on which teaching and learning can be grounded.

FIRST PRINCIPLE

1. *In all the operations of nature, development is from within.*

For example: in the case of a bird it is not the claws, or the feathers, or the skin that are first formed, but the inner parts; the outer parts are formed later, at the proper season.

2. *Deviation.* It is on this point that those teachers fall into error who, instead of thoroughly explaining the subjects of study to the boys under their charge, give them endless dictations, and make them learn their lesson off by heart. Even those who wish to explain the subject matter do not know how to do so, that is to say, do not know how to tend the roots or how to engraft the graft of knowledge. Thus they fatigue their pupils, and resemble a man who uses a club or a mallet, instead of a knife, when he wishes to make an incision in a plant.

3. *Rectification.* It therefore follows:

That the scholar should be taught first to understand things, and then to remember them, and that no stress should be laid on the use of speech or pen, till after a training on the first two points.

SECOND PRINCIPLE

1. *Nature, in its formative processes, begins with the universal and ends with the particular.*

For example: a bird is to be produced from an egg. It is not the head, an eye, a feather, or a claw that is first formed, but an outline of the shape of the whole bird (defining the parts that are to become the head, the wings, the feet, etc.).

2. *Deviation.* From this it follows that it is a mistake to teach the several branches of science in detail before a general outline of the whole realm of knowledge has been placed before the student, and that no one should be instructed in such a way to become proficient in any one branch of knowledge without thoroughly understanding its relation to all the rest.

3. *Rectification.* The remedy for this want of system is as follows: at the very commencement of their studies, boys should receive instruction in the first principles of general culture, that is to say, the subjects learned should be arranged in such a manner that the studies that come later introduce nothing new, but only ex-

pand the elements of knowledge that the boy has already mastered.

THIRD PRINCIPLE

1. *Nature carefully avoids obstacles and things likely to cause hurt.*

For example: when a bird is hatching eggs it does not allow a cold wind, much less rain or hail, to reach them. It also drives away snakes, birds of prey, etc.

2. *Deviation.* It is therefore folly to introduce a student to controversial points when he is just beginning a subject, that is to say, to allow a mind that is mastering something new to assume an attitude of doubt. What is this but to tear up a plant that is just beginning to strike root?

3. *Rectification.* Care should therefore be taken

(i) That the scholars receive no books but those suitable for their classes.

(ii) That these books be of such a kind that they can rightly be termed sources of wisdom, virtue, and piety.

(iii) That neither in the school nor in its vicinity the scholars are allowed to mix with bad companions.

FOURTH PRINCIPLE

1. *Nature begins by a careful selection of materials.*

For instance, for hatching a bird she selects fresh eggs and those that contain pure matter.

2. *Deviation.* It follows from this:

(i) That the result must be bad if a boy be instructed by several teachers at once, since it is scarcely possible for them all to use the same method, and, if they do not, the boy's mind is drawn first in one direction and then in another, and its development is thus hindered.

(ii) That it shows great lack of judgment if moral instruction be not made the first point when the education of children or of older boys is commenced; since, when they have been taught to control their feelings, they will be the more fit to receive other instruction. Horse tamers keep a horse under absolute control with an iron bit, and ensure its obedience before they teach it its paces. Rightly does Seneca say: "First learn virtue, and then wisdom, since without virtue it is difficult to learn wisdom." And Cicero says: "Moral philosophy makes the mind fit to receive the seeds of further knowledge."

3. *Rectification.* Therefore

(i) The pupil should not have more than one teacher in each subject.

(ii) Before anything else is done, the morals should be rendered harmonious by the master's influence.

FIFTH PRINCIPLE

1. *Nature prepares its material so that it actually strives to attain the form.*

Thus the chicken in the egg, when sufficiently formed, seeks to develop itself still further, moves, and bursts the shell or breaks through it with its beak. After escaping from its prison, it takes pleasure in the warmth and nutriment provided by its mother, opens its beak expectantly and swallows its food greedily. It rejoices to find itself under the open sky, exercises its wings, and later on, uses them with enjoyment.

2. *Deviation.* Therefore, those who drive boys to their studies, do them great harm. For what result can they expect? If a man have no appetite, but yet takes food when urged to do so, the result can only be sickness and vomiting, or at least indigestion and indisposition. On the other hand, if a man be hungry, he is eager to take food, digests it readily, and easily converts it into flesh and blood. Thus Isocrates says: "He who is eager to learn will also be learned." And Quintilian says: "The acquisition of knowledge depends on the will to learn, and this cannot be forced."

3. *Rectification.* Therefore

(i) The desire to know and to learn should be excited in boys in every possible manner.

(ii) The method of instruction should lighten the drudgery of learning, that there may be nothing to hinder the scholars or deter them from making progress with their studies.

4. The desire to learn is kindled by the teachers, if they are gentle and persuasive, and do not alienate their pupils from them by roughness, but attract them by fatherly sentiments and words; if they commend the studies that they take in hand on account

of their excellence, pleasantness, and ease; if they praise the industrious ones from time to time (to the little ones they may give apples, nuts, sugar, etc.); if they call the children to them, privately or in the class, and show them pictures of the things that they must learn, or explain to them optical or geometrical instruments, astronomical globes, and suchlike things that are calculated to excite their admiration; or again, if they occasionally give the children some message to carry to their parents. In a word, if they treat their pupils kindly they will easily win their affections, and will bring it about that they prefer going to school to remaining at home.

5. The school itself should be a pleasant place and attractive to the eye both within and without. Within, the room should be bright and clean, and its walls should be ornamented by pictures. These should be either portraits of celebrated men, geographical maps, historical plans, or other ornaments. Without, there should be an open place to walk and to play in (for this is absolutely necessary for children, as we shall show later), and there should also be a garden attached, into which the scholars may be allowed to go from time to time and where they may feast their eyes on trees, flowers, and plants. If this be done, boys will, in all probability, go to school with as much pleasure as to fairs, where they always hope to see and hear something new.

6. The subjects of instruction themselves prove attractive to the young, if they are suited to the age of the pupil and are clearly explained; especially if the explanation be relieved by a humorous or at any rate by a less serious tone. For thus the pleasant is combined with the useful.

SIXTH PRINCIPLE

1. *Nature develops everything from beginnings which, though insignificant in appearance, possess great potential strength.*

For instance, the matter out of which a bird is to be formed consists of a few drops, which are contained in a shell, that they may be easily warmed and hatched. But these few drops contain the whole bird potentially, since, later on, the body of the chicken is formed from the vital principle which is concentrated in them.

2. *Terrible deviation.* In direct opposition to this principle a terrible mistake is generally made in schools. Most teachers are at pains to place in the earth plants instead of seeds, and trees

instead of shoots, since, instead of starting with the fundamental principles, they place before their pupils a chaos of diverse conclusions or the complete texts of authors. And yet it is certain that instruction rests on a very small number of principles, just as the earth is composed of four elements (though in diverse forms); and that from these principles (in accordance with the evident limits of their powers of differentiation) an unlimited number of results can be deduced, just as, in the case of a tree, hundreds of branches, and thousands of leaves, blossoms, and fruits are produced from the original shoot.

3. *Rectification.*

(i) Every art must be contained in the shortest and most practical rules.

(ii) Each rule must be expressed in the shortest and clearest words.

(iii) Each rule must be accompanied by many examples, in order that the use of the rule may be quite clear when fresh cases arise.

SEVENTH PRINCIPLE

1. *Nature advances from what is easy to what is more difficult.*

For example: the formation of an egg does not begin with the hardest part, the shell, but with the contents.

2. *Deviation.* It is therefore wrong to teach the unknown through the medium of that which is equally unknown, as is the case:

If boys who are beginning Latin are taught the rules in Latin. This is just as if the attempt were made to explain Hebrew by Hebrew rules, or Arabic by Arabic rules.

3. *Rectification.* These errors may be avoided

(i) If the subject matter be so arranged that the pupils get to know, first, that which lies nearest to their mental vision, then that which lies moderately near, then that which is more remote, and lastly, that which is farthest off. Therefore, if boys are being taught something for the first time (such as logic or rhetoric), the illustrations should not be taken from subjects that cannot be grasped by the scholars, such as theology, politics, or poetry, but should be derived from the events of everyday life. Otherwise the boys will understand neither the rules nor their application.

(ii) If boys be made to exercise, first their senses (for this is the easiest), then the memory, then the comprehension, and finally the judgment. In this way a graded sequence will take place; for all knowledge begins by sensuous perception; then through the medium of the imagination it enters the province of the memory; then, by dwelling on the particulars, comprehension of the universal arises; while finally comes judgment on the facts that have been grasped, and in this way our knowledge is firmly established.

EIGHTH PRINCIPLE

1. *Nature does not hurry, but advances slowly.*

For example: a bird does not place its eggs in the fire, in order to hatch them quickly, but lets them develop slowly under the influence of natural warmth.

2. *Deviation.* For the young, therefore, it is torture

(i) If they are compelled to receive six, seven, or eight hours' class instruction daily, and private lessons in addition.

(ii) If they are overburdened with dictations, with exercises, and with the lessons that they have to commit to memory, until nausea and, in some cases, insanity is produced.

If we take a jar with a narrow mouth (for to this we may compare a boy's intellect) and attempt to pour a quantity of water into it violently, instead of allowing it to trickle in drop by drop, what will be the result? Without doubt the greater part of the liquid will flow over the side, and ultimately the jar will contain less than if the operation had taken place gradually. Quite as foolish is the action of those who try to teach their pupils, not as much as they can assimilate, but as much as they themselves wish; for the faculties need to be supported and not to be overburdened, and the teacher, like the physician, is the servant and not the master of nature.

3. *Rectification.* The ease and pleasantness of study will therefore be increased:

(i) If the class instruction be curtailed as much as possible, namely to four hours, and if the same length of time be left for private study.

(ii) If the pupils be forced to memorize as little as possible, that is to say, only the most important things; of the rest they need only grasp the general meaning.

(iii) If everything be arranged to suit the capacity of the pupil, which increases naturally with study and age.

NINTH PRINCIPLE

1. *Nature compels nothing to advance that is not driven forward by its own mature strength.*

For instance, a chicken is not compelled to quit the egg before its limbs are properly formed and set; is not forced to fly before its feathers have grown; is not thrust from the nest before it is able to fly well, etc.

2. *Deviation.* Now the faculties of the young are forced:

(i) If the boys are compelled to learn things for which their age and capacity are not yet suited.

(ii) If they are made to learn by heart or to do things that have not first been thoroughly explained and demonstrated to them.

3. *Rectification.* From what has been said, it follows

(i) That nothing should be taught to the young, unless it is not only permitted but actually demanded by their age and mental strength.

(ii) That nothing should be learned by heart that has not been thoroughly grasped by the understanding. Nor should any feat of memory be demanded unless it is absolutely certain that the boy's strength is equal to it.

(iii) That nothing should be set boys to do until its nature has been thoroughly explained to them, and rules for procedure have been given.

TENTH PRINCIPLE

1. *Nature assists its operations in every possible manner.*

For example: an egg possesses its own natural warmth; but this is assisted by the warmth of the sun and by the feathers of the bird that hatches it.

2. *Deviation.* It is therefore cruelty on the part of a teacher if he set his pupils work to do without first explaining it to them thoroughly, or showing them how it should be done, and if he do not assist them in their first attempts; or if he allow them to toil hard, and then loses his temper if they do not succeed in their endeavors.

What is this but to torture the young? It is just as if a nurse were to force a child to walk, while it is still afraid to stand on its legs, and beat it when it fails to do so. Nature's teaching is very different, and shows that we ought to have patience with the weak as long as their strength is insufficient.

3. *Rectification.* From this it follows:

(i) That no blows should be given for lack of readiness to learn (for, if the pupil do not learn readily, this is the fault of no one but the teacher, who either does not know how to make his pupil receptive of knowledge or does not take the trouble to do so).

(ii) That the subjects that have to be learned by the pupils should be so thoroughly explained to them, that they can understand them as well as they understand their five fingers.

(iii) That, as far as is possible, instruction should be given through the senses, that it may be retained in the memory with less effort.

ELEVENTH PRINCIPLE

1. *Nothing is produced by nature of which the practical application is not soon evident.*

For example: when a bird is formed it is soon evident that the wings are intended for flying and the legs for running.

2. *Imitation.* The task of the pupil will be made easier, if the master, when he teaches him anything, show him at the same time its practical application in everyday life. This rule must be carefully observed in teaching languages, dialectic, arithmetic, geometry, physics, etc. If it be neglected, the things that you are explaining will seem to be monsters from the new world, and the attitude of the pupil, who is indifferent whether they exist or no, will be one of belief rather than of knowledge. When things are brought under his notice and their use is explained to him, they should be put into his hands that he may assure himself of his knowledge and may derive enjoyment from its application.

Thoroughness in Teaching and Learning

It is a common complaint that there are few who leave school with a thorough education, and that most men retain nothing but a veneer, a mere shadow of true knowledge. This complaint is corroborated by facts.

The cause of this phenomenon appears on investigation to be twofold: either that the schools occupy themselves with insignificant and unimportant studies, to the neglect of those that are more weighty, or that the pupils forget what they have learned, since most of it merely goes through their heads and does not stick fast there. This last fault is so common that there are few who do not lament it. For if everything that we have ever read, heard, and mentally appreciated were always ready to hand in our memories, how learned we should appear! We do, it is true, make practical use of much that we have learned, but the amount that we recollect is unsatisfactory, and the fact remains that we are continually trying to pour water into a sieve.

But can no cure be found for this? Certainly there can, if once more we go to the school of nature, and investigate the methods that she adopts to give endurance to the beings which she has created.

FIRST PRINCIPLE

1. *Nature produces nothing that is useless.*

For example: nature, when commencing to form a bird, does not give it scales, gills, horns, four feet, or any other organs that it cannot use, but supplies a head, a heart, wings, etc. In the same way a tree is not given ears, eyes, down, or hair, but bark, bast, wood, and roots.

2. *And in schools:*

(i) Nothing should be studied, unless it be of undoubted use in this world and in the world to come—its use in the world to come being the more important (Jerome reminds us that knowledge, that is to be of service to us in heaven, must be acquired on earth).

(ii) If it be necessary to teach the young much that is of value solely in this world (and this cannot be avoided), care must be taken that while a real advantage is gained for our present life, our heavenly welfare be not hindered thereby.

3. Why then pursue worthless studies? What object is there in learning subjects that are of no use to those who know them and the lack of which is not felt by those who do not know them? subjects, too, which are certain to be forgotten as time passes on and the business of life becomes more engrossing? This short life of ours has more than enough to occupy it, even if we do not waste it on worthless studies. Schools must therefore be organized in such a way that the scholars learn nothing but what is of value.

SECOND PRINCIPLE

1. *Nature develops everything from its roots and from no other source.*

The wood, bark, leaves, flowers, and fruit of a tree come from the roots and from no other source. For although the rain may fall on the tree and the gardener may water it, the moisture must all be taken up through the roots, and then dispersed through the trunk, branches, boughs, leaves, and fruit.

2. *Terrible deviation in schools.* Hitherto the schools have not taught their pupils to develop their minds like young trees from their own roots, but rather to deck themselves with branches plucked from other trees, and, like Æsop's crow, to adorn themselves with the feathers of other birds; they have taken no trouble to open the fountain of knowledge that is hidden in the scholars, but instead have watered them with water from other sources. That is to say, they have not shown them the objective world as it exists in itself, but only what this, that, or the other author has written or thought about this or that object, so that he is considered the most learned who best knows the contradictory opinions which many men have held about many things. The result is that most men possess no information but the quotations, sentences, and opinions that they have collected by rummaging about in various authors, and thus piece their knowledge together like a patchwork quilt. "Oh you imitators, you slavish pack!" cries Horace. A slavish pack indeed, and accustomed to carry burdens that are not their own.

3. It is only too evident that the methods which are so faulty in this respect have not been rectified (1) since the education of many, if not of most men, consists of nothing but a string of names; that is to say, they can repeat the technical terms and the rules of the arts, but do not know how to apply them practically; (2) since the education of no man attains the position of universal knowledge that can give itself support, strength, and breadth, but in a heterogeneous compound of which one part is borrowed from one source and another from another, whose elements are joined together on no logical principle, and which therefore bears no worthy fruit. For the knowledge that consists of the collected sayings and opinions of various authors resembles the tree which peasants erect when they make holiday, and which, though covered with branches, flowers, fruit, garlands, and crowns, cannot grow or even last, because its ornamentation does not spring from its roots, but is only hung on. Such a tree bears no fruit, and the branches that are attached to it wither and fall off. But a man who is thoroughly educated resembles a tree which grows from its own roots and is nourished by its own sap, and which, on that

account, increases in size (and from day to day with more vigor), and puts forth leaves, blossoms, and fruit.

4. *Rectification.* We arrive therefore at the following conclusion: men must, as far as is possible, be taught to become wise by studying the heavens, the earth, oaks, and beeches, but not by studying books; that is to say, they must learn to know and investigate the things themselves, and not the observations that other people have made about the things. We shall thus tread in the footsteps of the wise men of old, if each of us obtain his knowledge from the originals, from things themselves, and from no other source. We may therefore lay it down as a law:

(i) That all knowledge should be deduced from the unchanging principles of the subject in question.

(ii) That no information should be imparted on the grounds of bookish authority, but should be authorized by actual demonstration to the senses and to the intellect.

THIRD PRINCIPLE

1. *Nature becomes fruitful and strong through constant movement.*

Thus, when a bird hatches eggs, it does not only warm them, but, in order that they may be warmed equally on all sides, it turns them round daily (this can be easily observed in the case of geese, hens, and doves, since these hatch their eggs under our very eyes).

2. *Imitation.* The saying, "He who teaches others, teaches himself," is very true, not only because constant repetition impresses a fact indelibly on the mind, but because the process of teaching in itself gives a deeper insight into the subject taught.

Following out this idea, the scholars, when they meet one another after school hours, or when they go for walks together, should compare notes and discuss information that they have recently acquired, or should converse on anything new that attracts their attention. It would be of great assistance, when a certain number of scholars meet for such discussion, if one of them (to be chosen either by lot or by vote) were to take the place of teacher, and control the proceedings. If the scholar thus selected by his companions refuse the position, he should be severely reprimanded. For, far from being rejected, such opportunities of teaching and of learning should be sought after and competed for.

The Evils of Education

Jean Jacques Rousseau
(1712–1778)

"Do precisely the opposite of what is usually done, and you will have hit on the right plan." This was Rousseau's prescription for reforming an educational system which seemed to him best designed to enfeeble the minds and warp the emotional development of young people. Comenius had denounced the schools of his time as "slaughterhouses of minds," but he had not questioned the fundamental premise that education was a matter of conveying a body of knowledge from the teacher to the student. Rousseau attempted a complete revolution by actually dethroning knowledge and placing the student—his needs, his impulses, his developing powers—at the center of education.

Rousseau believed that a child's natural impulses are good, and that intellectual training is futile before the child becomes capable of reason and can begin to teach himself. He thus proposed a "negative" education in his classic *Émile*. "Whatever lesson they may need," he advises, "be sure not to give it to them today if you can safely put it off till tomorrow." How long may learning be thus delayed? "For the first twelve years," answers Rousseau, "the educator must teach the child *nothing*." It was not Rousseau's intention to produce a "noble savage," however. He did not think that mere maturation would prepare Émile for life. Rather, Rousseau believed that education was a necessary evil, since the child will eventually have to be able to get along in society.

The proper primary education is one which prepares the child to benefit later from formal schooling. It is an education which inures him to the deceptions of an artificial culture and strengthens his natural moral sense to withstand the demands of society. Even when formal schooling begins, there is to be no prescribed curriculum. The child is to learn everything through firsthand sense experiences and spontaneous activities, rather than through books. The teacher is to guide the student's independent learning rather than instruct him in a body of knowledge. Only when the child has reached adolescence are books introduced—not books of abstract principles, but books like *Robinson Crusoe*—so that the youngster can learn vicariously through the experience of others.

It is important to realize that in *Émile* Rousseau concentrated on only two-thirds of the child's education: the natural or negative phase, and the social or moral phase. He also planned a civic or political phase which he described in *Considerations on the Government of Poland.* This "public" education was to be nationalistic, collectivist, uniform, and government supervised. Rousseau's educational program thus included both extremes of a "progressive" concern with the full development of individual powers, and a classical regimen of training for civic responsibility. The relationship of these two schemes is not satisfactorily resolved in either *Émile* or the *Considerations.* This resolution probably formed a part of a *Comparison Between Public and Private Education,* a manuscript written about 1764, which has not been preserved.

But Rousseau's enduring impact on our schools today has been through the picture of the ideal education of an inherently good child in *Émile.* It was Pestalozzi's chief inspiration. It was reaffirmed when Froebel, the originator of the kindergarten, asserted that the child "precisely and surely wills what is best for himself." John Dewey quoted from it at the beginning of almost every chapter in *Schools of To-Morrow.*

Jean Jacques Rousseau was the son of a Swiss watchmaker. His upbringing was haphazard; after an irregular and amorous youth in various cities he arrived in Paris at the age of 29 to make his fortune. He failed to distinguish himself until, at the age of 37, he won first prize in an essay contest held by the Academy of Dijon on the question: Has scientific and artistic progress contributed to the corruption or to the improvement of human conduct? Rousseau, arguing that men were good by nature and only became corrupted in society, was catapulted to immediate renown. During the next few years he produced a number of important works in philosophy, political theory, and belles-lettres, including *La Nouvelle Héloïse, The Social Contract,* and *Émile* (1762). But at the same time he alienated both his friends and the authorities with his erratic, probably paranoiac behavior. He was driven from a number of Swiss towns, lived with the philosopher David Hume for a time, and finally died at Ermenonville, near Paris. The following excerpts are from *Selections from Emilius,* in three volumes, published in Edinburgh in 1773.

All things are good as they come out of the hands of their Creator, but every thing degenerates in the hands of man. He compels one soil to nourish the productions of another, and one tree to bear the fruits of another. He blends and confounds elements, climates, and seasons: he mutilates his dogs, his horses, and his slaves: he defaces, he confounds everything: he delights in deformity and monsters. He is not content with anything in its natural state, not even with his own species. His very offspring must be trained up for him, like a horse in the ménage, and be taught to grow after his own fancy, like a tree in his garden.

Without this, matters would be still worse than they are, and our species would not be civilized but by halves. Should a man, in a state of society, be given up, from the cradle, to his own notions and conduct, he would certainly turn out the most preposterous of human beings. The influence of prejudice, authority, necessity, example, and all those social institutions in which we are immerged, would stifle in him the emotions of nature, and substitute nothing in their place. His humanity would resemble a shrub, growing by accident in the highway, which would soon be destroyed by the casual injuries it must receive from the frequent passenger. . . .

We are born weak, we have need of help; we are born destitute of everything, we stand in need of assistance; we are born stupid, we have need of understanding. All that we are not possessed of at our birth, and which we require when grown up, is bestowed on us by education.

This education we receive from nature, from men, or from circumstances. The constitutional exertion of our organs and faculties is the education of nature: the uses we are taught to make of that exertion, constitute the education given us by men; and in the acquisitions made by our own experience, on the objects that surround us, consists our education from circumstances.

We are formed, therefore, by three kinds of masters. The pupil in whom the effects of their different lessons are contradictory, is badly educated and can never be consistent with himself. He in whom they are perfectly consonant, and always tend to the same point, hath only attained the end of a complete education. His life and actions demonstrate this, and that he alone is well brought up.

Of these three different kinds of education, that of nature depends not on ourselves; and but in a certain degree that of circumstances: the third, which belongs to men, is that only we have in our power: and even of this we are masters only in imagination; for who can flatter himself, he will be able entirely to govern the discourse and actions of those who are about a child?

No sooner, then, doth education become an art, or profession, than it is almost impossible it should succeed, as the concurrent circumstances necessary to its success are not to be depended on. All that can be done with our utmost solicitude, is to approach as near as possible the end we aim at, attributing it to good fortune if it be attained.

If it be asked, what is this end? it may be answered, that of nature, which has been already proved. For, since the concurrence of three kinds of education is necessary to its perfection, it is by that one, which is entirely independent of us, we must regulate the two others. But perhaps this word, *Nature*, may appear vague and equivocal; let us therefore endeavor to give it a precise and determinate meaning.

Nature, it has been said, is only habit. But to what purpose is this said? Are there not habits, which are contracted only upon compulsion, and which can never suppress the tendency of nature? Such is, for example, the habitual growth of plants restrained from pursuing their vertical direction. Take off the restraint, and it is true, they preserve the inclination they have been compelled to take: but, you will find, the rise of the sap has not on that account changed its primitive direction; if the plant continues to vegetate, its future growth becomes still upwards.

It is the same with the inclinations and dispositions of mankind. While we remain in exactly the same situation in which they were acquired, we may retain even the most unnatural habits; but as soon as circumstances change, the force of habit ceases and that of nature exerts itself. Education itself is certainly nothing but habit: but some people fail to retain what they have been taught, while others do. Whence arises this difference? If it be pretended that by nature is only meant habits conformable to nature, the position itself is unmeaning and absurd. . . .

According to the order of nature, all men being equal, their common vocation is the profession of humanity; and whoever is well educated to discharge the duties of a man, cannot be badly prepared to fill up any of those offices that have a relation to him. It matters little to me, whether my pupil be designed for the army, the bar, or the pulpit. Nature has destined us to the offices of human life, antecedent to the destination of our parents concerning the part we are to act in society. To live is the profession I would teach him. When I have done with him, it is true, he will be neither a lawyer, a soldier, nor a divine. Let him first be a man; he will on occasion as soon become anything else, that a man ought to be, as any other person whatever. Fortune may remove him from one rank to another as she pleases, he will be always sound in his place. . . .

The education of a man commences at his birth: before he can speak, before he can understand, he is already instructed. Experience is the forerunner of precept; the moment he knows the features of his nurse, he may be said to have acquired considerable knowledge. Trace the progress of the most ignorant of mortals, from his birth to the present hour, and you will be astonished at the knowledge he has acquired. If we divide all human science into two parts, the one consisting of that which is common to all men, and the other of what is peculiar to the learned, the latter will appear insignificant and trifling in comparison with the other. But we think nothing of general acquisitions, because they are made insensibly, and even before we arrive at the age of reason; knowledge becomes conspicuous only in its difference on comparison; just as in working algebraic equations, common quantities are struck out and stand for nothing. . . .

The only habit in which a child should be indulged, is that of contracting none; he should not be permitted to exercise one arm more than the other; we should not accustom him to present his right hand oftener than his left, or to make use of one more than the other; he should not be used to eat, sleep, or do anything, at stated hours, or not to be left alone, whether in the day or night. Prepare early for his enjoyment of liberty, and the exercise of his natural abilities, by leaving him in full possession of them unrestrained by artificial habits, and by putting him in a situation to be always master of himself, and to do whatever his resolution prompts him, as soon as he is able to form one.

. . . .

Man, be humane! It is the first, the chief of moral duties, to exercise humanity to everything, of what age or condition soever, that is relative to man. What! is wisdom void of humanity? Have a tender regard for children; indulge them in their diversions, their pleasures, and in everything dictated by their harmless natures.

Who is there among us that has not, at times, looked back with regret on that period of our lives, wherein the countenance was always smiling, and the heart as constantly at ease. Why will you deprive the little innocents of the enjoyment of a season so short and transient? of a blessing so precious, which they cannot abuse? Why will you clog, with bitterness and sorrow, those rapid moments which will return no more for them than for you? Ye fathers, do you know when the stroke of death shall fall on your offspring? Lay not up in store, then, for your own sorrow, by depriving them of the enjoyment of the few moments nature has allotted them: as soon as they become sensible of the pleasures of existence, let them enjoy it, so that whenever it may please God to call them home, they may not die without tasting of life. . . .

He only performs the actions of his own will, who stands in no need of the assistance of others to put his designs in execution: and hence it follows, that the greatest of all blessings is not authority, but liberty. A man truly free, wills only what he is able to perform, and performs what he pleases. This is my fundamental maxim. It need only be applied to a state of infancy, and all the rules of education will naturally flow from it.

A wise man knows and will keep his place; but a child is ignorant of his, and therefore cannot confine himself to it. There are a thousand avenues through which he will be apt to escape: it belongs to those who have the care of his education, therefore, to prevent him; a task, by the way, which is not very easy. He should be neither treated as an irrational animal, nor as a man; but simply as a child: he should be made sensible of his weakness, but not abandoned to suffer by it: he should be taught dependence, and not merely obedience; he should be instructed to ask, and not to command. He is in a state of submission to others, only because of his wants, and because they know better than himself what is good or hurtful for him. No one hath a right, not even the father of a child, to command it to do anything that is useless. . . .

Excessive severity, as well as excessive indulgence, should be equally avoided. If you leave children to suffer, you expose their health, endanger their lives, and make them actually miserable; on the other hand, if you are too anxious to prevent their being sensible of any kind of pain and inconvenience, you only pave their way to feel much greater; you enervate their constitutions, make them tender and effeminate; in a word, you remove them out of their situation as men, into which they must hereafter return in spite of all your solicitude. In order not to expose them to the few evils nature would inflict on them, you provide for them many which they would otherwise never have suffered. . . .

We may reduce almost all the lessons of morality that have, or can be, formed for the use of children, to the following formula.

MASTER. You must not do so.

CHILD. And why must I not do so?

MASTER. Because it is naughty.

CHILD. Naughty! what is that being naughty?

MASTER. Doing what you are forbid.

CHILD. And what harm is there in doing what one is forbid?

MASTER. The harm is, you will be whipped for disobedience.

CHILD. Then I will do it so nobody shall know anything of the matter.

MASTER. Oh, but you will be watched.

CHILD. Ah! but then I will hide myself.

MASTER. Then you will be examined.

CHILD. Then I will tell a fib.

MASTER. But you must not tell fibs.

Child. Why must not I?

Master. Because it is naughty, etc.

Thus we go round the circle; and yet, if we go out of it, the child understands us no longer. Are not these very useful instructions, think you? I could be very curious to know what could be substituted in the place of this fine dialogue. Locke himself would certainly have been embarrassed had he been asked so puzzling a question. To distinguish between good and evil, to perceive the reasons on which our moral obligations are founded, is not the business, as it is not within the capacity, of a child.

Nature requires children to be children before they are men. By endeavoring to pervert this order, we produce forward fruits, that have neither maturity nor taste, and will not fail soon to wither or corrupt. Hence it is we have so many young professors and old children. Childhood hath its manner of seeing, perceiving, and thinking, peculiar to itself; nor is there anything more absurd than our being anxious to substitute our own in its stead. I would as soon require an infant to be five feet high, as a boy to have judgment at ten years of age. In fact, of what use would reason be to him at that age? Reason is given us as a check upon our power; a child has no need of such restraint. . . .

Treat your pupil according to his years. Put him at first into his place, and keep him there so strictly, that he may never afterwards be tempted to go from it. Thus, before he may have learned what prudence is, he will have practiced the most important of all its lessons. Never command him to do anything in the world. Let him not even imagine you pretend to have any authority over him. Let him only be made sensible that he is weak, and you are strong; that, from your situation and his, he lies necessarily at your mercy: let him know, let him learn to perceive this circumstance; let him early feel on his aspiring crest the hard yoke nature hath imposed on man, the heavy yoke of necessity under which every finite being must bow; let him see that necessity in the nature and constitution of things, and not in the caprices of mankind. The bridle of his restraint should be force, and not authority. As to doing those things from which he ought to abstain, forbid him not, but prevent him, without explanation or argument: whatever you indulge him in, grant it to his first request without solicitation or entreaty, and particularly without making any conditions. Grant with pleasure, and refuse with reluctance; but, I say again, let all your denials be irrevocable; let no importunity overcome your resolution; let the *no!* once pronounced, be as a brazen wall, against which when a child hath some few times exhausted his strength without making any impression, he will never attempt to overthrow it again. . . .

It is very strange, that, ever since mankind have taken it into their heads to trouble themselves so much about the education of children, they should never have thought of any other instruments to effect their purpose than those of emulation, jealousy, envy, pride, covetousness, and servile fear; all passions, the most dangerous, the most apt to ferment, and the most proper to corrupt the soul, even before the body is formed. With every premature instruction we instill into the head, we implant a vice in the bottom of the heart. Senseless preceptors, those, who think they work wonders, by making children actually vicious, in order to instruct them in the theory of virtue, and then gravely tell us, Such is man. Yes, such, indeed, is the man of your making.

Almost every method has been tried but one, and that the only one which can succeed, natural liberty duly regulated. No one ought to undertake the education of a child who cannot conduct him at pleasure, merely by the maxims of possibility and impossibility. The sphere of both being equally unknown to infancy, it may be extended or contracted as we please. A child may be equally excited or restrained, by the single plea of necessity, without murmuring: he may be rendered pliant and docile by the force of circumstance only, without ever giving occasion to sow the seeds of vice in his heart: for the passions will never be irritated so long as they must be exerted without effect. Give your pupil no kind of verbal instructions; he should receive none but from experience: inflict on him no kind of punishment, for he knows not what it is to be in fault: require him never to ask pardon, for he cannot offend you. As he is insensible of all moral obligation, he cannot do any thing morally evil, or that is deserving of punishment or reprimand. . . .

Let us lay down as an incontestable maxim, that the first emotions of nature are always right: there is no original perversity in the human heart. I will venture to say, there is not a single vice to be found there, that one could not say how and which way it entered. The only passion natural to man is the love of himself, or self-love taken in an extensive sense. This passion considered in itself, or as relative to us, is good and useful; and, as it has no necessary relation to anyone else, it is in that respect naturally indifferent: it becomes good or evil, therefore, from our application of it, and the several relations we give it. Till the guide of self-love, then, which is reason, appears, a child should do nothing merely because he is seen or heard, nothing from causes merely relative to others, but only those things which nature requires; and then he will never do wrong.

May I venture here to lay down the greatest, most important, and most useful rule of education? It is this: Not to gain time, but to lose it. The generality of readers will be so good as to excuse my paradoxes; there is an absolute necessity for them in making reflections: and, say what you will, I had rather be remarkable for hunting after a paradox, than for being misled by prejudice. The most critical interval of human life is that between the hour of our birth and twelve years of age. This is the time wherein vice and error take root, without our being possessed of any instrument to destroy them, and when the implement is found, they are so deeply grounded, that they are no longer to be eradicated. If children took a leap from their mother's breast, and at once arrived at the age of reason, the methods of education now usually taken with them would be very proper; but according to the progress of nature, they require those which are very different. We should not tamper with the mind, till it has acquired all its faculties: for it is impossible it should perceive the light we hold out to it while it is blind; or that it should pursue, over an immense plain of ideas, that route which reason hath so slightly traced as to be perceptible only to the sharpest sight.

The first part of education, therefore, ought to be purely negative. It consists neither in teaching virtue nor truth; but in guarding the heart from vice, and the mind from error. If you could be content to do nothing yourself, and could prevent anything being done by others; if you could bring up your pupil healthy and robust to the age of twelve years, without his being able to distinguish his right hand from his left, the eyes of his understanding would be open to reason at your first lesson; void both of habit and prejudice, his passions would not operate against your endeavors, and he would become, under proper instructions, the wisest of men. It is thus, by attempting nothing in the beginning, you might produce a prodigy of education.

Take the road directly opposite to that which is in use, and you will almost always do right. As we think it not enough children should be children, but it is expected they should be masters of arts; so fathers and preceptors think they can never have too many checks, corrections, reprimands, menaces, promises, instructions, fair speeches, and fine arguments. You will act wiser than all this, by being reasonable yourself, and never arguing with your child, particularly in striving to reconcile him to what he dislikes; for to use him to reason only upon disagreeable subjects, is the way to disgust him, and bring argument early into discredit with a mind incapable of understanding it. Exercise his corporeal organs, senses, and faculties, as much as you please; but keep his intellectual ones inactive as long as possible. Be cautious of all the sentiments he acquires previous to the judgment which should enable him to scrutinize them. Prevent or restrain all foreign impressions; and, in order to hinder the rise of evil, be not in too great a hurry to instill good; for it is only such when the mind is enlightened by reason. Look upon every delay as an advantage; it is gaining a great deal, to advance without losing anything: let the infancy of children therefore have time to ripen. In short, whatever instruction is necessary for them, take care not to give it them today, if it may be deferred without danger till tomorrow. . . .

The apparent facility with which children seem to learn, operates greatly to their prejudice, and, though we do not observe it, is a plain proof they learn nothing. The delicate texture of their brain reflects, like a mirror, every object presented to them; but nothing penetrates the substance, or remains behind. A child retains the words, but the ideas accompanying them are reflected back again; those who hear him repeat, may understand what he means; but he himself knows nothing of the matter.

Although the memory and judgment are two faculties essentially different; yet the one cannot unfold itself without the other. Before a child arrives at years of understanding, he entertains not the ideas, but simply the images, of things; the difference between which consists in that such images are only the direct paintings of perceptible objects, and ideas are the notions of such objects determined by their respective relations to each other. A single image may subsist in the mind that is sensible of it; but every idea necessarily supposes the concomitance of others. To simple imagination, or the mere formation of images, nothing more is necessary than to have seen objects; but to conceive anything about their existence, or to form ideas of them, it is required that we should be able to compare them. Our sensations are merely passive, whereas our perceptions, or the ideas formed in consequence of those sensations, rise from an active principle capable of judging of them. This will be hereafter demonstrated.

I say, therefore, that children, being incapable of forming a judgment of things, have no real memory. They retain, it is true, sounds, figures, and sensations; but seldom ideas, and still more seldom the connections between them. In objecting to what I advance, that children may be taught geometrical elements, this instance may be supposed to make against me; on the contrary, however, it makes for me. It may be shown, that, so far are they from being capable of reasoning of themselves, they are incapable of retaining the arguments of others; for, trace these little geometricians in the solving any problem, and you will see they retain only the exact impression of the figure, and the terms of the demonstration. On the least unforeseen objection, they are quite at a loss; vary the figure, and they are totally disconcerted; all their knowledge lies clearly in their sensations, and has not penetrated into the understanding. Their memory itself, however retentive, is as little perfect as their other faculties; as they are almost always obliged to learn, when they are grown up, the meaning of the words they got by rote in their childhood.

I am far, however, from thinking that children are capable of no kind of reasoning. On the contrary, I observe that they reason very well as to things they are acquainted with, and which regard their present and obvious interest. But it is in the depth of their knowledge we deceive ourselves, in attributing to them what they have not, and setting them to reason about things they cannot comprehend. We are still further deceived, in wanting to render them attentive to such considerations as cannot in any degree affect them, such as their future interest, their happiness when they come to be men, the esteem in which they will be held when grown up, and so forth; all which pleas, when made use of to beings void of all foresight, absolutely signify nothing, nor can serve to any good purpose. Now, all the studies imposed on these poor unfortunates, tend to such objects as are entirely foreign to their minds. Judge then of the attention they are like to bestow on them. . . .

It has been made a matter of great importance, to find out the best method of teaching children to read; to this end cards and other implements have been invented, so various and numerous, that they made the nursery resemble the workshop of a printer. Mr. Locke would have a child taught to read by means of letters carved on dice. Is not this an excellent invention! A more certain method than any of these, and that which is nevertheless always neglected, is to excite in children a desire to learn. Give a child this desire, and do as you will with your cards and dice; any method will then be sufficient.

The grand motive, indeed the only one that is certain and effectual, is present interest. Émile sometimes receives written invitations from his father, mother, and other friends, to dinner, to go on a party of pleasure, or to see some public entertainment. These invitations are short, plain, precise, and well written. When received, it is necessary for him to find somebody to read them to him: such a person is not always at hand, or complaisant enough to comply with his request. Thus the opportunity is lost: the billet, indeed, is read to him afterwards, but then it is too late to obey the summons. How ardently must he wish on such an occasion to be able to read himself! He receives others, equally short and interesting: he sets immediately about deciphering them; sometimes receiving assistance, and at others denied it. By stint of duty, he at length hammers out that he is invited to go tomorrow to eat cream; but where or with whom he cannot discover. How many efforts will he not make to find out the rest: Émile will learn to read by such means as these, without standing in need of horn books, cards, or dice. I might here speak of teaching him to write; but I am ashamed of descending to such trifling objects in a treatise on education. . . .

I am teaching the young preceptor a very difficult art; that of instructing without precepts, and of doing everything in the way of education by doing nothing. This art, I must confess, is not adapted to your age or views; it is not calculated to make an immediate display of your talents, nor to recommend you to the generality of fathers: it is the only one, however, in which you can succeed in the education of your pupil; you will never accomplish your design of forming sensible men, unless you begin by making playful children. This was the method of education among the Spartans: instead of tying down their sons to their books, they were taught to look out sharp for their dinner. Were they the greater blockheads for this when they grew up? The force and keenness of their repartees are, on the contrary, well known. Formed for universal conquest, they triumphed over their enemies in every kind of warfare; the talkative Athenians being equally afraid both of their tongues and their swords.

. . . .

The earth is the island on which mankind are cast, and the most striking object of their observation is the sun. As soon as our ideas begin to extend beyond ourselves, our attention will therefore naturally be engrossed between two such interesting subjects. Hence the philosophy of almost every savage nation is confined solely to the imaginary divisions of the earth, and the divinity of the sun. "What an excursion!" cries the reader. "We were but just now employed about objects that immediately surround us, and we are now traversing the globe, and soaring to the distant extremities of the universe." This excursion, however, is the simple effect of the progress of our faculties, and the bent of our understanding. During our infant state of weakness and incapacity, all our thoughts, influenced by self-preservation, are confined within ourselves. On the contrary, in a more advanced age, as our abilities increase, the desire of improving our existence carries us out of ourselves, and our ideas extend to their utmost limits. As the intellectual world, however, is as yet unknown to us, our thoughts cannot extend farther than we can see; but our comprehension dilates itself with the bounds of space.

Let us convert our sensations into ideas; but let us not fly at once from sensible to intellectual objects. It is by a due and rational attention to the former we can only attain the latter. In the first operations of the understanding, let our senses then always be our guide, the world our only book, and facts our sole preceptors. Children, when taught to read, learn that only; they never think; they gain no information; all their learning consists in words.

Direct the attention of your pupil to the phenomena of nature, and you will soon awaken his curiosity; but to keep that curiosity alive, you must be in no haste to satisfy it. Put questions to him adapted to his capacity, and leave him to resolve them. Let him take nothing on trust from his preceptor, but on his own comprehension and conviction: he should not learn, but invent the sciences. If ever you substitute authority in the place of argument, he will reason no longer; he will be ever afterwards bandied like a shuttlecock between the opinions of others.

. . . Talk not to children in a language they do not comprehend; make use of no pompous descriptions, no flowers of speech, no tropes and figures, no poetry; taste and sentiment are at present quite out of the question: simplicity, gravity, and precision are all that are yet required; the time will come but too soon when we must assume a different style.

A pupil educated agreeable to these maxims, and accustomed to receive no assistance till he has discovered his own inabilities, will examine every new object with a long and silent attention. He will be thoughtful without asking questions. Content yourself, therefore, with presenting proper objects opportunely to his notice, and when you see they have sufficiently excited his curiosity, drop some leading laconic questions, which may put him in the way of discovering the truth. . . .

When he asks a question, be your answer always calculated rather to keep alive than satisfy his curiosity; especially when you observe he has a mind to trifle rather than be instructed. You ought to pay less regard to the terms of interrogation, than to his motives for enquiry. This conduct becomes of the greatest importance when a child begins to reason.

The sciences are connected together by a series of propositions, all dependent on some general and common principles, which are gradually displayed. The philosophers make use of these; with us they are as yet out of the question. There is another chain of reasoning, of a different construction, by which every particular object is connected to some other, and points out that which succeeds it. This order of succession, which, from our natural curiosity, keeps alive our attention, is generally made use of by grown persons, and is peculiarly adapted to children. . . .

We acquire, without doubt, notions more clear and certain, of things we thus learn of ourselves, than of those we are taught by others. Another advantage also resulting from this method is, that we do not accustom ourselves to a servile submission to the authority of others; but, by exercising our reason, grow every day more ingenious in the discovery of the relations of things, in connecting our ideas, and in the contrivance of machines; whereas, by adopting those which are put into our hands, our invention grows dull and indifferent, as the man who never dresses himself, but is served in everything by his servants, and drawn about everywhere by his horses, loses by degrees the activity and use of his limbs. Boileau boasted that he had taught Racine to rhyme with much difficulty: among the many admirable methods taken to abridge the study of the sciences, we are in great want of one to make us learn them with difficulty.

The most obvious advantage of these slow and laborious researches, is to preserve, in the cultivation of speculative studies, the activity of the body; to preserve the suppleness of the limbs, and to be always busied in some manual operation, or employment, of use to mankind. The diversity of instruments, invented to direct us in our experiments and make up for the deficiency of our organs of sense, makes us neglect the exercise of the latter. A theodolite dispenses with our estimating the extent of angles; the eye, which is capable of measuring distances with great exactness, gives up the task to the chain; the steelyard excuses me from judging of the weight of anything by poising it in my hand. Thus the more ingenious and accurate our instruments, the more unsusceptible and inexpert become our organs: by assembling a heap of machinery about us, we find afterwards none in ourselves.

But when we set about the construction of these machines ourselves, and employ therein that sagacity and address which are required to do without them, we lose nothing: on the contrary, we gain everything; and, by adding the knowledge of art to nature, become more ingenious without being less dexterous. If, instead of keeping a boy poring over books, I employ him in a workshop, his hands will be busied to the improvement of his understanding; he will become a philosopher while he thinks himself only an artisan. In short, this practice hath other uses which I shall speak of hereafter, and show in what manner these philosophical amusements lead to the exercise of the proper functions of a man.

I have already observed, that the mere speculative part of science is by no means adapted to children, even when they approach adolescence; it is proper, nevertheless, though you do not enter with them too profoundly into the depth of physical theory, to connect their experiments by some chain of deduction, that they may arrange them in some order in their minds, for the sake of remembering them: for it is very difficult to retain separate and independent facts and conclusions long in the memory, without some leading clue for occasional recollection.

In your researches into the laws of nature, begin always with the most common and obvious phenomena; accustoming your pupil to look upon them always as mere facts. . . .

As soon as we are so far advanced as to give our pupil an idea of the word *useful*, we have attained a considerable influence over his future conduct; this term being very striking, provided the sense annexed to it be adapted to his years, and he see clearly its relation to his present welfare. Ordinary children are not affected by this term, because no care has been taken to affix to it an idea conformable to their understanding, and because others taking upon them to provide for them what is useful, they have no need to think of it themselves, and therefore remain ignorant of the meaning of utility.

What is the use of that? shall, for the future, be the determinate question between my pupil and me, on all occasions. On my part, I shall infallibly make use of it in answer to all his interrogatories, which may serve as a check to that multiplicity of silly, troublesome questions, with which children are incessantly teasing those about them, more for the sake of indulging themselves in a kind of imperiousness, than out of a desire of information. The child who is taught, as the most important lesson, to know nothing but what is useful to him, will interrogate with the views of a Socrates: he will not put a question, without having an answer ready to that which he knows will be put to him before his own is resolved. . . .

Never point out anything to a child which is beyond his views. While he is a stranger to the relations and duties of humanity, as you cannot raise his comprehension to the state of manhood, you should bring down the state of manhood to a level with his capacity. In projecting what may be useful to him hereafter, speak to him directly only of what is apparently useful to him at present. Beware, also, in general, of making comparisons between your pupil and other children; let him have no rival, no competitor, not even in his corporeal exercises, as soon as he begins to reason. I had much rather he should not learn at all whatever must be taught him by means of vanity or jealousy. I would content myself, in this respect, with remarking his annual progress, and comparing his situation and exploits in the present year with those of the past. I would say to him, You are grown so much since such a time; here is the ditch you leaped, the weight you lifted, the distance you threw a stone, so far you ran without fetching breath; let us see what you can do more at present. Thus would I excite him to emulation, without making him jealous or envious of a rival: he would be desirous indeed to excel himself, and so he ought to be; I see no inconvenience in this kind of emulation.

I hate books; they only teach people to talk about what they do not understand. It is said that Hermes engraved the elements of the sciences on columns, to secure his discoveries from being lost in the time of a general deluge. Had he imprinted them on the minds of men, they had been better preserved by tradition. The organs of the memory, duly prepared, are the monuments on which human science would be most indelibly engraven. . . .

The practice of simple manual arts, to the exercise of which the abilities of the individual are equal, leads to the invention of the arts of industry, the exercise of which requires the concurrence of many. The former may be practiced by hermits and savages; but the latter can be exercised only in a state of society, and render that state necessary. While man is subject only to the calls of physical necessity, he is capable of satisfying them himself; but, by the introduction of superfluous wants, the joint concern and distribution of labor become indispensable: for though a man by his own labor, when alone, procures only subsistence for an individual; yet a hundred men working in concert, will easily procure, in the same time, subsistence for double the number. As soon, therefore, as one part of mankind take upon themselves to live idle, it becomes necessary that the concurrent labor of numbers should supply the place of those who live without work.

Your greatest care should be to keep from your pupil the notions of those social relations which he is not in a capacity to comprehend; but when the connection of his ideas obliges you to speak of the mutual dependence of mankind, instead of presenting him at first the moral side of the question, divert his attention as much as possible to industry and the mechanical arts, which render men useful to one another. In going about with him to the workshops of various artisans, never let him see anything performed without lending a hand to the work, nor come out of the shop without perfectly understanding the reason of what he observes there. To this end you should work yourself, and in everything set him an example. To make him a master, be you in everything the apprentice; and reflect that he will learn more by one hour of manual labor, than he will retain from a whole day's verbal instructions.

The different arts are entitled to various proportions of public esteem, and that in an inverse ratio to their real use. This esteem is directly as their inutility, and so it politically ought to be. The most useful arts are those which are the worst paid for, or least rewarded; because the number of workmen is proportioned to the wants of the whole society, and the labor the poor must purchase must necessarily be at a low price. On the contrary, those important artisans, who, by way of distinction, are termed artists, and are employed only in the service of the rich and idle, set an arbitrary price on their workmanship; and as the excellence of their baubles is mere matter of opinion, their high price constitutes great part of their merit, and they are esteemed in proportion to what they cost. The value thus set upon them is not on account of any use they are of to the rich, but because they are too costly to be purchased by the poor.

What will become of your pupils, if you permit them to adopt this ridiculous prejudice, if you encourage it yourself, or see them, for example, enter with more respect the shop of a jeweler than that of a locksmith? What a judgment will they form of the real merit of the arts, and the intrinsic value of things, when they see whim and caprice universally opposed to real utility, and find the more a thing costs, the less it is worth? If ever such ideas as these take root in their minds, you as well give up at once the remaining part of their education; they will, in spite of all you can do, be educated like the rest of the world, and you will have taken, for fourteen years past, all your trouble for nothing. . . .

My child learn a trade! make my son a mechanic! consider, sir, what you advise.—I do, madam, I consider this matter better than you, who would reduce your child to the necessity of being a lord, a marquis, or a prince, or perhaps one day or other to be less than nothing. I am desirous of investing him with a title that cannot be taken from him, that will in all times and places command respect; and, I can tell you, whatever you may think of it, he will have fewer equals in this rank than in that he may derive from you.

The letter destroys, and the spirit maketh alive. I would not have him learn a trade, merely for the sake of knowing how to exercise it, but that he may overcome the prejudices usually conceived against it. You will never be reduced, you say, to work for your bread. So much the worse for you; I say, so much the worse. But, no matter; if you labor not through necessity, do it for reputation. Stoop to the situation of an artisan, that you may raise yourself above your own. To make fortune subservient to your will, you must begin by rendering yourself independent. To triumph in the opinion of the world, you must begin by despising that opinion.

Remember, I do not advise you to acquire a talent, but a trade; a mechanical art, in the exercise of which the hands are more employed than the head; an art by which you will never get a fortune, but may be enabled to live without one. . . .

All things duly considered, the trade I should like best my pupil should have a taste for, is that of a joiner. This is neat, useful, and may be carried on within doors: it is sufficiently laborious to keep the body in exercise, and requires both diligence and dexterity: at the same time, taste and elegance are not excluded from being displayed on the form and contrivance of the work.

If it should so happen, indeed, that your pupil has a natural turn for the speculative sciences, I should not blame you for teaching him a mechanical art conformable to his inclinations; let him learn, for example, to design and construct mathematical instruments, quadrants, telescopes, and the like.

When Émile learns a trade, I also will learn it with him; for I am convinced he will never learn, as should be, what we do not learn together. We will, therefore, both serve an apprenticeship; not affecting to be treated as gentlemen, but as real apprentices who are not trifling with a profession: nay, why should we not be so in reality? Czar Peter worked as a common ship carpenter in the yard, and served as a drummer in his own troops: do you think that prince was not your equal, at least either in birth or merit? The reader will observe, I do not ask Émile this question, but put it to everyone, of whatever rank he may happen to be.

If I have hitherto made myself understood, the reader will perceive, that, while I have accustomed my pupil to corporeal exercise and manual labor, I have given him insensibly a taste for reflection and meditation; in order to counterbalance that indolence which would be the natural result of his indifference for the opinions of mankind and the tranquility of his passions, it is necessary that he work like a peasant, and think like a philosopher, lest he become as idle as a savage. The great secret of education is, to make the exercises of the body and the mind serve as a relaxation to each other.

An Experiment in Education

Johann Heinrich Pestalozzi

(1746–1827)

Froebel, the great nineteenth-century German educator, described his mentor Pestalozzi as unable to give a coherent explanation of his own educational program. "Go and see for yourself," Pestalozzi would urge questioners, "it works splendidly."

This challenge was made with confidence, for Pestalozzi was certainly one of the greatest teachers in the history of pedagogy. He admitted, however, that he had been incapable of philosophic thought since the age of twenty. The theoreticians whom he inspired—Froebel and Herbart—were left with the task of translating Pestalozzi's intuitive practice into coherent theory.

Pestalozzi's contribution was largely to *do* what Rousseau and other educational reformers had merely talked about. He took literally Quintilian's injunction that the teacher should become a second father to his students, and insisted that those who teach must accept responsibility not only for what the pupils learn, but for what they become. This responsibility entailed the substitution of "continual benevolent supervision" for mere instructing. Pestalozzi's ideal school was to be based on the insight that "the essential principle of Education is not teaching but love."

This view of Pestalozzi's brings up the crucial question of the individual teacher's role in the educational process. If love is the essence of education, then no pedagogical method or system will be of real help. All will depend on the intuitive wisdom of individual teachers. This is certainly what Pestalozzi depended on; this is why he felt he had no method to impart. But are there enough "natural" teachers to provide mass education based on this principle?

Is it even useful to demand that all teachers strive for such an exalted ideal?

Pestalozzi developed more practical principles, of course. He based his method on an extraordinary understanding of the child's mind and its growth. Moreover, he worked out an orderly sequence of sensory experiences and spontaneous activities designed to strengthen the powers of the child's mind rather than fill it with facts.

Because it was the example of his actual teaching that had such widespread impact on education, it is appropriate to select from Pestalozzi's writings a description of an actual experimental school. In December, 1798, Pestalozzi was asked to take charge of about eighty Catholic children left destitute after French troops had destroyed their Swiss village. The difficulties he faced, the triumphs and failures he experienced, are typical of every project which he undertook. But this is more than a dramatic picture of the great teacher in action: Pestalozzi's classroom at Stanz contained the seeds of the modern public elementary school.

"All for others, nothing for himself" was the accurate epitaph which Pestalozzi's countrymen gave him. Forced to abandon his career as a minister because of radical political activities, he became a commercial farmer near Zurich. This enterprise failed in 1775, costing Pestalozzi everything but his home. His response was to turn the house into an orphanage and school. This project faltered after several years, but gave Pestalozzi the raw material for his first important book. *Leonard and Gertrude* portrayed how, amidst the mean and anarchic village life of contemporary Switzerland, a good woman educates her children in handicrafts and in the basic subjects.

In 1798 Pestalozzi took charge at Stanz, at the age of 52. But the experimental schools to which visitors came from all over the world were his later ones at Burgdorf, from 1800 to 1804, and at Yverdun from 1805 to 1825. This last, his most ambitious enterprise, collapsed due not to failures with the children, but because of dissension and rivalry among the staff. He retired to the farmhouse where he had begun, and died there in 1827. The following account of his experiment at Stanz in 1798, written to his friend Gessner, is from

John Russell's translation of De Guimp's *Histoire de Pestalozzi,* the first biography of the man.

My friend, once more I awake from a dream; once more I see my work destroyed, and my failing strength wasted.

But, however weak and unfortunate my attempt, a friend of humanity will not grudge a few moments to consider the reasons which convince me that some day a more fortunate posterity will certainly take up the thread of my hopes at the place where it is now broken. . . .

I once more made known, as well as I could, my old wishes for the education of the people. In particular, I laid my whole scheme before Legrand (then one of the Directors), who not only took a warm interest in it, but agreed with me that the Republic stood in urgent need of a reform of public education. He also agreed with me that much might be done for the regeneration of the people by giving a certain number of the poorest children an education which should be complete, but which, far from lifting them out of their proper sphere, would but attach them the more strongly to it.

I limited my desires to this one point, Legrand helping me in every possible way. He even thought my views so important that he once said to me: "I shall not willingly give up my present post till you have begun your work. . . ."

It was my intention to try to find near Zurich or in Aargau a place where I should be able to join industry and agriculture to the other means of instruction, and so give my establishment all the development necessary to its complete success. But the Unterwalden disaster (September, 1798) left me no further choice in the matter. The Government felt the urgent need of sending help to this unfortunate district, and begged me for this once to make an attempt to put my plans into execution in a place where almost everything that could have made it a success was wanting.

I went there gladly. I felt that the innocence of the people would make up for what was wanting, and that their distress would, at any rate, make them grateful.

My eagerness to realize at last the great dream of my life would have led me to work on the very highest peaks of the Alps, and, so to speak, without fire or water.

For a house, the Government made over to me the new part of

the Ursuline convent at Stanz, but when I arrived it was still uncompleted, and not in any way fitted to receive a large number of children. Before anything else could be done, then, the house itself had to be got ready. The Government gave the necessary orders, and Rengger pushed on the work with much zeal and useful activity. I was never indeed allowed to want for money.

In spite, however, of the admirable support I received, all this preparation took time, and time was precisely what we could least afford, since it was of the highest importance that a number of children, whom the war had left homeless and destitute, should be received at once.

I was still without everything but money when the children crowded in; neither kitchen, rooms, nor beds were ready to receive them. At first this was a source of inconceivable confusion. For the first few weeks I was shut up in a very small room; the weather was bad, and the alterations, which made a great dust and filled the corridors with rubbish, rendered the air very unhealthy.

The want of beds compelled me at first to send some of the poor children home at night; these children generally came back the next day covered with vermin. Most of them on their arrival were very degenerated specimens of humanity. Many of them had a sort of chronic skin disease, which almost prevented their walking, or sores on their heads, or rags full of vermin; many were almost skeletons, with haggard, careworn faces, and shrinking looks; some brazen, accustomed to begging, hypocrisy, and all sorts of deceit; others broken by misfortune, patient, suspicious, timid, and entirely devoid of affection. There were also some spoilt children amongst them who had known the sweets of comfort, and were therefore full of pretensions. These kept to themselves, affected to despise the little beggars their comrades and to suffer from this equality, and seemed to find it impossible to adapt themselves to the ways of the house, which differed too much from their old habits. But what was common to them all was a persistent idleness, resulting from their want of physical and mental activity. Out of every ten children there was hardly one who knew his A B C; as for any other knowledge, it was, of course, out of the question.

The entire absence of school learning was what troubled me least, for I trusted in the natural powers that God bestows on even the poorest and most neglected children. I had observed for a long time that behind their coarseness, shyness, and apparent incapacity are hidden the finest faculties, the most precious powers; and now, even amongst these poor creatures by whom I was surrounded at Stanz, marked natural abilities soon began to show themselves. I knew how useful the common needs of life are in teaching men the relations of things, in bringing out their natural intelligence, in forming their judgment, and in arousing faculties which, buried, as it were, beneath the coarser elements of their nature, cannot become active and useful till they are set free. It was my object then to set free these faculties, and bring them to bear on the pure and simple circumstances of domestic life, for I was convinced this was all that was wanting, and these natural faculties would show themselves capable of raising the hearts and minds of my pupils to all that I could desire.

I saw then how my wishes might be carried out; and I was persuaded that my affection would change the state of my children just as quickly as the spring sun would awake to new life the earth that winter had benumbed. I was not deceiving myself: before the spring sun melted the snow of our mountains my children were hardly to be recognized.

But I must not anticipate. Just as in the evening I often mark the quick growth of the gourd by the side of the house, so I want you to mark the growth of my plant; and, my friend, I will not hide from you the worm which sometimes fastens on the leaves, sometimes even on the heart.

I opened the establishment with no other helper but a woman servant. I had not only to teach the children, but to look after their physical needs. I preferred being alone, and, unfortunately, it was the only way to reach my end. No one in the world would have cared to enter into my views for the education of children, and at that time I knew scarcely anyone even capable of it.

In proportion as the men whom I might have called to my aid were highly educated just so far they failed to understand me, and were incapable of confining themselves even in theory to the simple starting points which I sought to come back to. All their views about the organization and requirements of the enterprise differed entirely from mine. What they specially objected to was the notion that the enterprise might be carried out without the aid of any artificial means, and simply by the influence of nature in the environment of the children, and by the activity aroused in them by the needs of their daily life.

And yet it was precisely upon this idea that I based all my hope of success; it was, as it were, a basis for innumerable other points of view.

Experienced teachers, then, could not help me; still less boorish, ignorant men. I had nothing to put into the hands of assistants to guide them, nor any results or apparatus by which I could make my ideas clearer to them. Thus, whether I would or no, I had first to make my experiment alone, and collect facts to illustrate the essential features of my system before I could venture to look for outside help. Indeed in my then position, nobody could help me. I knew that I must help myself and shaped my plans accordingly.

I wanted to prove by my experiment that if public education is to have any real value for humanity, it must imitate the means which make the merit of domestic education; for it is my opinion that if school teaching does not take into consideration the circumstances of family life, and everything else that bears on a man's general education, it can only lead to an artificial and methodical dwarfing of humanity.

In any good education, the mother must be able to judge daily, nay hourly, from the child's eyes, lips, and face, of the slightest change in his soul. The power of the educator, too, must be that of a father, quickened by the general circumstances of domestic life.

Such was the foundation upon which I built. I determined that there should not be a minute in the day when my children should not be aware from my face and my lips that my heart was theirs, that their happiness was my happiness, and their pleasures my pleasures.

Man readily accepts what is good, and the child readily listens to it; but it is not for you that he wants it, master and educator, but for himself. The good to which you would lead him must not depend on your capricious humor or passion; it must be a good which is good in itself and by the nature of things, and which the child can recognize as good. He must feel the necessity of your will in things which concern his comfort before he can be expected to obey it.

Whatever he does gladly, whatever gains him credit, whatever tends to accomplish his great hopes, whatever awakens his powers and enables him truly to say *I can,* all this he *wills.*

But this will is not aroused by words; it is aroused only by a kind of complete culture which gives feelings and powers.

Words do not give the thing itself, but only an expression, a clear picture, of the thing which we already have in our minds.

Before all things I was bound to gain the confidence and the love of the children. I was sure that if I succeeded in this all the rest would come of itself. Friend, only think how I was placed, and how great were the prejudices of the people and of the children themselves, and you will comprehend what difficulties I had to overcome. . . .

Think, my friend, of this temper of the people, of my weakness, of my poor appearance, of the ill will to which I was almost publicly exposed, and then judge how much I had to endure for the sake of carrying on my work.

And yet, however painful this want of help and support was to me, it was favorable to the success of my undertaking, for it compelled me to be always everything for my children. I was alone with them from morning till night. It was from me that they received all that could do them good, soul and body. All needful help, consolation, and instruction they received direct from me. Their hands were in mine, my eyes were fixed on theirs.

We wept and smiled together. They forgot the world and Stanz; they only knew that they were with me and I with them. We shared our food and drink. I had about me neither family, friends, nor servants; nothing but them. I was with them in sickness and in health and when they slept. I was the last to go to bed and the first to get up. In the bedroom I prayed with them and, at their own request, taught them till they fell asleep. Their clothes and bodies were intolerably filthy, but I looked after both myself and was thus constantly exposed to the risk of contagion.

This is how it was that these children gradually became so attached to me, some indeed so deeply that they contradicted their parents and friends when they heard evil things said about me. They felt that I was being treated unfairly and loved me, I think, the more for it. But of what avail is it for the young nestlings to love their mother when the bird of prey that is bent on destroying them is constantly hovering near?

However, the first results of these principles and of this line of action were not always satisfactory, nor, indeed, could they be so. The children did not always understand my love. Accustomed to idleness, unbounded liberty, and the fortuitous and lawless pleasures of an almost wild life, they had come to the convent in the expectation of being well fed, and of having nothing to do. Some of them soon discovered that they had been there long enough, and wanted to go away again; they talked of the school fever that attacks children when they are kept employed all day long. This dissatisfaction, which showed itself during the first months, resulted principally from the fact that many of them were ill, the consequence either of the sudden change of diet and habits, or of the severity of the weather and the dampness of the building in which we lived. We all coughed a great deal, and several children were seized with a peculiar sort of fever. This fever, which always began with sickness, was very general in the district. Cases of sickness, however, not followed by fever, were not at all rare, and were an almost natural consequence of the change of food. Many people attributed the fever to bad food, but the facts soon showed them to be wrong, for not a single child succumbed.

On the return of spring it was evident to everybody that the children were all doing well, growing rapidly, and gaining color. Certain magistrates and ecclesiastics, who saw them some time afterwards, stated that they had improved almost beyond recognition. . . .

Months passed before I had the satisfaction of having my hand grasped by a single grateful parent. But the children were won over much sooner. They even wept sometimes when their parents met me or left me without a word of salutation. Many of them were perfectly happy, and used to say to their mothers: "I am better here than at home." At home, indeed, as they readily told me when we talked alone, they had been ill-used and beaten and had often had neither bread to eat nor bed to lie down upon. And yet these same children would sometimes go off with their mothers the very next morning.

A good many others, however, soon saw that by staying with me they might both learn something and become something, and these never failed in their zeal and attachment. Before very long their conduct was imitated by others who had not altogether the same feelings.

Those who ran away were the worst in character and the least capable. But they were not incited to go till they were free of their vermin and their rags. Several were sent to me with no other purpose than that of being taken away again as soon as they were clean and well clothed.

But after a time their better judgment overcame the defiant hostility with which they arrived. In 1799 I had nearly eighty children. Most of them were bright and intelligent, some even remarkably so.

For most of them study was something entirely new. As soon as they found that they could learn, their zeal was indefatigable, and in a few weeks children who had never before opened a book, and could hardly repeat a *Pater Noster* or an *Ave,* would study the whole day long with the keenest interest. Even after supper, when I used to say to them, "Children, will you go to bed, or learn something?" they would generally answer, especially in the first month or two, "Learn something." It is true that afterwards, when they had to get up very early, it was not quite the same.

But this first eagerness did much towards starting the establishment on the right lines and making the studies the success they ultimately were, a success indeed which far surpassed my expectations. And yet great beyond expression were my difficulties. I did not as yet find it possible to organize the studies properly.

Neither my trust nor my zeal had been able to overcome either the intractability of individuals or the want of coherence in the whole experiment. The general order of the establishment, I felt, must be based upon order of a higher character. As this higher order did not yet exist, I had to attempt to create it; for without this foundation I could not hope to organize properly either the teaching or the general management of the place, nor should I have wished to do so. I wanted everything to result not from a preconceived plan, but from my relations with the children. The high principles and educating forces I was seeking, I looked for from the harmonious common life of my children, from their common attention, activity, and needs. It was not, then, from any external organization that I looked for the regeneration of which they stood so much in need. If I had employed constraint, regulations, and lectures, I should, instead of winning and ennobling my children's hearts, have repelled them and made them bitter, and thus been farther than ever from my aim. First of all, I had to arouse in them pure, moral, and noble feelings, so that afterwards in external things I might be sure of their ready attention, activity, and obedience. I had, in short, to follow the high precept of Jesus Christ, "Cleanse first that which is within, that the outside may be clean also"; and if ever the truth of this precept was made manifest, it was made manifest then.

My one aim was to make their new life in common, and their new powers, awaken a feeling of brotherhood amongst the children, and make them affectionate, just, and considerate.

I was successful in gaining my aims. Amongst these seventy wild beggar children there soon existed such peace, friendship, and cordial relations as are rare even between actual brothers and sisters.

The principle to which I endeavored to conform all my conduct was as follows: Endeavor, first, to broaden your children's sympathies and, by satisfying their daily needs, to bring love and kindness into such unceasing contact with their impressions and their activity, that these sentiments may be engrafted in their hearts; then try to give them such judgment and tact as will enable them to make a wise, sure, and abundant use of these virtues in the circle which surrounds them. In the last place, do not hesitate to touch on the difficult questions of good and evil, and the words connected with them. And you must do this especially in connection with the ordinary events of every day, upon which your whole teaching in these matters must be founded, so that the children may be reminded of their own feelings and supplied, as it were, with solid facts upon which to base their conception of the beauty and justice of the moral life. Even though you should have to spend whole nights in trying to express in two words what others say in twenty, never regret the loss of sleep.

I gave my children very few explanations; I taught them neither morality nor religion. But sometimes, when they were perfectly quiet, I used to say to them, "Do you not think that you are better and more reasonable when you are like this than when you are making a noise?" When they clung round my neck and called me their father, I used to say, "My children, would it be right to deceive your father? After kissing me like this, would you like to do anything behind my back to vex me?" When our talk turned on the misery of the country, and they were feeling glad at the thought of their own happier lot, I would say, "How good God is to have given man a compassionate heart!" . . . They perfectly understood that all they did was but a preparation for their future activity, and they looked forward to happiness as the certain result of their perseverance. That is why steady application soon became easy to them, its object being in perfect accordance with their wishes and their hopes. Virtue, my friend, is developed by this agreement, just as the young plant thrives when the soil suits its nature, and supplies the needs of its tender shoots.

I witnessed the growth of an inward strength in my children, which, in its general development, far surpassed my expectations, and in its particular manifestations not only often surprised me, but touched me deeply.

When the neighboring town of Altdorf was burnt down, I gathered the children round me, and said, "Altdorf has been burnt down; perhaps, at this very moment, there are a hundred children there without home, food, or clothes; will you not ask our good Government to let twenty of them come and live with us?" I still seem to see the emotion with which they answered, "Oh, yes, yes!" "But, my children," I said, "think well of what you are asking! Even now we have scarcely money enough, and it is not at all certain that if these poor children came to us, the Government would give us any more than they do at present, so that you might have to work harder, and share your clothes with these children, and sometimes perhaps go without food. Do not say, then, that you would like them to come unless you are quite prepared for all these consequences." After having spoken to them in this way as seriously as I could, I made them repeat all I had said, to be quite sure that they had thoroughly understood what the consequences of their request would be. But they were not in the least shaken in their decision, and all repeated, "Yes, yes, we are quite ready to work harder, eat less, and share our clothes, for we want them to come."

Some refugees from the Grisons having given me a few crowns for my poor children, I at once called them and said, "These men are obliged to leave their country; they hardly know where they will find a home tomorrow, yet, in spite of their trouble, they have given me this for you. Come and thank them." And the emotion of the children brought tears to the eyes of the refugees.

It was in this way that I strove to awaken the feeling of each virtue before talking about it, for I thought it unwise to talk to children on subjects which would compel them to speak without thoroughly understanding what they were saying.

I followed up this awakening of the sentiments by exercises intended to teach the children self-control, so that all that was good in them might be applied to the practical questions of everyday life.

It will easily be understood that, in this respect, it was not possible to organize any system of discipline for the establishment; that could only come slowly, as the general work developed.

Silence, as an aid to application, is perhaps the great secret of such an institution. I found it very useful to insist on silence when I was teaching, and also to pay particular attention to the attitude of my children. I succeeded so well that the moment I asked for silence, I could teach in quite a low voice. The children repeated my words all together; and as there was no other sound, I was able to detect the slightest mistakes of pronunciation. It is true that this was not always so. Sometimes, whilst they repeated sentences after me, I would ask them as if in fun to keep their eyes fixed on their middle fingers. It is hardly credible how useful simple things of this sort sometimes are as means to the very highest ends.

One young girl, for instance, who had been little better than a savage, by keeping her head and body upright, and not looking about, made more progress in her moral education than anyone would have believed possible.

These experiences have shown me that the mere habit of carrying oneself well does much more for the education of the moral sentiments than any amount of teaching and lectures in which this simple fact is ignored.

Thanks to the application of these principles, my children soon became more open, more contented and more susceptible to every good and noble influence than anyone could possibly have foreseen when they first came to me, so utterly devoid were they of ideas, good feelings, and moral principles. As a matter of fact, this lack of previous instruction was not a serious obstacle to me; indeed, it hardly troubled me at all. I am inclined even to say that, in the simple method I was following, it was often an advantage, for I had incomparably less trouble to develop those children whose minds were still blank, than those who had already acquired inaccurate ideas. The former, too, were much more open than the latter to the influence of all pure and simple sentiments.

But when the children were obdurate and churlish, then I was severe, and made use of corporal punishment. My dear friend, the pedagogical principle which says that we must win the hearts and minds of our children by words alone without having recourse to corporal punishment, is certainly good, and applicable under favorable conditions and circumstances; but with children of such widely different ages as mine, children for the most part beggars, and all full of deeply rooted faults, a certain amount of corporal punishment was inevitable, especially as I was anxious to arrive surely, speedily, and by the simplest means at gaining an influence over them all, for the sake of putting them all in the right road. I was compelled to punish them, but it would be a mistake to suppose that I thereby, in any way, lost the confidence of my pupils.

It is not the rare and isolated actions that form the opinions and feelings of children, but the impressions of every day and every hour. From such impressions they judge whether we are kindly disposed towards them or not, and this settles their general attitude towards us. Their judgment of isolated actions depends upon this general attitude.

This is how it is that punishments inflicted by parents rarely make a bad impression. But it is quite different with schoolmasters and teachers who are not with their children night and day and have none of those relations with them which result from life in common.

My punishments never produced obstinacy; the children I had beaten were quite satisfied if a moment afterwards I gave them my hand and kissed them, and I could read in their eyes that the final effect of my blows was really joy. The following is a striking instance of the effect this sort of punishment sometimes had. One day one of the children I liked best, taking advantage of my affection, unjustly threatened one of his companions. I was very indignant, and my hand did not spare him. He seemed at first almost brokenhearted and cried bitterly for at least a quarter of an hour. When I had gone out, however, he got up and going to the boy he had ill-treated begged his pardon and thanked him for having spoken about his bad conduct. My friend, this was no comedy; the child had never seen anything like it before.

It was impossible that this sort of treatment should produce a bad impression on my children, because all day long I was giving them proofs of my affection and devotion. They could not misread my heart, and so they did not misjudge my actions. It was not the same with the parents, friends, strangers, and teachers who visited us; but that was natural. But I cared nothing for the whole world, provided my children understood me.

I always did my best, therefore, to make them clearly understand the motives of my actions in all matters likely to excite their attention and interest. This, my friend, brings me to the consideration of the moral means to be employed in a truly domestic education.

Elementary moral education, considered as a whole, includes three distinct parts: the children's moral sense must first be aroused by their feelings being made active and pure; then they must be exercised in self-control, so that they may give themselves to that which is right and good; finally they must be brought to form for themselves, by reflection and comparison, a just notion of the moral rights and duties which are theirs by reason of their position and surroundings.

So far, I have pointed out some of the means I employed to reach the first two of these ends. They were just as simple for the third; for I still made use of the impressions and experiences of their daily life to give my children a true and exact idea of right and duty. When, for instance, they made a noise, I appealed to their own judgment, and asked them if it was possible to learn under such conditions. I shall never forget how strong and true I generally found their sense of justice and reason, and how this sense increased and, as it were, established their good will.

I appealed to them in all matters that concerned the establishment. It was generally in the quiet evening hours that I appealed to their free judgment. When, for instance, it was reported in the village that they had not enough to eat, I said to them, "Tell me, my children, if you are not better fed than you were at home? Think, and tell me yourselves, whether it would be well to keep you here in such a way as would make it impossible for you afterwards, in spite of all your application and hard work, to procure what you had become accustomed to. Do you lack anything that is really necessary? Do you think that I could reasonably and justly do more for you? Would you have me spend all the money that is entrusted to me on thirty or forty children instead of on eighty as at present? Would that be just?"

In the same way, when I heard that it was reported that I punished them too severely, I said to them: "You know how I love you, my children; but tell me, would you like me to stop punishing you? Do you think that in any other way I can free you from your deeply rooted bad habits, or make you always mind what I say?" You were there, my friend, and saw with your own eyes the sincere emotion with which they answered, "We don't complain about your hitting us. We wish we never deserved it. But we want to be punished when we do wrong."

Many things that make no difference in a small household could not be tolerated where the numbers were so great. I tried to make my children feel this, always leaving them to decide what could or could not be allowed. It is true that in my intercourse with them I never spoke of liberty or equality; but, at the same time, I encouraged them as far as possible to be free and unconstrained in my presence, with the result that every day I marked more and more that clear open look in their eyes which, in my experience, is the sign of a really liberal education. I could not bear the thought of betraying the trust in me which I saw shining in their eyes; I strove constantly to strengthen it and at the same time their free individuality, that nothing might happen to trouble those angel eyes, the sight of which caused me the most intense delight. But I could not endure frowns and anxious looks; I myself smoothed away the frowns; then the children smiled, and even among themselves they took care not to show frowning faces.

By reason of their great number, I had occasion nearly every day to point out the difference between good and evil, justice and injustice. Good and evil are equally contagious amongst so many children, so that, according as the good or bad sentiments spread, the establishment was likely to become either much better or much worse than if it had only contained a smaller number. About this, too, I talked to them frankly. I shall never forget the impression that my words produced when, in speaking of a certain disturbance that had taken place among them, I said, "My children, it is the same with us as with every other household; when the children are numerous, and each gives way to his bad habits, the disorder becomes such that the weakest mother is driven to take sensible measures in bringing up her children, and make them submit to what is just and right. And that is what I must do now. If you do not willingly assist in the maintenance of order, our establishment cannot go on, you will fall back into your former condition, and your misery — now that you have been accustomed to a good home, clean clothes, and regular food — will be greater than ever. In this world, my children, necessity and conviction alone can teach a man to behave; when both fail him, he is hateful. Think for a moment what you would become if you were safe from want and cared nothing for right, justice, or goodness. At home there was always someone who looked after you, and poverty itself forced you to many a right action; but with convictions and reason to guide you, you will rise far higher than by following necessity alone."

I often spoke to them in this way without troubling in the least whether they each understood every word, feeling quite sure that they all caught the general sense of what I said. . . .

Here are a few more thoughts which produced a great impression on my children: "Do you know anything greater or nobler than to give counsel to the poor, and comfort to the unfortunate? But if you remain ignorant and incapable, you will be obliged, in spite of your good heart, to let things take their course; whereas, if you acquire knowledge and power, you will be able to give good advice, and save many a man from misery."

I have generally found that great, noble, and high thoughts are indispensable for developing wisdom and firmness of character.

Such an instruction must be complete in the sense that it must take account of all our aptitudes and all our circumstances; it must be conducted, too, in a truly psychological spirit, that is to say, simply, lovingly, energetically, and calmly. Then, by its very nature, it produces an enlightened and delicate feeling for everything true and good, and brings to light a number of accessory and dependent truths, which are forthwith accepted and assimilated by the human soul, even in the case of those who could not express these truths in words.

I believe that the first development of thought in the child is very much disturbed by a wordy system of teaching, which is not adapted either to his faculties or the circumstances of his life. According to my experience, success depends upon whether what is taught to children commends itself to them as true through being closely connected with their own personal observation and experience. . . .

I knew no other order, method, or art, but that which resulted naturally from my children's conviction of my love for them, nor did I care to know any other.

Thus I subordinated the instruction of my children to a higher aim, which was to arouse and strengthen their best sentiments by the relations of everyday life as they existed between themselves and me. . . .

As a general rule I attached little importance to the study of words, even when explanations of the ideas they represented were given.

I tried to connect study with manual labor, the school with the workshop, and make one thing of them. But I was the less able to do this as staff, material, and tools were all wanting. A short time only before the close of the establishment, a few children had begun to spin; and I saw clearly that, before any fusion could be effected, the two parts must be firmly established separately—study, that is, on the one hand, and labor on the other.

But in the work of the children I was already inclined to care less for the immediate gain than for the physical training which, by developing their strength and skill, was bound to supply them later with a means of livelihood. In the same way I considered that what is generally called the instruction of children should be merely an exercise of the faculties, and I felt it important to exercise the attention, observation, and memory first, so as to strengthen these faculties before calling into play the art of judging and reasoning; this, in my opinion, was the best way to avoid turning out that sort of superficial and presumptuous talker, whose false judgments are often more fatal to the happiness and progress of humanity than the ignorance of simple people of good sense.

Guided by these principles, I sought less at first to teach my children to spell, read, and write than to make use of these exercises for the purpose of giving their minds as full and as varied a development as possible. . . .

In natural history they were very quick in corroborating what I taught them by their own personal observations on plants and animals. I am quite sure that, by continuing in this way, I should soon have been able not only to give them such a general acquaintance with the subject as would have been useful in any vocation, but also to put them in a position to carry on their education themselves by means of their daily observations and experiences; and I should have been able to do all this without going outside the very restricted sphere to which they were confined by the actual circumstances of their lives. I hold it to be extremely important that men should be encouraged to learn by themselves and allowed to develop freely. It is in this way alone that the diversity of individual talent is produced and made evident.

I always made the children learn perfectly even the least important things, and I never allowed them to lose ground; a word once learnt, for instance, was never to be forgotten, and a letter once well written never to be written badly again. I was very patient with all who were weak or slow, but very severe with those who did anything less well than they had done it before.

The number and inequality of my children rendered my task easier. Just as in a family the eldest and cleverest child readily shows what he knows to his younger brothers and sisters, and feels proud and happy to be able to take his mother's place for a moment, so my children were delighted when they knew something that they could teach others. A sentiment of honor awoke in them, and they learned twice as well by making the younger ones repeat their words. In this way I soon had helpers and collaborators amongst the children themselves. When I was teaching them to spell difficult words by heart, I used to allow any child who succeeded in saying one properly to teach it to the others. These child helpers, whom I had formed from the very outset, and who had followed my method step by step, were certainly much more useful to me than any regular schoolmasters could have been.

I myself learned with the children. Our whole system was so simple and so natural that I should have had difficulty in finding a master who would not have thought it undignified to learn and teach as I was doing. . . .

You will hardly believe that it was the Capuchin friars and the nuns of the convent that showed the greatest sympathy with my work. Few people, except Truttman, took any active interest in it. Those from whom I had hoped most were too deeply engrossed with their high political affairs to think of our little institution as having the least degree of importance.

Such were my dreams; but at the very moment that I seemed to be on the point of realizing them, I had to leave Stanz.

What Knowledge Is of Most Worth?

Herbert Spencer
(1820–1903)

The title of Herbert Spencer's famous essay, "What Knowledge Is of Most Worth?" suggests why the essay is a high point in the literature of education. It signals a reaction against the two themes which had dominated educational thought since the Renaissance—the denigration of knowledge as the core of education and the shift of emphasis onto the individual student's growth and development. For Spencer the essential question in education is *not* the nature of the student, but the "relative values of knowledges." The school's task is to prepare the new generation to sustain and improve the existing material society, rather than to create new men who can revolutionize society along spiritually better lines.

Spencer's criterion of true education was utilitarian. "Of what use is it?" he asked of every subject the schools were teaching. His answers required him to turn upside down the classical curriculum which still dominated the schools of nineteenth-century England despite reformers like Pestalozzi. The "cultural" subjects then paramount were toppled to the bottom in Spencer's suggested curriculum. "As they occupy the leisure part of life," he unflinchingly concluded, "so should they occupy the leisure part of education."

Spencer's basic approach was first formulated by Locke. That philosopher write: "Since it cannot be hoped he (the pupil) should have time and strength to learn all things, most pains should be taken about that which is most necessary, and that principally looked after which will be of most frequent use to him in the world." Today when curriculum specialists design courses of study by conducting surveys of what the students will need to know in later life, they are following Locke's and Spencer's principles.

With the advent of mass education, publicly supervised and publicly supported, the "common-sense" ideas of the man in the street have increasingly affected educational theory and practice. The man in the street can understand Spencer more readily than he can follow the mystical and idealistic tradition stretching from Comenius to Pestalozzi. After all, he agrees, unless men are trained to do the world's work and provide for their essential needs, there won't be any higher culture to transmit. Though he cannot express it with Spencer's satiric bite and incisive clarity, the average man responds instinctively to the argument that education must be useful. Consider the current emphasis on science and scientific method, the training in vocational and professional skills, the preparation for parenthood and for citizenship, and most important of all, the axiomatic acceptance of usefulness in everyday life as the criterion for deciding what shall be taught in schools and colleges. Many of these developments have been attributed to the influence of John Dewey; yet all of them can be traced at least in part to Spencer. Moreover, the recent reaction against progressivism has encouraged laymen and professional educators to apply, often unconsciously, Spencer's principles of utilitarian education.

But by concentrating on education for use—education in the scientific techniques by which industrial civilization is created and maintained—we run the risk of growing stupid about the *ends* of our productive activities. Moreover, in an age of automation, with leisure coming to dominate most men's lives, the liberal arts may well turn out to be the most useful education for an adult life devoted more to cultural than to vocational pursuits.

Herbert Spencer was born in Derby, England, in 1820. He began his career as a civil engineer, but later rejected the profession to become a writer and subeditor of *The Economist*. During his later years he devoted himself to study and to writing numerous books and essays which formed a comprehensive system of philosophy and sociology based on the theory of evolution. The following is an abridged version of the first chapter of his 1860 volume, *Education: Intellectual, Moral, and Physical.*

Among mental as among bodily acquisitions, the ornamental comes before the useful. Not only in times past, but almost as much in our own era, that knowledge which conduces to personal well-being has been postponed to that which brings applause. In the Greek schools, music, poetry, rhetoric, and a philosophy which, until Socrates taught, had but little bearing upon action, were the dominant subjects; while knowledge aiding the arts of life had a very subordinate place. And in our own universities and schools at the present moment the like antithesis holds. We are guilty of something like a platitude when we say that throughout his aftercareer a boy, in nine cases out of ten, applies his Latin and Greek to no practical purposes. The remark is trite that in his shop, or his office, in managing his estate or his family, in playing his part as director of a bank or a railway, he is very little aided by this knowledge he took so many years to acquire—so little, that generally the greater part of it drops out of his memory; and if he occasionally vents a Latin quotation, or alludes to some Greek myth, it is less to throw light on the topic in hand than for the sake of effect. If we inquire what is the real motive for giving boys a classical education, we find it to be simply conformity to public opinion. Men dress their children's minds as they do their bodies, in the prevailing fashion. As the Orinoco Indian puts on his paint before leaving his hut, not with a view to any direct benefit, but because he would be ashamed to be seen without it; so, a boy's drilling in Latin and Greek is insisted on, not because of their intrinsic value, but that he may not be disgraced by being found ignorant of them—that he may have "the education of a gentleman"—the badge marking a certain social position, and bringing a consequent respect. . . .

Thoroughly to realize the truth that with the mind as with the body the ornamental precedes the useful, it is needful to glance at its rationale. This lies in the fact that, from the far past down even to the present, social needs have subordinated individual needs, and that the chief social need has been the control of individuals. It is not, as we commonly suppose, that there are no governments but those of monarchs, and parliaments, and constituted authorities. These acknowledged governments are supplemented by other unacknowledged ones, that grow up in all circles, in which every man or woman strives to be king or queen or lesser dignitary. To get above some and be reverenced by them, and to propitiate those who are above us, is the universal struggle in which the chief energies of life are expended. By the accumulation of wealth, by style of living, by beauty of dress, by display of knowledge or intellect, each tries to subjugate others; and so aids in weaving that ramified network of restraints by which society is kept in order. It is not the savage chief only, who, in formidable war paint, with scalps at his belt, aims to strike awe into his inferiors; it is not only the belle who, by elaborate toilet, polished manners, and numerous accomplishments, strives to "make conquests"; but the scholar, the historian, the philosopher, use their acquirements to the same end. We are none of us content with quietly unfolding our own individualities to the full in all directions; but have a restless craving to impress our individualities upon others, and in some way subordinate them. And this it is which determines the character of our education. Not what knowledge is of most real worth, is the consideration; but what will bring most applause, honor, respect—what will most conduce to social position and influence—what will be most imposing. As, throughout life, not what we are, but what we shall be thought, is the question; so in education, the question is, not the intrinsic value of knowledge, so much as its extrinsic effects on others. And this being our dominant idea, direct utility is scarcely more regarded than by the barbarian when filing his teeth and staining his nails.

If there needs any further evidence of the rude, undeveloped character of our education, we have it in the fact that the comparative worths of different kinds of knowledge have been as yet scarcely even discussed—much less discussed in a methodic way with definite results. Not only is it that no standard of relative values has yet been agreed upon; but the existence of any such standard has not been conceived in any clear manner. And not only is it that the existence of any such standard has not been clearly conceived; but the need for it seems to have been scarcely even felt. Men read books on this topic, and attend lectures on that; decide that their children shall be instructed in these branches of knowledge, and shall not be instructed in those; and all under the guidance of mere custom, or liking, or prejudice; without ever considering the enormous importance of determining in some rational way what things are really most worth learning. It is true that in all circles we have occasional remarks on the importance of this or the other order of information. But whether the degree of its importance justifies the expenditure of the time needed to acquire it; and whether there are not things of more importance to which the time might be better devoted; are queries which, if raised at all, are disposed of quite summarily, according to personal predilections. It is true also, that from time to time, we hear revived the standing controversy respecting the comparative merits of classics and mathematics. Not only, however, is this controversy carried on in an empirical manner, with no reference to an ascertained criterion; but the question at issue is totally insignificant when compared with the general question of which it is part. To suppose that deciding whether a mathematical or a classical education is the best, in deciding what is the proper *curriculum*, is much the same thing as to suppose that the whole of dietetics lies in determining whether or not bread is more nutritive than potatoes!

The question which we contend is of such transcendent moment, is, not whether such or such knowledge is of worth, but what is its *relative* worth? When they have named certain advantages which a given course of study has secured them, persons are apt to assume that they have justified themselves: quite forgetting that the adequateness of the advantages is the point to be judged. There is, perhaps, not a subject to which men devote attention that has not *some* value. A year diligently spent in getting up heraldry, would very possibly give a little further insight into ancient manners and morals, and into the origin of names. Anyone who should learn the distances between all the towns in England, might, in the course of his life, find one or two of the thousand facts he had acquired of some slight service when arranging a journey. Gathering together all the small gossip of a county, profitless occupation as it would be, might yet occasionally help to establish some useful fact—say, a good example of hereditary transmission. But in these cases, everyone would admit that there was no proportion between the required labor and the probable benefit. No one would tolerate the proposal to devote some years of a boy's time to getting such information, at the cost of much more valuable information which he might else have got. . . . Before devoting years to some subject which fashion or fancy suggests, it is surely wise to weigh with great care the worth of the results, as compared with the worth of various alternative results which the same years might bring if otherwise applied.

In education, then, this is the question of questions, which it is high time we discussed in some methodic way. The first in importance, though the last to be considered, is the problem—how to decide among the conflicting claims of various subjects on our attention. Before there can be a rational *curriculum*, we must settle which things it most concerns us to know; or, to use a word of Bacon's, now unfortunately obsolete—we must determine the relative values of knowledges.

To this end, a measure of value is the first requisite. And happily, respecting the true measure of value, as expressed in general terms, there can be no dispute. Everyone in contending for the worth of any particular order of information, does so by showing its bearing upon some part of life. . . .

How to live?—that is the essential question for us. Not how to live in the mere material sense only, but in the widest sense. The general problem which comprehends every special problem is—the right ruling of conduct in all directions under all circumstances. In what way to treat the body; in what way to treat the mind; in what way to manage our affairs; in what way to bring up a family; in what way to behave as a citizen; in what way to utilize all those sources of happiness which nature supplies—how to use all our faculties to the greatest advantage of ourselves and others—how to live completely? And this being the great thing needful for us to learn, is, by consequence, the great thing which education has to teach. To prepare us for complete living is the function which education has to discharge; and the only rational mode of judging of any educational course is, to judge in what degree it discharges such function. . . .

Our first step must obviously be to classify, in the order of their importance, the leading kinds of activity which constitute human life. They may be naturally arranged into: 1. Those activities which directly minister to self-preservation; 2. Those activities which, by securing the necessaries of life, indirectly minister to self-preservation; 3. Those activities which have for their end the rearing and discipline of offspring; 4. Those activities which are involved in the maintenance of proper social and political relations; 5. Those miscellaneous activities which make up the leisure part of life, devoted to the gratification of the tastes and feelings.

That these stand in something like their true order of subordination, it needs no long consideration to show. The actions and precautions by which, from moment to moment, we secure personal safety, must clearly take precedence of all others. Could there be a man, ignorant as an infant of all surrounding objects and movements, or how to guide himself among them, he would pretty certainly lose his life the first time he went into the street; notwithstanding any amount of learning he might have on other matters. And as entire ignorance in all other directions would be less promptly fatal than entire ignorance in this direction, it must be admitted that knowledge immediately conducive to self-preservation is of primary importance.

That next after direct self-preservation comes the indirect self-preservation which consists in acquiring the means of living, none will question. That a man's industrial functions must be considered before his parental ones, is manifest from the fact that, speaking generally, the discharge of the parental functions is made possible only by the previous discharge of the industrial ones. The power of self-maintenance necessarily preceding the power of maintaining offspring, it follows that knowledge needful for self-maintenance has stronger claims than knowledge needful for family welfare—is second in value to none save knowledge needful for immediate self-preservation.

As the family comes before the State in order of time—as the bringing up of children is possible before the State exists, or when it has ceased to be, whereas the State is rendered possible only by the bringing up of children; it follows that the duties of the parent demand closer attention than those of the citizen. Or, to use a further argument—since the goodness of a society ultimately depends on the nature of its citizens; and since the nature of its citizens is more modifiable by early training than by anything else; we must conclude that the welfare of the family underlies the welfare of society. And hence knowledge directly conducing to the first, must take precedence of knowledge directly conducing to the last.

Those various forms of pleasurable occupation which fill up the leisure left by graver occupations—the enjoyments of music, poetry, painting, etc.—manifestly imply a pre-existing society. Not only is a considerable development of them impossible without a long-established social union; but their very subject matter consists in great part of social sentiments and sympathies. Not only does society supply the conditions to their growth; but also the ideas and sentiments they express. And, consequently, that part of human conduct which constitutes good citizenship is of more moment than that which goes out in accomplishments or exercise of the tastes; and, in education, preparation for the one must rank before preparation for the other. . . .

Of course the ideal of education is — complete preparation in all these divisions. But failing this ideal, as in our phase of civilization everyone must do more or less, the aim should be to maintain *a due proportion* between the degrees of preparation in each. Not exhaustive cultivation in any one, supremely important though it may be (not even an exclusive attention to the two, three, or four divisions of greatest importance, but an attention to all) greatest where the value is greatest, less where the value is less, least where the value is least. For the average man (not to forget the cases in which peculiar aptitude for some one department of knowledge rightly makes that one the breadwinning occupation) for the average man, we say, the desideratum is, a training that approaches nearest to perfection in the things which most subserve complete living, and falls more and more below perfection in the things that have more and more remote bearings on complete living. . . .

These, then, are the general ideas with which we must set out in discussing a *curriculum:* Life as divided into several kinds of activity of successively decreasing importance; the worth of each order of facts as regulating these several kinds of activity, intrinsically, quasi-intrinsically, and conventionally; and their regulative influences estimated both as knowledge and discipline.

Happily, that all-important part of education which goes to

secure direct self-preservation, is in great part already provided for. Too momentous to be left to our blundering, Nature takes it into her own hands. While yet in its nurse's arms, the infant, by hiding its face and crying at the sight of a stranger, shows the dawning instinct to attain safety by flying from that which is unknown and may be dangerous; and when it can walk, the terror it manifests if an unfamiliar dog comes near, or the screams with which it runs to its mother after any startling sight or sound, shows this instinct further developed. . . . Being thus, as we say, so well cared for by Nature, this fundamental education needs comparatively little care from us. What we are chiefly called upon to see, is that there shall be free scope for gaining this experience, and receiving this discipline. . . .

This, however, is by no means all that is comprehended in the education that prepares for direct self-preservation. Besides guarding the body against mechanical damage or destruction, it has to be guarded against injury from other causes—against the disease and death that follow breaches of physiologic law. For complete living it is necessary, not only that sudden annihilations of life shall be warded off; but also that there shall be escaped the incapacities and the slow annihilation which unwise habits entail. As, without health and energy, the industrial, the parental, the social, and all other activities become more or less impossible; it is clear that this secondary kind of direct self-preservation is only less important than the primary kind; and that knowledge tending to secure it should rank very high. . . .

We infer that as vigorous health and its accompanying high spirits are larger elements of happiness than any other things whatever, the teaching how to maintain them is a teaching that yields in moment to no other whatever. And therefore we assert that such a course of physiology as is needful for the comprehension of its general truths, and their bearings on daily conduct, is an all-essential part of a rational education.

Strange that the assertion should need making! Stranger still that it should need defending! Yet are there not a few by whom such a proposition will be received with something approaching to derision. Men who would blush if caught saying Iphigénia instead of Iphigenía, or would resent as an insult any imputation of ignorance respecting the fabled labors of a fabled demigod, show not the slightest shame in confessing that they do not know where the Eustachian tubes are, what are the actions of the spinal cord, what is the normal rate of pulsation, or how the lungs are inflated. While anxious that their sons should be well up in the superstitions of two thousand years ago, they care not that they should be taught anything about the structure and functions of their own bodies—nay, would even disapprove such instruction. So overwhelming is the influence of established routine! So terribly in our education does the ornamental override the useful!

We need not insist on the value of that knowledge which aids indirect self-preservation by facilitating the gaining of a livelihood. This is admitted by all; and, indeed, by the mass is perhaps too exclusively regarded as the end of education. But while everyone is ready to endorse the abstract proposition that instruction fitting youths for the business of life is of high importance, or even to consider it of supreme importance; yet scarcely any inquire what instruction will so fit them. It is true that reading, writing, and arithmetic are taught with an intelligent appreciation of their uses; but when we have said this we have said nearly all. While the great bulk of what else is acquired has no bearing on the industrial activities, an immensity of information that has a direct bearing on the industrial activities is entirely passed over.

For, leaving out only some very small classes, what are all men employed in? They are employed in the production, preparation, and distribution of commodities. And on what does efficiency in the production, preparation, and distribution of commodities depend? It depends on the use of methods fitted to the respective natures of these commodities; it depends on an adequate knowledge of their physical, chemical, or vital properties, as the case may be; that is, it depends on science. This order of knowledge, which is in great part ignored in our school courses, is the order of knowledge underlying the right performance of all those processes by which civilized life is made possible. Undeniable as is this truth, and thrust upon us as it is at every turn, there seems to be no living consciousness of it: its very familiarity makes it unregarded. . . .

Thus, to all such as are occupied in the production, exchange, or distribution of commodities, acquaintance with science in some of its departments is of fundamental importance. Whoever is immediately or remotely implicated in any form of industry (and few are not) has a direct interest in understanding something of the mathematical, physical, and chemical properties of things; perhaps, also, has a direct interest in biology; and certainly has in sociology. Whether he does or does not succeed well in that indirect self-preservation which we call getting a good livelihood, depends in a great degree on his knowledge of one or more of these sciences: not, it may be, a rational knowledge; but still a knowledge, though empirical. For what we call learning a business, really implies learning the science involved in it; though not perhaps under the name of science. And hence a grounding in science is of great importance, both because it prepares for all this, and because rational knowledge has an immense superiority over empirical knowledge. Moreover, not only is it that scientific culture is requisite for each, that he may understand the *how* and the *why* of the things and processes with which he is concerned as maker or distributor; but it is often of much moment that he should understand the *how* and the *why* of various other things and processes. In this age of joint-stock undertakings, nearly every man above the laborer is interested as capitalist in some other occupation than his own; and, as thus interested, his profit or loss often depends on his knowledge of the sciences bearing on this other occupation. . . .

That which our school courses leave almost entirely out, we thus find to be that which most nearly concerns the business of life. All our industries would cease, were it not for that information which men begin to acquire as they best may after their education is said to be finished. And were it not for this information, that has been from age to age accumulated and spread by unofficial means, these industries would never have existed. Had there been no teaching but such as is given in our public schools, England would now be what it was in feudal times. That increasing acquaintance with the laws of phenomena which has through successive ages enabled us to subjugate Nature to our needs, and in these days gives the common laborer comforts which a few centuries ago kings could not purchase, is scarcely in any degree owed to the appointed means of instructing our youth. The vital knowledge—that by which we have grown as a nation to what we are, and which now underlies our whole existence, is a knowledge that has got itself taught in nooks and corners; while the ordained agencies for teaching have been mumbling little else but dead formulas.

We come now to the third great division of human activities—a division for which no preparation whatever is made. If by some strange chance not a vestige of us descended to the remote future save a pile of our schoolbooks or some college examination papers, we may imagine how puzzled an antiquary of the period would be on finding in them no indication that the learners were ever likely to be parents. "This must have been the *curriculum* for their celibates," we may fancy him concluding. "I perceive here an elaborate preparation for many things: especially for reading the books of extinct nations and of coexisting nations (from which indeed it seems clear that these people had very little worth reading in their own tongue); but I find no reference whatever to the bringing up of children. They could not have been so absurd as to omit all training for this gravest of responsibilities. Evidently then, this was the school course of one of their monastic orders."

Seriously, is it not an astonishing fact, that though on the treatment of offspring depend their lives or deaths, and their moral welfare or ruin; yet not one word of instruction on the treatment of offspring is ever given to those who will hereafter be parents? Is it not monstrous that the fate of a new generation should be left to the chances of unreasoning custom, impulse, fancy — joined with the suggestions of ignorant nurses and the prejudiced counsel of grandmothers? If a merchant commenced business without any knowledge of arithmetic and bookkeeping, we should exclaim at his folly, and look for disastrous consequences. Or if, before studying anatomy, a man set up as a surgical operator, we should wonder at his audacity and pity his patients. But that parents should begin the difficult task of rearing children without ever having given a thought to the principles—physical, moral, or intellectual—which ought to guide them, excites neither surprise at the actors nor pity for their victims. To tens of thousands that are killed, add hundreds of thousands that survive with feeble constitutions, and millions that grow up with constitutions not so strong as they should be; and you will have some idea of the curse inflicted on their offspring by parents ignorant of the laws of life. . . .

Equally great are the ignorance and the consequent injury, when we turn from physical training to moral training. Consider the young mother and her nursery legislation. . . . See her with an unfolding human character committed to her charge—see her profoundly ignorant of the phenomena with which she has to deal, undertaking to do that which can be done but imperfectly even with the aid of the profoundest knowledge. She knows nothing about the nature of the emotions, their order of evolution, their functions, or where use ends and abuse begins. She is under the impression that some of the feelings are wholly bad, which is not true of any one of them; and that others are good, however far they may be carried, which is also not true of any one of them. And then, ignorant as she is of that with which she has to deal, she is equally ignorant of the effects that will be produced on it by this or that treatment. What can be more inevitable than the disastrous results we see hourly arising? Lacking knowledge of mental phenomena, with their causes and consequences, her interference is frequently more mischievous than absolute passivity would have been. This and that kind of action, which are quite normal and beneficial, she perpetually thwarts; and so diminishes the child's happiness and profit, injures its temper and her own, and produces estrangement. Deeds which she thinks it desirable to encourage, she gets performed by threats and bribes, or by exciting a desire for applause; considering little what the inward motive may be, so long as the outward conduct conforms; and thus cultivating hypocrisy, and fear, and selfishness, in place of good feeling. While insisting on truthfulness, she constantly sets an example of untruth, by threatening penalties which she does not inflict. While inculcating self-control, she hourly visits on her little ones angry scoldings for acts that do not call for them. She has not the remotest idea that in the nursery, as in the world, that alone is the truly salutary discipline which visits on all conduct, good and bad, the natural consequences—the consequences, pleasurable or painful, which in the nature of things such conduct tends to bring. Being thus without theoretic guidance, and quite incapable of guiding herself by tracing the mental processes going on in her children, her rule is impulsive, inconsistent, mischievous, often, in the highest degree; and would indeed be generally ruinous, were it not that the overwhelming tendency of the growing mind to assume the moral type of the race, usually subordinates all minor influences.

And then the culture of the intellect—is not this, too, mismanaged in a similar manner? Grant that the phenomena of intelligence conform to laws; grant that the evolution of intelligence in a child also conforms to laws; and it follows inevitably that education can be rightly guided only by a knowledge of these laws. To suppose that you can properly regulate this process of forming and accumulating ideas, without understanding the nature of the process, is absurd. How widely, then, must teaching as it is, differ from teaching as it should be; when hardly any parents, and but few teachers, know anything about psychology. As might be expected, the system is grievously at fault, alike in matter and in manner. While the right class of facts is withheld, the wrong class is forcibly administered in the wrong way and in the wrong order. With that common limited idea of education which confines it to knowledge gained from books, parents thrust primers into the hands of their little ones years too soon, to their great injury. Not recognizing the truth that the function of books is supplementary—that they form an indirect means to knowledge when direct means fail—a means of seeing through other men what you cannot see for yourself; they are eager to give secondhand facts in place of firsthand facts. Not perceiving the enormous value of that spontaneous education which goes on in early years—not perceiving that a child's restless observation, instead of being ignored or checked, should be diligently administered to, and made as accurate and complete as possible; they insist on occupying its eyes and thoughts with things that are, for the time being, incomprehensible and repugnant. Possessed by a superstition which worships the symbols of knowledge instead of the knowledge itself, they do not see that only when his acquaintance with the objects and processes of the household, the streets, and the fields, is becoming tolerably exhaustive—only then should a child be introduced to the new sources of information which books supply: and this, not only because immediate cognition is of far greater value than mediate cognition; but also, because the words contained in books can be rightly interpreted into ideas, only in proportion to the antecedent experience of things. Observe next, that this formal instruction, far too soon commenced, is carried on with but little reference to the laws of mental development. Intellectual progress is of necessity from the concrete to the abstract. But regardless of this, highly abstract subjects, such as grammar, which should come quite late, are begun quite early. Political geography, dead and uninteresting to a child, and which should be an appendage of sociological studies, is commenced betimes; while physical geography, comprehensible and comparatively attractive to a child, is in great part passed over. Nearly every subject dealt with is arranged in abnormal order: definitions, and rules, and principles being put first, instead of being disclosed, as they are in the order of nature, through the study of cases. And then, pervading the whole, is the vicious system of rote learning—a system of sacrificing the spirit to the letter. See the results. What with perceptions unnaturally dulled by early thwarting, and a coerced attention to books—what with the mental confusion produced by teaching subjects before they can be understood, and in each of them giving generalizations before the facts of which these are the generalizations—what with making the pupil a mere passive recipient of other's ideas, and not in the least leading him to be an active inquirer or self-instructor—and what with taxing the faculties to excess; there are very few minds that become as efficient as they might be. Examinations being once passed, books are laid aside; the greater part of what has been acquired, being unorganized, soon drops out of recollection; what remains is mostly inert—the art of applying knowledge not having been cultivated; and there is but little power either of accurate observation or independent thinking. To all which add, that while much of the information gained is of relatively small value, an immense mass of information of transcendent value is entirely passed over.

Thus we find the facts to be such as might have been inferred *a priori*. The training of children—physical, moral, and intellectual—is dreadfully defective. And in great measure it is so, because parents are devoid of that knowledge by which this training can alone be rightly guided. What is to be expected when one of the most intricate of problems is undertaken by those who have given scarcely a thought to the principles on which its solution depends? For shoemaking or housebuilding, for the management of a ship or a locomotive engine, a long apprenticeship is needful. Is it, then, that the unfolding of a human being in body and mind, is so comparatively simple a process, that anyone may superintend and regulate it with no preparation whatever?

Thus we see that for regulating the third great division of human activities, a knowledge of the laws of life is the one thing needful. Some acquaintance with the first principles of physiology and the elementary truths of psychology is indispensable for the right bringing up of children. We doubt not that this assertion will by many be read with a smile. That parents in general should be expected to acquire a knowledge of subjects so abstruse, will seem to them an absurdity. And if we proposed that an exhaustive knowledge of these subjects should be obtained by all fathers and mothers, the absurdity would indeed be glaring enough. But we do not. General principles only, accompanied by such detailed illustrations as may be needed to make them understood, would suffice. And these might be readily taught—if not rationally, then dogmatically. Be this as it may, however, here are the indisputable facts—that the development of children in mind and body rigorously obeys certain laws; that unless these laws are in some degree conformed to by parents, death is inevitable; that unless they are in a great degree conformed to, there must result serious physical and mental defects; and that only when they are completely conformed to, can a perfect maturity be reached. Judge, then, whether all who may one day be parents, should not strive with some anxiety to learn what these laws are.

From the parental functions let us pass now to the functions of the citizen. We have here to inquire what knowledge best fits a man for the discharge of these functions. It cannot be alleged, as in the last case, that the need for knowledge fitting him for these functions is wholly overlooked; for our school courses contain certain studies which, nominally at least, bear upon political and social duties. Of these the only one that occupies a prominent place is history.

But, as already more than once hinted, the historic information commonly given is almost valueless for purposes of guidance. Scarcely any of the facts set down in our school histories, and very few even of those contained in the more elaborate works written for adults, give any clue to the right principles of political action. The biographies of monarchs (and our children commonly learn little else) throw scarcely any light upon the science of society. Familiarity with court intrigues, plots, usurpations, or the like, and with all the personalities accompanying them, aids very little in elucidating the principles on which national welfare depends. We read of some squabble for power, that it led to a pitched battle; that such and such were the names of the generals and their leading subordinates; that they had each so many thousand infantry and cavalry, and so many cannon; that they arranged their forces in this and that order; that they maneuvered, attacked, and fell back in certain ways; that at this part of the day such disasters were sustained, and at that such advantages gained; that in one particular movement some leading officer fell, while in another a certain regiment was decimated; that after all the changing fortunes of the fight, the victory was gained by this or that army; and that so many were killed and wounded on each side, and so many captured by the conquerors. And now, out of the accumulated details which make up the narrative, say which it is that helps you in deciding on your conduct as a citizen. . . .

The only history that is of practical value, is what may be called descriptive sociology. And the highest office which the historian can discharge, is that of so narrating the lives of nations, as to furnish materials for a comparative sociology; and for the subsequent determination of the ultimate laws to which social phenomena conform.

But now mark, that even supposing an adequate stock of this truly valuable historical knowledge has been acquired, it is of comparatively little use without the key. And the key is to be found only in science. Without an acquaintance with the general truths of biology and psychology, rational interpretation of social phenomena is impossible. Only in proportion as men obtain a certain rude, empirical knowledge of human nature, are they enabled to understand even the simplest facts of social life: as, for instance, the relation between supply and demand. And if not even the most elementary truths of sociology can be reached until some knowledge is obtained of how men generally think, feel, and act under given circumstances; then it is manifest that there can be nothing like a wide comprehension of sociology, unless through a competent knowledge of man in all his faculties, bodily and mental. Consider the matter in the abstract, and this conclusion is self-evident. Thus: Society is made up of individuals; all that is done in society is done by the combined actions of individuals; and therefore, in individual actions only can be found the solutions of social phenomena. But the actions of individuals depend on the laws of their natures; and their actions cannot be understood until these laws are understood. These laws, however, when reduced to their simplest expression, are found to depend on the laws of body and mind in general. Hence it necessarily follows, that biology and psychology are indispensable as interpreters of sociology. . . . Thus, then, we see that for the regulation of this fourth division of human activities, we are, as before, dependent on science. Of the knowledge commonly imparted in educational courses, very little is of any service in guiding a man in his conduct as a citizen. Only a small part of the history he reads is of practical value; and of this small part he is not prepared to make proper use. He commonly lacks not only the materials for, but the very conception of, descriptive sociology; and he also lacks that knowledge of the organic sciences, without which even descriptive sociology can give him but little aid.

And now we come to that remaining division of human life which includes the relaxations, pleasures, and amusements filling leisure hours. After considering what training best fits for self-preservation, for the obtainment of sustenance, for the discharge of parental duties, and for the regulation of social and political conduct; we have now to consider what training best fits for the miscellaneous ends not included in these—for the enjoyments of nature, of literature, and of the fine arts, in all their forms. Postponing them as we do to things that bear more vitally upon human welfare; and bringing everything, as we have, to the test of actual value; it will perhaps be inferred that we are inclined to slight these less essential things. No greater mistake could be made, however. We yield to none in the value we attach to aesthetic culture and its pleasures. Without painting, sculpture, music, poetry, and the emotions produced by natural beauty of every kind, life would lose half its charm. So far from thinking that the training and gratification of the tastes are unimportant, we believe the time will come when they will occupy a much larger share of human life than now. When the forces of nature have been fully conquered to man's use, when the means of production have been brought to perfection, when labor has been economized to the highest degree, when education has been so systematized that a preparation for the more essential activities may be made with comparative rapidity, and when, consequently, there is a great increase of spare time; then will the poetry, both of art and nature, rightly fill a large space in the minds of all.

But it is one thing to admit that aesthetic culture is in a high degree conducive to human happiness; and another thing to admit that it is a fundamental requisite to human happiness. However important it may be, it must yield precedence to those kinds of culture which bear more directly upon the duties of life. As before hinted, literature and the fine arts are made possible by those activities which make individual and social life possible; and manifestly, that which is made possible, must be postponed to that which makes it possible. A florist cultivates a plant for the sake of its flower; and regards the roots and leaves as of value, chiefly because they are instrumental in producing the flower. But while, as an ultimate product, the flower is the thing to which everything else is subordinate, the florist very well knows that the root and leaves are intrinsically of greater importance; because on them the evolution of the flower depends. He bestows every care in rearing a healthy plant; and knows it would be folly if, in his anxiety to obtain the flower, he were to neglect the plant. Similarly in the case before us. Architecture, sculpture, painting, music, poetry, etc., may be truly called the efflorescence of civilized life. But even supposing them to be of such transcendent worth as to subordinate the civilized life out of which they grow (which can hardly be asserted), it will still be admitted that the production of a healthy civilized life must be the first consideration; and that the knowledge conducing to this must occupy the highest place.

And here we see most distinctly the vice of our educational system. It neglects the plant for the sake of the flower. In anxiety for elegance, it forgets substance. While it gives no knowledge conducive to self-preservation, while of knowledge that facilitates gaining a livelihood it gives but the rudiments, and leaves the greater part to be picked up anyhow in afterlife, while for the discharge of parental functions it makes not the slightest provision, and while for the duties of citizenship it prepares by imparting a mass of facts, most of which are irrelevant, and the rest without a key; it is diligent in teaching everything that adds to refinement, polish, éclat. However fully we may admit that extensive acquaintance with modern languages is a valuable accomplishment, which, through reading, conversation, and travel, aids in giving a certain finish; it by no means follows that this result is rightly purchased at the cost of that vitally important knowledge sacrificed to it. Supposing it true that classical education conduces to elegance and correctness of style; it cannot be said that elegance and correctness of style are comparable in importance to a familiarity with the principles that should guide the rearing of children. Grant that the taste may be greatly improved by reading all the poetry written in extinct languages; yet it is not to be inferred that such improvement of taste is equivalent in value to an acquaintance with the laws of health. Accomplishments, the fine arts, belles-lettres, and all those things which, as we say, constitute the efflorescence of civilization, should be wholly subordinate to that knowledge and discipline in which civilization rests. As they occupy the leisure part of life, so should they occupy the leisure part of education.

. . . .

Thus to the question with which we set out—What knowledge is of most worth?—the uniform reply is—science. This is the verdict on all the counts. For direct self-preservation, or the maintenance of life and health, the all-important knowledge is—science. For that indirect self-preservation which we call gaining a livelihood, the knowledge of greatest value is—science. For the due discharge of parental functions, the proper guidance is to be found only in—science. For that interpretation of national life, past and present, without which the citizen cannot rightly regulate his conduct, the indispensable key is—science. Alike for the most perfect production and highest enjoyment of art in all its forms, the needful preparation is still—science. And for purposes of discipline—intellectual, moral, religious—the most efficient study is, once more—science. The question which at first seemed so perplexed, has become, in the course of our inquiry, comparatively simple. We have not to estimate the degrees of importance of different orders of human activity, and different studies as severally fitting us for them; since we find that the study of science, in its most comprehensive meaning, is the best preparation for all these orders of activity. We have not to decide between the claims of knowledge of great though conventional value, and knowledge of less though intrinsic value; seeing that the knowledge which we find to be of most value in all other respects, is intrinsically most valuable: its worth is not dependent upon opinion, but is as fixed as is the relation of man to the surrounding world. Necessary and eternal as are its truths, all science concerns all mankind for all time. Equally at present, and in the remotest future, must it be of incalculable importance for the regulation of their conduct, that men should understand the science of life, physical, mental, and social; and that they should understand all other science as a key to the science of life.

And yet the knowledge which is of such transcendent value is that which, in our age of boasted education, receives the least attention. While this which we call civilization could never have arisen had it not been for science; science forms scarcely an appreciable element in what men consider civilized training. Though to the progress of science we owe it, that millions find support where once there was food only for thousands; yet of these millions but a few thousands pay any respect to that which has made their existence possible. Though this increasing knowledge of the properties and relations of things has not only enabled wandering tribes to grow into populous nations, but has given to the countless members of those populous nations comforts and pleasures which their few naked ancestors never even conceived, or could have believed, yet is this kind of knowledge only now receiving a grudging recognition in our highest educational institutions. To the slowly growing acquaintance with the uniform coexistences and sequences of phenomena—to the establishment of invariable laws, we owe our emancipation from the grossest superstitions. But for science we should be still worshipping fetishes; or, with hecatombs of victims, propitiating diabolical deities. And yet this science, which, in place of the most degrading conceptions of things, has given us some insight into the grandeurs of creation, is written against in our theologies and frowned upon from our pulpits.

Paraphrasing an Eastern fable, we may say that in the family of knowledges, science is the household drudge, who, in obscurity, hides unrecognized perfections. To her has been committed all the work; by her skill, intelligence, and devotion, have all the conveniences and gratifications been obtained; and while ceaselessly occupied ministering to the rest, she has been kept in the background, that her haughty sisters might flaunt their fripperies in the eyes of the world. The parallel holds yet further. For we are fast coming to the denouement, when the positions will be changed; and while these haughty sisters sink into merited neglect, science, proclaimed as highest alike in worth and beauty, will reign supreme.

The Revolution in Education

Mortimer J. Adler and Milton Mayer

(1902–   ) (1908–   )

When we look back over the educational landmarks of our Western tradition, two questions naturally arise. First, is there a common body of theory and practice which has characterized education from Plato to Spencer? Second, if there is, can it really help us to cope with our current problems, or is the modern world so radically different from any previous age that we must find new techniques to reach new ends in our schools? These are the questions to which philosopher Mortimer Adler and writer Milton Mayer address themselves in this essay.

Mayer and Adler begin by extracting from the tradition of Western educational thought "the principles upon which Plato taught Aristotle in Athens and Mentor Graham taught Abraham Lincoln in Sangamon County, Illinois." As the authors point out, these principles deserve our careful consideration, for they produced the best minds of previous ages. But Mayer and Adler are well aware that the unique developments in the world since the middle of the nineteenth century—secularism, scientism, industrialism, democratization—have meant that "in certain critical respects our situation cuts us off from the past altogether." For the first time the challenge to the schools is to prepare *all* the people for lives of political responsibility, substantial leisure, and the continued learning necessary to keep pace with a fast-changing world. This essay thus looks both to the past and to the future—backward to the educational principles which have proved themselves through trial and error in the Western tradition, forward to the formulation of new principles needed for a contemporary world which is largely cut off from all traditions and precedents.

Mortimer Adler was born in New York City in 1902. After graduating from Columbia University, he taught law and philosophy of law at the University of Chicago and was also on the faculty at Columbia University. He was an associate editor of the Great Books of the Western World. Adler's own books include *Art and Prejudice, How to Read a Book, A Dialectic of Morals, How to Think About War and Peace, The Capitalist Manifesto,* and most recently, *The Idea of Freedom.* This last two-volume work, a dialectical examination of the "Great Debate" over freedom in the Western tradition, is the product of the Institute for Philosophical Research, of which Dr. Adler is director.

Mortimer Adler has been a prominent critic of the progressive movement in American education. He maintains an Aristotelian position related to those of Robert Hutchins, Stringfellow Barr, and Mark Van Doren. His basic premise is that the aim of education should be the same for all men in all times and places.

Milton Mayer has taught at the University of Chicago, William Penn College, and the Institute for Social Research, Frankfort University. He wrote *They Thought They Were Free,* a study of Nazi Germany.

The following selection is from the book *The Revolution in Education* published by the University of Chicago Press in 1958.

There were, in the centuries that preceded 1850, great crises in education, but there was still greater continuity. The pre-scientific, pre-industrial societies—sacred or secular—were concerned with the schooling of the few and with them alone. The polity might be a republic, an aristocracy, an oligarchy, or even a tyranny; its basic concern was the same: to prepare the leisured few for the learned or holy vocations and, in later times, for the highest ranks of commerce and government. The pattern was no more altered by the phenomenon of the student beggars of the Continental universities at the end of the Middle Ages than it was by the English "charity schools," the pre-Revolutionary "pauper schools" in America, or the appearance of an occasional hayseed at Henry Adams' Harvard.

The two great educational crises of the ages past were not educational crises at all but religious. The first occurred with the transition from Greek and Roman antiquity to pre-medieval Christendom. The ideal function of education in the Greek city-states was defined by Plato in the *Republic* and the *Laws* and was practiced in greater or lesser degree before and after his time: the preparation of the elite few for the service of the state and its governance. The absolute supremacy of the state may have been worse abused in later ages, but it has never been better praised than it was in ancient Greece. Lycurgus, the lawgiver of Sparta, was, so Plutarch recites, "of a persuasion that children were not so much the property of their parents as of the whole commonwealth." Accordingly, "he bred up his citizens in such a way that they neither would nor could live by themselves; they were to make themselves one with the public good, and, clustering like bees around their commander, be by their zeal and public spirit carried all but out of themselves, and devoted wholly to their country." So single-minded was their education that they were not allowed to learn of governments different from their own. Some four hundred years later Aristotle was glorifying the Spartans for making education "the business of the state." "The citizen," he said, "should be molded to suit the form of government under which he lives . . . if the laws are democratic, democratically, or oligarchically, if the laws are oligarchical."

This classic doctrine had its echoes a few decades ago in the cry of "adjustment." The business of education was the adjustment of the child to his environment. But the "adjustment" school—or, at least, its slogan—passed from favor with the rise of the modern totalitarian state whose educational system adjusted the child to an environment which Americans thought abominable. Then came the Second World War and the Cold War, and Aristotle, and even Lycurgus, were heard again. "The overarching objective," says Dr. Wilbur A. Yauch, chairman of the Department of Education at Northern Illinois State Teachers College, "the objective for which schools primarily exist, is to indoctrinate for democracy."

The Spartans, the Athenians, and later the Romans espoused indoctrination of the young in the name of education partly to ward off subversive ideas and partly to secure the state, through the will and training of its citizens, against attack from without.

In the face of the Communist threat the role of education in national security has come to the fore in our own time, as many of the speakers at the 1955 White House Conference on Education indicated. Citing the Soviet Union's lead in training scientists and engineers, Vice-President Nixon told the Conference that "it is apparent that our national security has a tremendous stake in our educational system." Neil H. McElroy, then president of Procter and Gamble Company and chairman of the President's Committee for the White House Conference (and subsequently Secretary of Defense of the United States) went further: "In this highly technical era, education has become as much a part of our system of defense as the Army, the Navy, or the Air Force. We must have good schools, not only because of our ideals, but for survival."

Another participant in the Conference was worried by the integration of education into the survival of the state. Speaking on "What Should Our Schools Accomplish?" President James R. Killian of the Massachusetts Institute of Technology said: "In Nazi and communistic societies there isn't much doubt about that question—their schools are arranged to shape youth to the needs of the state. It is of course a tradition in our own country to consider the individual paramount; we would not think of subordinating the educational desires of an individual to the needs of the state. . . . And we cling to this freedom for the individual even though it looks at times as though the welfare of the nation were suffering from it.

"For instance," President Killian went on, "we need science teachers in our schools today even more desperately than we need other kinds of teachers, but there is no way in which we can impress students into programs which would prepare them to be science teachers. . . . In an age when science is essential to our safety and our economic welfare, it might be argued that a shortage of science teachers and of scientists and engineers is a clear and present danger to the nation. I, for one, am convinced that it is just that."

Presumably, Nazi and Communist education—and Greek and Roman—would sacrifice freedom to the national danger. President Killian thinks it is not necessary: "Personal opportunities are often created by national needs—the national shortage of engineers has led to good jobs for young engineers and, as a consequence, can bring about an increase in the number of students seeking training as engineers." President Killian's hope might be realized, but what if there were a national shortage of, say, sonnet writers or saints, and the job market did not respond by raising salaries in those professions? The question has been asked before. Plato thought the state was short of philosophers, for whom personal opportunities were scarce and wages low. He offered the classical answer—which in principle seems to be the Nazi and Communist answer: Man belonged to the state, and education was to mold him to its service and survival.

The revival of the ancient doctrine under modern stress is still attacked. As long ago as 1917, with England at war, Bertrand Russell, in his *Why Men Fight*, excoriated the "molding" principle of education as the highest treason to the child: "What is considered in education is hardly ever the boy or girl, the young man or young woman, but almost always, in some form, the maintenance of the existing order. . . . Hardly anything is done to foster the inward growth of mind and spirit." And Canon Bernard Iddings Bell, in the midst of Cold War, wants the university to be "a breeding place of rebels, a sender forth of graduates who, unadjusted and unadjustable, would try to turn the world upside down"; a far and forlorn cry from the reaction to the successful launching of the Soviet Union's earth satellites in 1957, when Americans in high quarters and low called for an all-out effort by the educational system to overtake the totalitarians' lead in the production of scientists and engineers for national defense.

The aim of education remained the same throughout antiquity: to "mold" the good man and the good citizen, the two being generally held identical. The means were the inculcation of patriotism or the service of the state, the cultivation of the intellect, and (to whatever degree it might be achieved through schooling) the discipline of the passions in the direction of the classical ideal of moderation. But the school did not exist as we know it, and, until the last few centuries of Rome, it did not exist in any form. Instruction was private, or in very small groups, and peripatetic. In a world where nearly all labor was done by slaves, the students were members of that minority destined by birth or fortune (usually by both) to live a life of leisure or, in any case, of intellectual and not necessitous toil.

But Athens and Rome did not wholeheartedly follow the utopian precepts of Plato and Aristotle and make education "the business of the state." The young citizen's father directed his education and sent him with a specially designated slave, a παιδαγωγός, a "child-accompanier," from which the word "pedagogue" is derived, to hear lectures. The Romans placed more (and, in earlier periods, all) of their emphasis on the father's education of the son, directly and as supervisor of the teaching slaves (who were usually Greeks). The home was the school, and family example the primary tool of instruction. In the first century A.D., Quintilian (who kept a school of rhetoric and is sometimes called "the first public school teacher" because he was the first whose wages were paid by the emperor) grievously lamented the withering away of familial education.

Whatever adjustments were made in content and method from place to place and epoch to epoch in the ancient world, the curriculum that evolved was substantially the same. It consisted of what Cicero called "the liberal arts" of grammar (including folk literature), logic or dialectic (the art of argument), and rhetoric (the art of persuasion, which included law and lawmaking). These, plus geometry (including geography and natural history), astronomy, arithmetic, and music, were distinguished as the arts of liberty or the life of freedom, the political freedom of the citizens or ruling class and the economic freedom of the leisured to engage themselves in political, intellectual, or aesthetic activity. They were the arts (in contrast with the "servile" or mechanical) that freed man from the ignorance to which the slave was condemned by the conditions of economic production to perform his primitive labors.

Religion played an increasingly perfunctory role as classical culture developed, except in times of public crisis. At their height the pagan civilizations of the northern and eastern Mediterranean treated their gods ceremonially, as symbolic representations of the state and its prowess; and the symbolic representations of the state, in turn, were deified. The golden eagles of the Roman legions "were placed in a chapel in the camp," says Gibbon, "and with the other deities received the religious worship of the troops." Of course mythology—combining religion and education—was integral to the education of the child. But theology as we know it was nonexistent, and philosophy had no concern with the antics of the gods.

Far from repudiating the Greco-Roman construction of education—based on the liberal arts—the early Greek Fathers of the Church, such as Clement and Origen, regarded Christianity as a kind of ultimate philosophy. An uneducated man might be a Christian, but liberal education was the means of actually understanding the mysteries of faith. Even Augustine and Jerome advocated the liberal arts, whose ends were worldly, insisting only that they be subordinated to the Christian life, whose ends were other than worldly. It was not until the Middle Ages that the cleavage between the two objectives was sharpened into a revulsion against the intellectualism of pagan education isolated from Christian faith. But the liberal arts, preserved through the Dark Ages in the monasteries, were never rejected; with a religious foundation beneath them, they continued to dominate the medieval curriculum as they had the classical. The continuity of Western education was not interrupted by the religiously oriented schooling of medieval Christendom.

The Renaissance broke the religious pattern of the Middle Ages but not the educational continuum that began in Greece and Rome. On the contrary; re-emphasizing the secular ends of classical humanism, the Renaissance accepted the education of antiquity, rejecting only the aim of the service of the state as it rejected the medieval aim of the service of God. But the schools—such as they were—were rooted in the church, and, in spite of the progressive secularization of the university curriculum and the opening of schools under civil control in the Hanseatic towns in the fifteenth and sixteenth centuries, nearly all schooling remained in the care of the churches for another three hundred years. The churches, originally interested in augmenting the priesthood, always provided an educational opportunity for a limited number of poor boys; such a purpose in part motivated the establishment of Winchester, Eton, and St. Paul's in England between the fourteenth and sixteenth centuries. But the motivation was soon lost or submerged, and the schools became aristocratic. Education remained, from the Renaissance to the second quarter of the nineteenth century, in America no less than in Europe, the prerogative of the advantaged few, its graduates trained for the highest affairs, its basic content that of late antiquity plus religion variously emphasized in various periods.

To say that education remained substantially the same for

twenty-five centuries is not to say that there was unanimity in educational philosophy. Nor does it mean that great variations, in both theory and practice, did not appear from place to place and from time to time at the level of the organization of schooling or its duration, the method of instruction, or the exact content of the curriculum. Nearly all the great contributors to educational thought and action disagreed in respect to one or another of these issues. But they agreed on the fundamental convictions which maintained the continuity, from age to age, of the insights of Greece and Rome.

There were exceptions, of course, among educational philosophers, but the marvel is that among men whose general philosophies were incompatible (men like Aristotle, Augustine, Montaigne, Erasmus, and Benjamin Franklin) there were so few dissents from the prevailing philosophy of education. The list of exceptions is pretty well exhausted by Rousseau's emphasis upon naturalism and the cultivation of the instincts and, less radically if no less prophetically, by Locke's and Spencer's advocacy of vocational training in connection with general schooling and Bacon's plans for intensive specialization at the university level. But these dissents did not seriously affect educational practice during the centuries in which they were voiced; they have appeared in general practice only during the last hundred years.

The common practice—and the common theory—of every age preceding our own reduces, in summary, to five fundamental concepts. Upon these the institution of education rested undisturbed in Western history up to the middle of the last century.

First, the aim of education is the cultivation of the individual's capacities for mental growth and moral development. It is intended to help him acquire the intellectual techniques and aesthetic sensibilities, the knowledge, understanding, and wisdom requisite for a good human life spent publicly in political and professional action and privately in the worthiest use of leisure. As a secondary function, which it shares with other institutions, it concerns itself with the training of the body and the maturation of the emotions; this last objective (inculcated in part by rational emphasis on the "golden mean" and in part by discipline and personal concern) is viewed as a contribution to moral development. Specifically Christian education, of course, orients all these temporal objectives to the life of grace.

It was thought, in the second place, that basic schooling, given these objectives, must be "liberal" education. The corollaries of this concept were, generally, that basic schooling is the same for all who go to school, with due allowance for the varying dispositions of the normal individual; that training in the particular skills required for productive tasks is outside the area of basic schooling and is best acquired by apprenticeship; and that specialized education, after the completion of basic schooling, is to be given in only those vocations that are essentially liberal in character—namely, the learned professions.

Third, it was thought that education does not end with the completion of schooling, even of professional schooling, but, rather, that the pursuit of knowledge involves the effort of a lifetime and is one of the principal activities of those with time for leisure-work. Adult education was rarely discussed as such, partly because the stages of schooling were not so sharply defined by age level as they are now and partly, no doubt, because its pursuit, among the leisured few, was (correctly or incorrectly) assumed. But it was explicitly maintained that only the beginning of education can occur in youth because of the limitations intrinsic to immaturity and the limitations of any subject matter appropriate to immature study. To Seneca's dictum that "an old man who has still to learn his lessons is a shameful and ridiculous object; training and preparation are for the young, action for the old," Aristotle replies (three hundred years earlier!) that child prodigies may be found in mathematics and harmony, but never in morals or politics, which require the experience of life for their comprehension.

The fourth fundamental concept of education down the ages was that the profession of teaching is not only a learned profession, involving special preparation in the liberal arts and the skill of transmitting them, but also a profession of learning, in which the teacher not only practices his art but improves it by the continuous study of the subjects he teaches. The teacher is a lifelong learner.

Finally, the advancement of learning, upon which the vitality of education in any society depends, requires scholarship, or investigation and research, apart from the dissemination and acquisition of the learning already available; and scholarship is likely to flourish in a community of scholars (whether or not they are organized as the faculties of educational institutions) cooperating and communicating across the separate fields of learning which, since their common goal is truth, are implicitly related to one another.

These concepts are enumerated as five for the sake of discussion here; they might be condensed or extended. What is important is that, historically, they represent together the basic principles of educational theory and practice of every epoch preceding our own. They were education's answers to the questions asked of it by the social situation of twenty-five pre-scientific and pre-technological centuries, in which what was required of education was to produce a small class of educated men. The differences and disagreements which arose in theory and in practice occurred within the general framework of these suppositions.

The fact that almost all educators and educational philosophers concurred in these general principles does not establish their validity. The fact that it was Cicero or Aquinas or Kant—or all of them together—who held these views does not mean that they were right. What it does mean is that they were held, and nearly universally held, by the best minds we have known from age to age. They do not, for that reason, command our assent, but they do command, in the name of common humility, our consideration.

Anyone who undertakes to judge their validity—for their time and place—has to consider one stupendous historical fact: These are the principles upon which the men responsible for our culture were educated, generation after generation, century after century. They are the principles upon which Plato taught Aristotle in Athens and Mentor Graham taught Abraham Lincoln in Sangamon County, Illinois. For better or for worse, this is the outline of the education which (to whatever extent education civilizes) gave us our civilization.

Among these thinkers, for all their agreement, the effectiveness of education as a civilizing agency was moot, as it still is and, it seems probable, as it always will be. The question asked in the first recorded discussion of education has not been answered: "Can you tell me, Socrates, whether virtue is acquired by teaching or by practice . . . or in what other way?" Schooling, which is what we are here concerned with, is only a part of the civilizing (or educational) process; it is that part dealing formally and primarily with the cultivation of the mind and only indirectly with the formation or fortification of moral character.

The Platonic adage that "the city educates the man" sobers the enthusiast for more and better schooling. There are other forces at work—the home, the church, the organization of society and the form of government (and the government itself), the streets and the playgrounds, and in a modern society the newspapers, magazines, and books (including comic books), and the cinema, the radio, and the television screen. These, too, are educational agencies in the general sense of the term. So are the economic order and the conditions of labor, housing, diet, and medical care. So are the genes and chromosomes; we are the omnibuses, said Oliver Wendell Holmes, in which our ancestors ride, and sometimes one of them sticks his head out the window and makes a terrible fuss. The school—in a word—is just *one* contributor to the education of men.

Of this particular institution the free man is the end product. While there are certainly such men who have not been schooled, the purpose of liberal education is to contribute to the production of such a man. We may agree that moral training is central to the development of the free man, but whether such training is within the primary competence of the institution of secular education is arguable; not, however, here. What is unarguable—at least historically—is that the direct and overt objective of liberal education is the liberation of the intellect from ignorance and its cultivation as a critical instrument.

The wisest men of whom we have record agreed generally that the principles upon which education was conducted up to a century ago better fulfilled the limited objective of such education than any other principle or set of principles. Were we living today in one of the many societies in which they lived, we might follow their consensus with confidence. But we are not. We are living in a society which none of these men of imagination ever imagined.

However imperfectly the ideal of universal suffrage is realized in the United States—and it is realized more perfectly every day—its embodiment in the basic law of the land makes "every man a king," every American adult the sovereign ruler of the state, holding, like the king he is, its highest and only permanent office, that of citizen. But the king must be educated, and he must be educated to rule. A truly democratic state without compulsory education at public expense would be an anomaly. Universal education is an inescapable corollary of universal suffrage.

With the emancipation of the chattel slaves came their enfranchisement a few years later. With their enfranchisement came the desperate necessity to convert them from their condition of general illiteracy to one of adequate education. Southern demagogues—and many other men, thoroughly sincere—argued against emancipation on the ground that, even if slavery were morally indefensible, the country would not survive the ravages of uneducated freedmen at the polls, and on this point the Great Emancipator agreed with them. Nor would it have, for long; the freedman had to be given the educational opportunity of a ruler.

In 1920 almost half the adults in the United States became, for the first time, full citizens: the women. They had, of course, played a progressively freer role in society for a century, and their status was reflected in the changed character of "female education," which was steadily becoming indistinguishable from that of the adolescent male. In all ages past, women, along with slaves, had been foreclosed from liberal education. In Jefferson's time no American college admitted them. The first college for women (Wesleyan Female College, in Macon, Georgia) and the first college to become coeducational (Oberlin College, in Ohio) have the same founding date—1837. Previously, girls of the wealthy class were instructed by private tutor or in seminaries or finishing schools in reading, writing, and ciphering for household management, in cooking, needlework, and music, and sometimes in the care of minor medical emergencies in the home. Since the adoption of the Nineteenth Amendment and the removal of the last disabled segment of our people from political ineligibility, the lines between "male" and "female" education have disappeared.

It took almost two centuries to establish in this country the principle of free education for every future citizen and almost a century more before our people agreed that schooling had to be the full-time occupation of the child and that even eight years of elementary education were insufficient for his preparation for intelligent citizenship and the blessings of private life. But then the change was rapid. In 1875 there were only 500 high schools in the

United States, and in 1900 this country had a smaller proportion of its population in school than any country of western Europe except Italy. But in 1925 there were 16,000 high schools, and in 1950, 71.3 per cent of all American children between fourteen and seventeen years of age were in school. In 1900 there were about 500,000 boys and girls in all the high schools of this country, or about 10 per cent of those who were eligible. Today there are over 7,000,000 or approximately 85 per cent of all the children between fourteen and seventeen years of age. No other country attempts to give secondary schooling to more than 20 per cent of its youth.

The school-leaving age rises every year now; today almost as many high-school graduates go on to college as do not. Under conditions of advanced industrial production, the campaign for child-labor laws and a child-labor amendment to the Constitution has subsided, except in very limited areas; mechanization, which in its early stages produced the frightful torture of children in factories, mills, and mines, has finally produced, in anything like normal conditions, an adult-labor "surplus" that makes child labor unnecessary even in nonmoral terms. Automation promises to make the whole adult population "surplus labor" in increasing degree. Under present and presently projected conditions of industry, it is economically possible from a manpower standpoint for compulsory basic schooling to be lengthened to a fourteen- or even sixteen-year period; the absorption of eighteen-year-olds into the peacetime army did not retard production.

Along with the reduction of labor time, the industrial economy has vitiated the age-old distinction between a leisured class and a laboring class. With exceptions that are rapidly becoming spectacular, every adult is both a worker and a man of leisure. Not only are the idle rich disappearing, but it is not in the least uncommon, where the five-day week prevails, to find the employer working longer hours than his employees. What is more, under public and private pension systems the employer is likelier than his employee to go on working in his advanced age. The divisions of American society today—and no one supposes that the direction of change will be reversed—are no longer divisions into distinct classes. They are, rather, a division of the time of every adult into distinct activities—those of labor and those of leisure, the one devoted to wealth or the goods of subsistence, the other devoted to the creation of civilization or the goods of the human spirit.

The increase of time available for leisure activities with the shortening of the work day, the work week, and the work years has opened the possibility of continuing education to almost every adult who wants it. The adult-education movement in this country once had two primary purposes—first (still common in Europe), to provide opportunity for adults to make up for insufficient basic schooling in childhood; second, to orient non-English-speaking immigrants. With the lengthening of the period of compulsory education and the closing of mass immigration, there is less and less need for compensatory or orientation schooling for adults. Adult education tends now to become the kind of education which sustains and advances learning after adequate basic schooling has been completed in youth.

With the political, productive, and scientific revolution of the past century fully developed, the problems of education in mid-twentieth-century America can be seen by examining the realities of the present against the background of one fairly reliable assumption about the past, the assumption that the traditional principles of education (enumerated above) were valid for an undemocratic, nonindustrial, and pre-scientific society. Acceptance of this assumption leads at once to the two questions upon which the discussion of our present problems may be sharply focused: Are the traditional principles valid for a modern industrial democracy, with, of course, such adaptations as contemporary circumstances indicate? And if they are not, what is now to be the meaning of education and its fundamental aim and procedure? The serious educational controversies of the last two or three generations—the generations that have begun to feel the full impact of the great change in society—have revolved around these two questions.

If the traditional principles are valid, and by one or another means adaptable to modern conditions, certain subordinate questions are immediately raised. Do we know how to apply them so that what was once the education of the few can be made the education of all? Can the teacher, under the increased pressures of the modern profession and of modern life, be expected to go on learning? Can the community of scholars that was once thought to be an indispensable condition for the advancement of learning coexist with intense specialization in an era of science and technology?

And if the traditional principles are held to have been valid under past historical conditions, but no longer, to what criteria are we to turn for the judgment of alternative principles? What is the ideal to be substituted for the liberal education of the few who were to be free and responsible citizens, when every man and woman is to be free and responsible? What kind of men and women (in so far as education contributes to their development) do we want in order to maintain and perfect the kind of society we want, and how may education proceed to contribute to their development?

The extremist view—that the traditional principles were invalid even for their own time and irrelevant and even misleading for ours—is matched at the other extreme by the view that the traditional principles of education can be applied whole, without amendment or adaptation, to our new kind of society. This view, like its equal and opposite, is rarely advanced in contemporary discussion. In between, the two more moderate positions more or less adequately embrace those who have made a sustained and conscientious effort to think about education for our time.

Each of the two moderate positions has a different obstacle to overcome. The first, or traditionalist, position must discover and formulate the means whereby the same quality of liberal education that was once the privilege of the few can be extended to all, both in school and (given the advance of leisure) in adult life. The second, or nontraditionalist, position must redefine the aims of education to conform to the realities of an industrial democracy in an age of science, but without making it any less appropriate for all the men who are now citizens and men of leisure than the education of past ages was for the ruling few of the leisure class.

As we examine current educational controversy of an earnest—rather than a polemical—nature, we are likely to find that the two moderate positions are not wholly irreconcilable. This does not mean that there are not basic disagreements among the protagonists. It means only that their disagreements might be more manageable if they were seen in the light of their common rejection of both the extremist positions. Unfortunately, the educational literature of the last fifty years has, in bulk, tended to foist each of the appropriate extremes upon each of the moderate positions. The consequence has been more conflict than controversy. The character of the conflict has not only obscured the real issues; it has diverted attention from them, and especially the attention of each side from the difficulties of its own position. The chance of surmounting these difficulties—and of solving the problems of education in a scientific and industrial democracy—might be greater if the problems themselves could be clarified. . . .

The real differences in philosophy of education in our time are the consequence of the social revolution of 1850–1950. In the face of that revolution education could not continue in its historic forms. It could not, and it did not. The forms fell apart, or were burst by the forces generated by the democratic, industrial, and scientific revolution in America. Education went on, in any and every which way. Both of the moderate positions in the current controversy call for principled reforms in the prevalent practices of the schools, and for this reason both of them are opposed, or, rather, blindly rejected, by those (not all of whom are outside the field of education) who do not wish to be disturbed.

But they are being disturbed, willy-nilly. Parents are challenging the popular practices—or demanding to know exactly what they are and what they are for. Civic organizations are challenging them. Even pupils are, in their own often inarticulate way, challenging them by "delinquent" behavior. In the midst of the hullabaloo, harried schoolmen, who did not bargain for all the criticism the schools are getting, are heard saying plaintively that they have troubles enough without being asked, "Why?" and "What for?" The motto of all old institutions is, "Don't rock the boat." A distinguished Englishman once said that in educational reform the time is never ripe until it is rotten.

There is another, perhaps more tangible if less potent, source of opposition to both moderate positions. The traditionalists and the nontraditionalists accept the revolution of the past century and welcome it. They stand together against those who do not, against those who think either that democratic government is wrong or that the dispersion of the fruits of technology and industrial production, in the form of higher living standards and increasing leisure for the whole of our people, is deplorable. Democracy and mechanization of labor are here, and they are here together. Whatever their shortcomings in practice, they present the human race for the first time in human history with the possibility of the good life for all men and the equitable organization of human society.

The demands which modern democracy makes upon education cannot be avoided. To meet these demands in our own country—the most radically transformed of all modern societies—educational philosophers cannot bicker indefinitely. The problems are critical, and they must be faced with a view to their resolution in the best interests of our country and its people and their form of government and their aspirations. Businessmen and poets can, if they are financially independent, refine their techniques to their hearts' content before they go into production. Educators cannot; they are "producing" members of society whether or not they are ready to.

There is more, much more, at stake in educational controversy than the preservation of a point of view at any cost or the maintenance of prestige and position in an area of argument which, perhaps because educators are so often on the defensive in an activist culture, sometimes degenerates into polysyllabic fishwifery. Education needs to know what it is doing and why, and to be aggressive about it. "The keystone of the arch of our government," Jefferson called it. What the thinking of the past was able, at its best, to do for society of some, the thinking of the present must try to do for society of all.

Education in the Perspective of History

Arnold J. Toynbee

(1889–)

Education is older than Western civilization; it is characteristic of human society at all times and in all places. We need a broad perspective to understand the perennial role of schools: a perspective going back before classical times and reaching beyond Western Europe. Few men are as well-qualified to offer such a view as historian Arnold J. Toynbee. In this essay Toynbee applies to our educational problems conclusions drawn from a comparative study of education's role in fifteen civilizations. He considers most of the challenges with which the remaining writers represented in this volume wrestle: industrialism, the scientific revolution, social mobility, the explosion of knowledge, and rising expectations in underdeveloped nations. Toynbee does not hesitate to focus also on such peculiarly American problems as the status of teachers, our disgraceful incompetence in foreign languages, and the growing imbalance between research and teaching at our colleges and universities.

Toynbee urges the Western nations to face up to the challenge of aiding the underdeveloped regions of the world by helping to educate their people. But he warns that previous attempts to unify the world through education have failed. In weighing our chances of succeeding in this task, Toynbee neglects one perhaps critical consideration. Although he sees the extraordinary development of science and technology as creating many of the distinctive problems of modern education, such as the explosion of knowledge, Toynbee does not consider the possibility that we might solve some of these problems by applying technology to the educational process itself. We might ask whether worldwide television, teaching machines, and cheap printed materials may not offer us some historically unique advantages over previous civilizations, such as the Chinese and Roman, which have assayed the great task of educating mankind.

Arnold Joseph Toynbee, born in 1889, was educated at Oxford where he remained as a tutor and fellow until 1915. After the First World War he became professor of Greek language and history at the University of London, and in 1925 was appointed research professor and director of studies at the Royal Institute of International Affairs. He stayed there for thirty years.

Toynbee achieved international renown with his ten-volume *A Study of History*, in which he considers the problems of history in terms of great cultural and ethical groups rather than in terms of nations. His thesis is that the development and decay of a civilization depends upon its ability to respond to the challenges which face it from without and within.

The following essay was first published as the concluding chapter of *Education in the Perspective of History*, by Professor Edward D. Myers, published by Harper & Brothers in 1960.

Education is a specifically human activity. Unlike other animals, man inherits something over and above what is transmitted to him automatically by physical and psychic heredity. He inherits a culture which the members of the rising generation acquire, not as an automatic birthright, but through being inducted into it by their elders. Human culture is not built into human minds; it is a mental tool that is transmitted, held, and operated by them, and it is detachable and variable. Our minds are like handles to which alternative systems of culture can be fitted. Our culture does resemble our physical and psychic constitution in that it changes in the course of transmission; but its rate of change is incomparably faster than nature's. Even when the intentions of all concerned are conservative, the transmitting generation never succeeds in handing on its cultural heritage in quite the form in which it received it from its predecessors; and the time span of one generation is infinitesimally short compared to the age of the human race.

In most human societies in most times and places so far, education, in the broad sense of the transmission of a cultural heritage, has been unself-conscious and unorganized activity. People have mostly acquired their ancestral culture in the way in which they learn their mother tongue. They associate with their elders and learn from them unconsciously, while the elders, on their side, are hardly more conscious of being teachers.

This unsophisticated kind of education continues to play an important part even in societies in process of civilization in which organized and formal systems of education have come to be established. Even in educational institutions in which the official staple is book learning, the forming of habits and the training of character are still largely left to be taken care of by the spontaneous effects of the social relations between the rising generation and its elders; and what the child brings with him from his home may count for as much as what is deliberately impressed upon him at school. The importance of the home's contribution comes to light when an educational institution that has been the preserve of some privileged minority is thrown open to a wider public. One of the most effective privileges hitherto has been the privilege of being heir to a richer cultural heritage than is accessible to the unprivileged majority, and this richer heritage is transmitted through the family as well as through schools and colleges. This becomes apparent when children with a poorer cultural heritage are admitted to the minority's schools. They find it difficult to obtain as much benefit as their privileged schoolfellows obtain from the same course of formal education, because they bring less with them. To him that hath shall be given. This is not just, but it is one of the facts of life. It takes more than one generation for a family that has made its way out of a less privileged into a more privileged social class to acquire the full cultural heritage of the class to which it has won admission.

A society enters on the process of civilization as soon as it can afford to maintain a minority, however small, whose time and energy is not wholly taken up in producing food and the other primary necessities of life. This leisured minority is the social milieu in which an unorganized and unself-conscious apprenticeship in the older generation's way of life comes to be supplemented, more and more, by the organized and self-conscious kind of instruction which is what we commonly mean today in our society when we use the word "education." This development, which is one of the accompaniments of civilization, is what makes possible the enrichment of the cultural heritage that the word "civilization" implies. But the introduction of formal education has several awkward consequences.

One consequence is that education becomes a burden on the mind. In the act of making it formal we make it cumulative. The successive cultural achievements of successive generations are recorded and handed on, while the capacity of a single human mind in a single lifetime remains within constant natural limits. How is a limited human mind to cope with a cultural heritage that is perpetually increasing in bulk? This problem is aggravated when people begin deliberately to extend the range of human knowledge by systematic research. There will be a temptation to try to facilitate the acquisition of the growing heritage by simplifying its content at the cost of impoverishing it. For educational purposes the culture may be reduced to a conventional form in which it will tend to become impersonal, secular, and abstract; and in this process the living essence of the culture may slip out of the educational net. The apprenticeship for life may be ousted by a course of instruction set by syllabus. Ordeals that are initiations into successive stages of life may shrivel into examinations in arbitrarily selected bodies of cut-and-dried knowledge.

Another consequence of formalizing education is to make it esoteric. When poetry, sacred or secular, is preserved over a series of generations by being committed to memory or to writing, the work of art "freezes" the language in which it is conveyed. Of all man's cultural tools, his living language is perhaps the one that changes most rapidly. It quickly parts company with the language of a work that has become a classic, and the classical language soon becomes archaic and finally ceases to be intelligible to anyone who has not had the leisure to devote himself to the study of it. Mastery of a language that still enjoys high cultural prestige but is at the same time a "dead" language for all but a learned minority gives this minority a monopoly that carries power with it and that may therefore come to be prized and clung to for its own sake.

This may happen even when the transmission of a classical literature is still oral. History shows that in societies in which the human mind's natural powers of memory have not been weakened by dependence on written records, large bodies of literature can be handed down, word perfect, for centuries by memorization, unaided by writing. And indeed, many societies, long after they have acquired the art of writing, have cherished a strong and persistent prejudice against committing to writing anything that is felt to be of social and cultural value—for instance, laws and, still more, liturgies. Writing seems usually to have come into use first of all for prosaic practical purposes such as the recording of inventories, contracts, and correspondence. It has to become well established and familiar before people can bring themselves to use it for higher cultural ends.

The earliest scripts have been the clumsiest and the most complicated and therefore the most difficult to learn to read and write. So, when the scribe's monopoly of understanding a classical language is reinforced by a monopoly of manipulating an archaic script, he becomes doubly entrenched in his position of privilege, and acquires a vested interest in opposing the literary use of the vulgar tongue of his own day conveyed in a system of writing which is easily mastered.

The Egyptian hieroglyphic script, the Sumerian cuneiform, and above all, the vast array of Chinese characters are examples of scripts that have been misused to defeat the purpose of the art of writing by making it a barrier to communication instead of a channel for it. For this reason the invention of the alphabet has been a turning point in the history of education, if we think of this history as being the story of the effort to make formal, as well as spontaneous, education one of the fundamental rights of all men instead of leaving it to remain the privilege of a minority. Yet, during 3,000 years since the discovery of the principle of analyzing the sounds of human speech into their elements, by the unknown genius to whom the invention of the alphabet is due, this principle has never been applied with complete rationality. Every known version of the alphabet retains letters that are superfluous because they are duplicates or compounds, and lacks letters required for conveying some of the sounds that occur in the language to which this version of the alphabet has been geared.

Successive breaches in the scribe's monopoly have been made from various motives. For instance, the government of a wide-spread empire, embracing all, and perhaps more than all, the domain of an entire civilization, may find the traditional privileged minority inadequate or unsuitable for supplying the imperial government with the administrators that it needs; and then this government may deliberately call into existence a new class of educated people to fill or supplement the ranks of its administrative hierarchy. In China at the turn of the second and the last century B.C., the imperial government entered into an alliance with the Confucian school of philosophers, whose literary stock-in-trade was the classics that Confucius had canonized. The result was a considerable extension of the educated class in China and a concomitant broadening of this class's social basis. A wholly new "intelligentsia" may be called into existence by an imperial government that has become converted to an alien culture or has brought an alien culture in with it. This was one of the effects of the "reception" of Western culture in Russia after the reign of Peter the Great, and of the introduction of Western culture into India by the British raj.

Missionary religions, again, have called into existence new corporations of educated clerics in their zeal to propagate themselves to the ends of the earth; and their leaders, looking upon the whole human race as prospective converts, have been perhaps the first people in the world to conceive of universal education. In China, in particular, the inventions of printing and paper appear to have been stimulated by the eagerness of Buddhist missionaries to bring spiritual enlightenment within the reach of the masses.

This vision of universal education was caught by the higher religions before the economic means had been provided for translating it from an ideal into a reality. During these first 5,000 years of the history of civilization, one of the most characteristic, and most ugly, features of this new way of life has been the monopoly of its amenities, spiritual as well as material, by a small minority of the members of societies in process of civilization. This blot on the scutcheon of civilization during its first phase has not been due solely to the selfishness of the ruling minority. Even if all the members of this group had succeeded in rising above their natural human egotism and had tried with all their might to share their cultural heritage with the unprivileged majority of their fellow human beings, they would have been defeated, before the Industrial Revolution, by the smallness of the economic surplus remaining in hand after the satisfaction of elementary economic needs. This revolution started in the Western world about two hundred years ago and, since then, has been increasing in momentum and communicating itself from the Western peoples to the rest of mankind.

In a pre-industrial agricultural economy, in which human and animal muscle power has not been reinforced by mechanical power, all but a small minority of the members of society are condemned to live as a peasantry whose puny production cannot provide amenities beyond such common necessities as food, clothing, and shelter for more than a small minority. This injustice was made intolerable by the appearance in the world of higher religions that divined and proclaimed the infinite spiritual values of every human soul, irrespective of the social class in which it has been placed by the accident of birth. An injustice that has long since been intolerable has now been made unnecessary by the Industrial Revolution, which has brought it within our economic power at last to provide the amenities of civilization for mankind in the mass—always supposing that we do not use the new power generated by the progress of technology for the self-destruction of the human race.

Our present Industrial Revolution is, of course, only one in a long series of technological advances; but it is perhaps the first since the invention of agriculture that has been potent enough to provide appreciable social and cultural benefits for all members of a society that has made it. At the dawn of civilization, the agricultural yield was increased in the river valleys of Southwest Asia and Egypt by the invention of water control. In the seventh and sixth centuries B.C., the quality of the yield was increased in Greece by the invention of specialization in luxury crops to be traded in exchange for staple foodstuffs and raw materials. These too were brilliant economic revolutions, but they were comparatively minor ones in their material effect. Our present-day Industrial Revolution is the first that has opened up the prospect of providing the material means for raising the standard of living of the world's vast peasantry above the neolithic level that was attained round the rim of the Fertile Cresent during the age preceding the dawn of civilization there. This present possibility of bringing the benefits of civilization to the whole of the great unprivileged majority of the human race carries with it a moral command to execute the act of justice that is now at last within our power. This is the new requirement with which mankind, and consequently the ancient human institution of education, is confronted today. The educational problems involved are of the same order of magnitude as the requirement itself.

One problem is presented by the unalterable and inescapable fact that a human being has a strictly limited capacity. The maximum natural endowment of ability and energy that can be in action over the maximum effective life span is something that is fixed within very narrow limits of marginal variability. On the other hand, human knowledge is cumulative in science and technology. In the humanities as well, knowledge tends to accumulate within the time spans of particular civilizations and higher religions, and sometimes outlives the disintegration and disappearance of these social matrices of humane culture. This accumulation of culture confronts the givers and receivers of formal education with a Psyche's task of ever-increasing difficulty; and this difficulty confronts all individuals alike, in every civilization and in every social class.

In modern times Western civilization has been sensationally successful in deliberately and systematically extending the bounds of knowledge and in applying its knowledge of nonhuman nature to the practical purpose of increasing human power over man's nonhuman environment. One of the devices by which these successes have been achieved has been specialization. And there is a temptation to carry specialization to still greater lengths as a possible means of coping with the overwhelming mass of new knowledge that specialization has won for us. At the present time this temptation is reinforced by the new demand of governments and nongovernmental corporations and foundations for specialists in natural science and technology, now that technological and scientific knowledge is expected to count for more than military prowess and administrative skill in the arena of international power politics.

Any state or people that succumbs to this temptation seems likely to defeat its own purpose. The modern marriage of technology with science has proved fruitful because science has been pursued primarily for its own sake, without any immediate view to a practical application of its discoveries. And even the disinterested pursuit of science becomes sterile if it runs in narrow ruts. Specialization in particular branches of natural science soon runs dry if it is cut off from its source in comprehensive and philosophical scientific thinking. Moreover, even a scientist who takes the whole of nonhuman nature into his purview cannot afford to leave human nature out of it. "The proper study of mankind is man" because man's dealings with himself and with his human neighbors are the part of man's business in which he has been conspicuously unsuccessful thus far; and the penalty for failure here becomes heavier, the greater the power over nonhuman nature that the advance of natural science places in man's hands for him to wield, in his perversity, against himself. The need for balancing an education in natural science and technology with an education in the humanities has been recognized and acted upon by, for instance, the Massachusetts Institute of Technology, one of the most distinguished educational institutions of the present day; and the wisdom of this broad-minded policy has been recognized in the educational world. This should be noted and taken to heart by the advocates of extreme specialization in the various branches of technology and natural science, who suppose such specialization to be a key to dominance in the competition for power between states.

Meanwhile, the ocean of knowledge has grown to an immeasurable size, not only in natural science but in the humanities as well. In the past, when various civilizations were living more or less in isolation from one another, a humane education demanded no more than mastery of the "classical" language, literature, and philosophy of some single civilization—for example, the Chinese classics for the peoples of Eastern Asia and the Greek and Latin classics for the peoples of the West. Since modern Western civilization has made its impact on the rest of the world, however, the children of other civilizations have been finding that a mastery of their own ancestral culture is no longer enough to enable them to hold their own. If they are to survive "under the strenuous conditions of modern life" (to quote a phrase from the Covenant of the League of Nations), they must now learn something about the West, to whom new knowledge has given a temporary dominance over other peoples. Under Western pressure, the non-Western peoples have been stealing a march on the Westerners in broadening the traditional range of their education in the humanities. And the West, in its turn, is going to have to follow its unintended pupils' example. For, in our lifetime, we are seeing the West rapidly losing its recently won supremacy, as one non-Western people after another acquires the Western technological and scientific know-how and thereby begins to recapture its normal position in the world, a position that was temporarily lost when the modern West took the world by storm through taking it by surprise.

The non-Western peoples' self-education in Western knowledge may be proving effective, for the moment, as a key to the recovery of power, but it is a shallow knowledge, compared to their traditional education in their ancestral humanities, and this new knowledge will prove a poor exchange for the old unless it is deepened. The typical Westernized—or, as he might prefer to say, modernized—non-Westerner of today has qualified himself for the exercise of some modern Western profession—say, medicine or engineering—and he has learned his profession in some Western language, but he is likely to be ignorant of the Greek and Latin classics, which are the source of the modern West's secular culture, and ignorant of Christianity, which is the source of an agnostic or atheist Westerner's spiritual outlook, as well as of his ethical principles. So the non-Western convert to Western civilization will have abandoned his own ancestral cultural heritage without having succeeded in acquiring its Western equivalent. But the peoples of the world cannot learn to understand each other if they confine their attention to the present surface of life and ignore the historical depths. We cannot truly know a person, a people, a civilization, or a religion without knowing something about its history; and here, by yet another route we are again brought face to face with the problem created by the inordinate increase in the quantity of our knowledge.

Today our knowledge of the past is increasing at an unprecedented rate, and this at both ends of its ever lengthening vista. The archeologists are making history by exhuming buried and forgotten civilizations as fast as the politicians are making it by taking new action for contemporary historians to study. The public records produced in the United Kingdom during the Second World War, which lasted less than six years, are said to equal in quantity all the surviving records produced previously by the

United Kingdom and its component states, the kingdoms of England and Scotland. The wartime records of one single government department in London would extend, it is said, for seventeen miles if the files were stacked on edge and placed in a row as tightly as they could be packed. The records of archeological excavations are also formidably extensive; and, in between, our knowledge of comparatively well-known periods in the histories of the civilizations and the religions has been increased and, in the process, transformed by the study of previously unknown or neglected documents and by the reinterpretation of previously familiar ones.

In the meantime, economics has opened up the study of an aspect of human activity that was previously ignored; anthropology and sociology have opened up the study of the structure of human society and the nature of human culture at all levels, from the most primitive to the least uncivilized. And psychology has added a new dimension to the study of human nature. The Greek sciences of epistemology, logic, and ethics had explored the rational and purposeful surface of the human psyche; psychology is probing the irrational and emotional depths; and here, once more, the questing human mind finds itself confronted by infinity. To borrow a phrase from the Gospel according to St. John, "the World itself could not contain the books that should be written" by a competent psychologist if he were to set himself to make an exhaustive record of all the psychic events that occur in a single psyche within the shortest period of time that the subtlest recording instruments can measure.

This immense and growing mass of knowledge about man and his nonhuman environment daunts the minds that are exposed to it and throws them on the defensive. In self-defense we are tempted to ask ourselves again whether our institutions for formal education cannot simply reject the greater part of this formidable load, or, short of that, divide it up into packages that can be distributed among different pairs of shoulders without risk of breaking any backs. The reply to this cry of distress has to be in the negative: "*Homo sum, humani nihil a me alienum puto*" ("I am a human being, so I cannot be indifferent to anything that has to do with human life and human nature"). Every man, woman, and child alive today is living in a world in which mankind is faced with the extreme choice between learning to live together as one family and committing genocide on a planetary scale. Neither the human race nor any living member of it can afford to ignore the present human situation. We must cope with it if we are not to destroy ourselves; in order to cope with it we must understand it; and trying to understand it commits each and all of us to making some acquaintance with at least three vast realms of knowledge: a knowledge of nonhuman nature; a knowledge of human nature; and a knowledge of the characters and histories of the local and temporary cultures—some relatively primitive, others relatively advanced—that man has created and transmitted and modified and discarded in the course of the ages that have passed since his prehuman ancestors became human. Formal education's minimum task has thus become a big undertaking in our day; and every child will have a strenuous course of formal as well as informal education to run in order to grow up into being an effective citizen of our new world.

How, then, are our educational institutions to convey this overwhelmingly massive heritage of knowledge to a puny and ephemeral human mind? The task would be an intimidating one even if we could confine it to the education of the privileged heirs of the Western cultural tradition. These, if anyone, should be receptive to an education of this comprehensive kind; for it is they who have called into existence the world-wide social framework within which the whole human race is now living. This has started as a Western framework (though, no doubt, it will turn into a very different one); and the privileged minority in the Western society has played the chief part in giving it its present shape. Thus they, if anyone, ought to feel at home in it. Yet how hard it is, today, to educate even this favored minority to cope with what is its own heritage! And before we have seen our way to solving even this limited educational problem, we have to plunge on into the still more difficult problems of educating the unprivileged majority of Westerners and the huge non-Western majority of the human race, for whom the present Western framework of their life is something alien and uncongenial. Clearly this educational task is a tremendous one. Yet we cannot afford to shy away from it or to exclude any part of the human race from its scope. We have to help mankind to educate itself against the danger of its destroying itself; and this is a duty that we dare not repudiate.

This is not the first time that an educational task of this nature, and even of something like this magnitude, has confronted human beings who have found themselves responsible for the destinies of large portions of the human race. It may be true that the whole human race, in all the habitable regions on the surface of the globe, has never been drawn together into a single world-wide society before this was achieved, in the course of the last few centuries, by Western initiative. All the same, in the past, there have been unifications on a scale that, short of being truly ecumenical, has been great enough to seem ecumenical to the people involved. Nineteen hundred years ago the Chinese Empire seemed to the inhabitants of the Chinese Empire, and the Roman Empire to the inhabitants of the Roman Empire, to embrace virtually the whole of the civilized world. Both societies were mistaken in their picture of themselves—as is demonstrated by the mere fact that these two "ecumenical" empires were coexisting, almost unknown to each other, at opposite ends of the same continent. Nevertheless, the educational problems that these predecessors of ours encountered as a result of unification on a subcontinental scale are sufficiently like our own truly ecumenical problem of the present day to be worth our notice. A glance at these partial precedents may perhaps at least give us warning of some of the pitfalls that we have to avoid, even if it does not throw as much light on the positive educational policies that we ought to pursue.

In the Chinese Empire in its first bout, under the Ts'in and Han Dynasties, as well as in the Roman Empire, there was an attempt to extend the range of formal education from the privileged minority that had previously monopolized it to a wider circle. In both cases this attempt miscarried, in the sense that it failed to teach the whole population of an "ecumenical" empire how to live together permanently as a single family. Both empires went to pieces (though both were put together again temporarily after an interregnum). In both cases, the same two reasons for miscarriage can be discerned within the field of education—though of course these reasons are only part of the explanation of what happened.

One reason was that the former privileged minority's traditional system of education was impoverished in the process of being disseminated. It degenerated into a formal education in book learning, divorced from a spontaneous apprenticeship for life. The test of having been initiated into the traditional culture came to be the mastery of an arbitrarily selected and canonized corpus of classical literature, and the test of this mastery came to be an ability to imitate the original. In fact, the art of playing with words was substituted for the art of living.

A second reason for the miscarriage was that the range of formal education was limited, in both cases, to the humanities. Though both the Greeks and the Chinese of the "classical" age had made additions to mankind's technological equipment, and the Greeks had also been pioneers in the discovery of pure mathematics and physical science, an aristocratic prejudice against "the useful arts" outlived the aristocratic regime in both societies. Accordingly, nothing was done in either society to try to raise the economy above the purely agricultural level at which it had always remained in Eastern Asia and to which it had been reduced again in the Greco-Roman world when the effects of the agricultural revolutions in Greece in the sixth century B.C. and in Italy in the second century B.C. had been offset by the incorporation into the Greco-Roman world of large economically backward areas in Northwest Africa and in the European hinterlands of the Mediterranean. The same aristocratic prejudice inhibited the Greeks from making that marriage between science and technology which was consummated in the modern Western world in and after the seventeenth century with such fruitful results. The consequence, in both the Greco-Roman world and Eastern Asia, was that a swollen educated class remained parasitic on a peasantry whose productivity had not been stepped up to carry the additional load; and this increase in the peasantry's social burden was not compensated for by any cultural benefits that the peasantry could appreciate. The cut-and-dried book learning in the classics, to which the privileged minority's culture had been reduced, was not made accessible to the peasants, and if it had been, it would probably not have proved attractive to them. In these circumstances it is not surprising that in both cases the peasantry revolted and that the "ecumenical" empire and the civilization embodied in it, collapsed. In this story from the past there are lessons for us today.

One lesson is that we must try to keep the several essential subjects of education in balance with each other. Undoubtedly the most important subject of all is man. The human race could not survive if, in each generation, we did not learn from our predecessors at least a modicum of the art of managing our relations with our fellow human beings and with ourselves. This is the essence of a humane education, but it cannot be learned just from a study of "the humanities" in book form. In the present-day world, it is true, a considerable amount of book learning has come to be a necessary part of everyone's education. At the same time, the essence of a humane education has still to be acquired mainly through the informal apprenticeship that is the heart of education in all societies and all social classes at all levels. This is what makes and keeps us human. Book learning in "the humanities" can be a valuable supplement to it, but can never be a substitute for it. And it must be remembered that while an apprenticeship in the art of living with one's fellows is an indispensable part of the education of every human being born into the world, the bookish supplement to it originally came into existence as a vocational education for administrative officials in government service and for ministers of the higher religions. These are two highly specialized occupations; and, though the range of "the liberal professions" has considerably increased *pari passu* with the increasing complexity of civilization in the modern age, these walks of life seem unlikely ever to provide employment for more than a small fraction of the human race or to find more than a small fraction willing and able to seek its vocation in them.

If we were to try to force mankind in the mass to undergo a formal literary education, not merely up to the elementary or the secondary stage, but up to the standard required in order to qualify for one of the liberal professions, we should ruin the higher levels of this branch of education in trying to bring them down to within the capacity of people with no special aptitude for rising to them, and at the same time we should be running the risk of alienating the mass of mankind from the idea of formal education of any kind. We must recognize that there is a diversity in human gifts, and that this diversity is valuable to society. Natural-born "intellectuals" are divided into those who are attracted to the humanities and those who are attracted to natural science. But "intellectuals" of both types are a rather small minority in every class, society, and race. What line of higher education an individual should follow ought to be a matter, not of privilege, but of personal aptitude. Most human beings in all races, societies, and classes are born with a practical bent, and these, when they reach the stage of more advanced education, will feel most at home if they turn from book learning toward an apprenticeship in technology, irrespective of what their family's social position may happen to be.

This does not, of course, mean that formal education should be depreciated or neglected; for, in a world in which peoples inheriting widely different ways of life have suddenly to learn how to live as one family, there are obvious tasks for formal education in the spheres of technology, science, and the humanities. Our first need is to communicate effectively with each other; and, in a world that is still a babel of mutually unintelligible languages, every child should be expected, whatever his vocation is going to be, to learn at least one other language besides his mother tongue. This is not an excessive demand, as is shown by the fact that in Switzerland every child does already learn two other languages, and in Holland three, as a matter of course. The incentive is greatest for those, like the Dutch, whose mother tongue happens not to be a world language, so that they will be strangers in the wide world if they do not make the effort to become polyglots. The English-speaking peoples tend to be spoiled by the handicap of happening to speak a world language as their mother tongue.

Americans also tend to think of the rest of the human race as being potential immigrants whose business it is to learn how to live the American way of life, and the first step toward this, as Americans see it, is to learn the English language. Today, however, it is the Americans' turn to come on to other peoples' ground if America is to hold her own in her world-wide competition with Russia. Since the Second World War, an important new profession has made its appearance in American life. There are now hundreds of thousands of Americans working abroad in the service, not only of the United States Government, but of the great American commercial corporations and cultural foundations. These American citizens on service in non-English-speaking countries have been caught at a disadvantage by the traditional American aversion to the learning of foreign languages. On the other hand, Russia enjoys the advantage of a traditional mastery of foreign languages up to almost Swiss and Dutch standards, and this tradition seems now to have revived in Russia after a lapse during the early years after the revolution of 1917. It looks as if the Russians are likely to be the unintentional promoters of a new movement in the United States to make the learning of foreign languages one of the staples of American education. But it is not only the English-speaking peoples who need a stimulus in this direction. In a world that has to be "one world" now if it is to continue to exist, there is room for improvement even in those countries in which the standard of proficiency in learning foreign languages stands at its highest today in all classes.

But the world cannot become "one world" in spirit merely by improving its means of intercommunication. Closer acquaintance may produce hostility instead of friendship so long as different peoples, and different classes within the same community, have such unequal shares in the amenities of civilization as they still have. This inequality has been the consequence of poverty; poverty has been the consequence of technological backwardness; and this backwardness has been overcome by the modern marriage of technology with science. The world needs to educate its scientific-minded "intellectuals" and the technological-minded majority of its people to work together with a view to raising the minimum standard of material life for all mankind to a hitherto undreamed-of level. Now that we have discovered how to tap atomic energy, there is no reason why every Indian peasant should not soon be as well off as a present-day Illinois farmer. A rise in material well-being of this magnitude might perhaps not be altogether good for the peasant's soul; but without a considerable rise above his present depressingly low level of material existence he will be unable to achieve the spiritual welfare that is the true end of man.

The greatest blessing that technological progress has in store for mankind is not, of course, an accumulation of material possessions. The amount of these that can be enjoyed effectively by one individual in one lifetime is not great. But there is not the same narrow limit to the possibilities of the enjoyment of leisure. The gift of leisure may be abused by people who have had no experience of making use of it. Yet the creative use of leisure by a minority of the leisured minority in societies in process of civilization has been the mainspring of all human progress beyond the primitive level. In our still archaic industrial society, leisure continues to be thought of, by all but a privileged minority, in its negative aspect of "unemployment" in gainful labor; and for the industrial worker, the prospect of unemployment is at present a nightmare because it carries with it a loss of income and, worse still, a loss of self-respect. In our world an unemployed worker feels as if he were an outcast from the working community. The Greeks had a truer vision in seeing in leisure the greatest of all human goods; and they did indeed use leisure for worthy ends—as is witnessed by the fact that the Greek word for leisure has provided most of the modern Western languages with their word for "school." In our world, the dawning age of automation is soon going to provide ample leisure for all industrial workers without loss of income or self-respect or social esteem.

No doubt, if this unheard-of leisure is thrust into their hands suddenly, they will partly misuse it to begin with. But sooner or later we shall surely be able to salvage some of it for employment on adult education of a formal kind. Our informal apprenticeship in life is, of course, lifelong; our experience of life educates us, whether we will this or not. But, in the poverty-stricken civilizations of these first few thousand years, formal education, even for a privileged minority, has usually come to an end at the close of adolescence, if not earlier; and this has had an unfortunate consequence. The student has been surfeited with book learning at a stage of life at which he has not yet acquired the experience to take advantage of this, and he has then been starved for book learning at a later stage in which, if he had been given the opportunity, he could have made much more of it in the light of his growing experience. In the rich society of the future, we shall be able to afford to offer part-time adult education to every man and woman at every stage of grown-up life. Already, in Denmark, a highly civilized people that has had the intelligence to carry out an agricultural revolution has used some of its modest profits, Greek fashion, for providing voluntary adult higher education for itself in the admirable Danish high schools (which are schools for grown-up persons, not for children). A Danish farmer will save money for years to enable himself to take a six-months' or a twelve-months' course, and he will make it a point of honor to choose his subject with an eye to raising the level of his culture and not with an eye to improving his economic position. In this present-day Danish institution we have a foretaste of an educational advance that will be open to the whole of mankind in the coming age of "atoms for peace," automation, and the leisure that will be generated by an abundance of scientifically directed mechanical power.

But the quality of education of all kinds depends on the quality of the people who give it, and there has been a paradoxical tendency for quality to deteriorate as the formal element in education has increased in importance. The spontaneous apprenticeship in life, which was the only form of education known to early man, was given by the leaders of the community. The child received it from his parents, and the young man from the community's priests and captains. The educational functions of these leaders were inseparable and indistinguishable from the rest of their activities, and therefore shared in their general prestige. But when a separate formal kind of education makes its appearance, it brings into existence a new class of professional teachers who work, like other professional men and women, for pay; and, in most societies in process of civilization thus far, both the pay and the status of the professional teacher have been lower than has been warranted by the lip service that society has paid to the value of formal education. This has sometimes set up a vicious circle, in which the depression and discontent of the teaching profession has deterred able people from entering it, and has thereby led to a further lowering of its standards and status, leading in turn to deeper depression and discontent. The lowness of the status of the teaching profession in the present-day Western world has been satirized in George Bernard Shaw's trenchant and telling epigram: "If you can, do; if you can't, teach."

It is true that, in the Western world, the status of the teaching profession varies appreciably from country to country. In Austria a professor's wife used to rank with a colonel's, while in Prussia she ranked with a major's. If anyone had thought of grading her in England, she probably would have ranked no higher than a captain's wife there, whereas in Scotland she certainly would have ranked as high as a major general's. Before the salaries of professors in the United Kingdom were evened out by subventions from the public purse to counteract the effects of inflation, poor Scotland used to pay her professors higher salaries than rich England cared to dole out in remuneration for the same work. Today, an English professor no longer gains an increase in monetary income if he is posted to a Scottish university; but his wife is still astonished at the deference—out of all proportion to her slender purchasing power—with which she is treated in the stores that she honors with her distinguished patronage.

Perhaps one reason why the status of professors remains high in

Scotland, is that they still trail some clouds of glory from an ecclesiastical past. Until recently, the ambition of every Scottish peasant family was to send a son into the Presbyterian ministry. The enterprise called for immense effort and self-sacrifice; and the professor was the good genius who won the whole family's gratitude by helping the aspiring student on his arduous road. This cannot, however, be the whole explanation, for the status of professors has also been comparatively high in France and Germany, where the professor has been, not a semiecclesiastical hierophant, but the civil servant of a secular state. And anyway, in the modern Western world, these instances of a relatively high status for teachers are exceptional. The relatively low status to which they have been depressed in most English-speaking countries outside Scotland is more typical of their status in the Western world as a whole.

What, then, can be done today to raise the Western teaching profession's status and standards? Here Russia may be doing the West another unintentional service by giving Western observers the impression that she treats her professors as grandees. Perhaps this impression, whether or not it is correct, may spur America into raising the status of the American teaching profession as an inescapable move in her competition with Russia for world power. This is not the best conceivable motive for an educational reform; but it is to be welcomed if it does move the American people to give American teachers large increases of salary and of leisure. America can already afford to be generous to her teachers, without needing to wait for the superabundance that is to be expected from "atoms for peace."

But a substantial improvement in the teaching profession's material conditions of life would not be enough in itself. It would merely be an enabling condition to open the way for a rise in the degree of esteem in which teachers are held in their own estimation as well as in the public's. This esteem cannot be high unless both the public and the profession become convinced of two things: first, that the teaching profession is performing a valuable public service, and, second, that it is maintaining a high professional standard in its work. The first of these two conditions will be fulfilled if it is realized that, in the present critical chapter of history, the teaching profession does have an indispensable part to play in helping the human race save itself from self-destruction by helping it to grow into one family in which the odious traditional division between the privileged and the unprivileged will have been abolished. Here is a field in which the teacher of languages and the teacher of technology can both prove their worth. As for the professional standard to which the teacher can rise, this will depend on the amount of leisure that is granted to him and on the use to which he puts it.

Since man in process of civilization first deliberately set himself to extend the bounds of human knowledge by purposeful and systematic research, it has been recognized that a university teacher must be given the opportunity to be a part-time researcher too if he is to retain his intellectual vitality and to communicate it to his pupils. We now have enough material resources to be able to offer the same opportunity to teachers not only at the university level but also at all levels below it. Nothing could do more to increase the teaching profession's efficiency, prestige, and self-respect. When we think of research, we should, of course, think of it in the widest terms. In the field of research into physical nature, no one would dispute the contention that the telescope is as valuable and as honorable an instrument as the microscope. In the field of the humanities, there has recently been a tendency for the microscopists to claim a monopoly of the label "research" for their own kind of work and to refuse the title to their brethren the telescopists. Yet it is surely obvious that the Newtons and the Einsteins have done no less to increase our knowledge and understanding of the universe than their fellow scientists who have discovered previously undetected planets or galaxies. It is also obvious that this truism holds good for the humanities as well as for physical science.

Research, of whatever kind, is good for teaching, because it sets a standard of precision and thoroughness which the researcher-teacher will exact from himself and demand from his pupils. But here, as so often before, we are brought back to the problem set by the limits of the capacity of human minds. Even if formal education is to become lifelong, how can a single mind in a single lifetime acquire an education that will be exact and at the same time comprehensive? We cannot do without either of these conditions in a world that has become "one world" and that has also become scientific in its intellectual standards. Perhaps the solution will be for everybody—pupil and teacher, researcher and "practical" man or woman alike—to operate in two intellectual dimensions simultaneously.

Everybody needs a glimpse of the bird's-eye view, with a radius of hundreds of miles, that one catches from a jet plane flying in the stratosphere. Everybody also needs to have a glimpse of the worm's-eye view, with the depth of thousands of feet, that one catches by sifting the successive strata that are brought to the surface by an oil-prospector's drill as it burrows into the bowels of the earth. The capacity of a single human mind is narrowly circumscribed; it can never succeed either in surveying the whole surface of the globe or in probing the globe's interior to the center. Yet at least it need not confine itself to either of these intellectual quests exclusively. It can sample both, and such intellectual catholicity will be a liberal education. Let our students survey the history of all mankind all over the face of the planet since the age when man's pre-human ancestors first became human; but at the same time let them scrutinize the history of some local short-lived tribe or parish. Let them learn to communicate with their neighbors in languages that are not their own mother tongues; but at the same time let them master in detail the structure of some particular language and the art of some particular poet. This dual approach to the problem of education seems the most promising that we can make in the huge and complex new world into which we are being carried today by the rushing current of history.

Progressive Education: The Ideal and the Reality

John Dewey
(1859–1952)

In the context of American education at the beginning of the twentieth century, John Dewey was indeed a revolutionary force. But within the tradition of Western educational thought since the Renaissance, he is more a synthesizer than an innovator. He accepted and developed four great themes which had been introduced by Comenius, extrapolated by Rousseau and practiced by Pestalozzi. These four themes were: (1) education should be based on the inherent nature of the child; (2) it should proceed largely through direct experiences rather than books; (3) it should aim higher than mere academic or vocational learning ("Life is the trade I would teach him," wrote Rousseau); and (4) it should operate to democratize culture by reaching the lower classes through special teaching techniques.

Of course, Dewey restated these classic principles in contemporary terms and he sought scientific confirmation for them. His concept of the child's development was based on the experimental findings of modern psychology, for example, and he wanted the direct experiences which constitute education to inculcate the scientific point of view. But the important thing is that he managed to combine in a unified theory the new respect for the nature of the child and the new conception of what kinds of activities would truly educate him. Dewey climaxes the Western tradition of reform in educational theory and classroom practice.

The span of John Dewey's life encompassed the great changes in American and Western civilization which inspired his philosophy. He was born in Burlington, Vermont, in the year that Darwin published *The Origin of Species,* the work which signaled the triumph of the modern scientific outlook. Dewey was educated at the University of Vermont and Johns Hopkins. He taught at the Universities of Minnesota, Michigan, Chicago, and finally Columbia, from which he retired in 1930.

The thesis of Dewey's philosophy has been well stated by Professor Gail Kennedy of Amherst: "A general application of the methods of science, to every possible field of inquiry, is the only adequate means of solving the problems of an industrial democracy." In addition to his contributions to technical philosophy, Dewey was a practical educator and an active participant in movements for social welfare, political reform, and the protection of academic freedom.

This selection consists of two essays. The first, "My Pedagogic Creed," was published in 1897, when the reform movement in American education was just getting up steam. Some of its general statements were later to be seriously misinterpreted and misapplied in the schools by Dewey's early followers. But the document itself succinctly stated the ideas about the schools and society which underlay progressive education. Dewey fused those ideas into a unity rarely achieved during the movement's heyday in the twenties and thirties.

The second essay is from the small volume *Experience and Education,* Dewey's most interesting work for the general reader. Published in 1938, when the movement was beginning to flag, the book is a critique of progressive ideas as distorted by the schools. In dissociating himself from the dogmatic excesses of progressivism, Dewey reasserted the principles of the "new" education: principles remarkably similar to those which led the seventeenth-century reformers to attack the formal training of the Renaissance schoolmasters.

My Pedagogic Creed

Article One—What Education Is

I believe that all education proceeds by the participation of the individual in the social consciousness of the race. This process begins unconsciously almost at birth, and is continually shaping the individual's powers, saturating his consciousness, forming his habits, training his ideas, and arousing his feelings and emotions. Through this unconscious education the individual gradually comes to share in the intellectual and moral resources which humanity has succeeded in getting together. He becomes an inheritor of the funded capital of civilization. The most formal and technical education in the world cannot safely depart from this general process. It can only organize it or differentiate it in some particular direction.

The only true education comes through the stimulation of the child's powers by the demands of the social situations in which he finds himself. Through these demands he is stimulated to act as a member of a unity, to emerge from his original narrowness of action and feeling, and to conceive of himself from the standpoint of the welfare of the group to which he belongs. Through the responses which others make to his own activities he comes to know what these mean in social terms. The value which they have is reflected back into them. For instance, through the response which is made to the child's instinctive babblings the child comes to know what those babblings mean; they are transformed into articulate language, and thus the child is introduced into the consolidated wealth of ideas and emotions which are now summed up in language.

This educational process has two sides—one psychological and one sociological—and neither can be subordinated to the other, or neglected, without evil results following. Of these two sides, the psychological is the basis. The child's own instincts and powers furnish the material and give the starting point for all education. Save as the efforts of the educator connect with some activity which the child is carrying on of his own initiative independent of the educator, education becomes reduced to a pressure from without. It may, indeed, give certain external results, but cannot truly be called educative. Without insight into the psychological structure and activities of the individual, the educative process will, therefore, be haphazard and arbitrary. If it chances to coincide with the child's activity it will get a leverage; if it does not, it will result in friction, or distintegration, or arrest of the child-nature.

Knowledge of social conditions, of the present state of civilization, is necessary in order properly to interpret the child's powers. The child has his own instincts and tendencies, but we do not know what these mean until we can translate them into their social equivalents. We must be able to carry them back into a social past and see them as the inheritance of previous race activities. We must also be able to project them into the future to see what their outcome and end will be. In the illustration just used, it is the ability to see in the child's babblings the promise and potency of a future social intercourse and conversation which enables one to deal in the proper way with that instinct.

The psychological and social sides are organically related, and that education cannot be regarded as a compromise between the two, or a superimposition of one upon the other. We are told the psychological definition of education is barren and formal —that it gives us only the idea of a development of all the mental powers without giving us any idea of the use to which these powers are put. On the other hand, it is urged that the social definition of education, as getting adjusted to civilization, makes of it a forced and external process, and results in subordinating the freedom of the individual to a preconceived social and political status.

Each of these objections is true when urged against one side isolated from the other. In order to know what a power really is we must know what its end, use, or function is, and this we cannot know save as we conceive of the individual as active in social relationships. But, on the other hand, the only possible adjustment which we can give to the child under existing conditions is that which arises through putting him in complete possession of all his powers. With the advent of democracy and modern industrial conditions, it is impossible to foretell definitely just what civilization will be twenty years from now. Hence it is impossible to prepare the child for any precise set of conditions. To prepare him for the future life means to give him command of himself; it means so to train him that he will have the full and ready use of all his capacities; that his eye and ear and hand may be tools ready to command, that his judgment may be capable of grasping the conditions under which it has to work, and the executive forces be trained to act economically and efficiently. It is impossible to reach this sort of adjustment save as constant regard is had to the individual's own powers, tastes, and interests—that is, as education is continually converted into psychological terms.

In sum, I believe that the individual who is to be educated is a social individual, and that society is an organic union of individuals. If we eliminate the social factor from the child we are left only with an abstraction; if we eliminate the individual factor from society, we are left only with an inert and lifeless mass. Education, therefore, must begin with a psychological insight into the child's capacities, interests, and habits. It must be controlled at every point by reference to these same considerations. These powers, interests, and habits must be continually interpreted—we must know what they mean. They must be translated into terms of their social equivalents—into terms of what they are capable of in the way of social service.

Article Two—What the School Is

I believe that the school is primarily a social institution. Education being a social process, the school is simply that form of community life in which all those agencies are concentrated that will be most effective in bringing the child to share in the inherited resources of the race, and to use his own powers for social ends.

Education, therefore, is a process of living and not a preparation for future living.

The school must represent life, life as real and vital to the child as that which he carries on in the home, in the neighborhood, or on the playground.

That education which does not occur through forms of life, forms that are worth living for their own sake, is always a poor substitute for the genuine reality, and tends to cramp and to deaden.

The school, as an institution, should simplify existing social life; should reduce it, as it were, to an embryonic form. Existing life is so complex that the child cannot be brought into contact with it without either confusion or distraction; he is either overwhelmed by the multiplicity of activities which are going on, so that he loses his own power of orderly reaction, or he is so stimulated by these various activities that his powers are prematurely called into play and he becomes either unduly specialized or else disintegrated.

As such simplified social life, the school should grow gradually out of the home life; it should take up and continue the activities with which the child is already familiar in the home.

It should exhibit these activities to the child, and reproduce them in such ways that the child will gradually learn the meaning of them, and be capable of playing his own part in relation to them.

This is a psychological necessity, because it is the only way of securing continuity in the child's growth, the only way of giving a background of past experience to the new ideas given in school.

It is also a social necessity because the home is the form of social life in which the child has been nurtured and in connection with which he has had his moral training. It is the business of the school to deepen and extend his sense of the values bound up in his home life.

Much of present education fails because it neglects this fundamental principle of the school as a form of community life. It conceives the school as a place where certain information is to be given, where certain lessons are to be learned, or where certain habits are to be formed. The value of these is conceived as lying largely in the remote future; the child must do these things for the sake of something else he is to do; they are mere preparations. As a result they do not become a part of the life experience of the child and so are not truly educative.

The moral education centers upon this conception of the school as a mode of social life, that the best and deepest moral training is precisely that which one gets through having to enter into proper relations with others in a unity of work and thought. The present educational systems, so far as they destroy or neglect this unity, render it difficult or impossible to get any genuine, regular moral training.

The child should be stimulated and controlled in his work through the life of the community.

Under existing conditions far too much of the stimulus and control proceeds from the teacher, because of neglect of the idea of the school as a form of social life.

The teacher's place and work in the school is to be interpreted from this same basis. The teacher is not in the school to impose certain ideas or to form certain habits in the child, but is there as a member of the community to select the influences which shall affect the child and to assist him in properly responding to these influences.

The discipline of the school should proceed from the life of the school as a whole and not directly from the teacher.

The teacher's business is simply to determine, on the basis of larger experience and riper wisdom, how the discipline of life shall come to the child.

All questions of the grading of the child and his promotion should be determined by reference to the same standard. Examinations are of use only so far as they test the child's fitness for social life and reveal the place in which he can be of the most service and where he can receive the most help.

Article Three—The Subject Matter of Education

I believe that the social life of the child is the basis of concentration, or correlation, in all his training or growth. The social life gives the unconscious unity and the background of all his efforts and of all his attainments.

The subject matter of the school curriculum should mark a gradual differentiation out of the primitive unconscious unity of social life.

We violate the child's nature and render difficult the best ethical results by introducing the child too abruptly to a number of special studies, of reading, writing, geography, etc., out of relation to this social life.

The true center of correlation on the school subjects is not science, nor literature, nor history, nor geography, but the child's own social activities.

Education cannot be unified in the study of science, or so-called nature study, because apart from human activity, nature itself is not a unity; nature in itself is a number of diverse objects in space and time, and to attempt to make it the center of work by itself is to introduce a principle of radiation rather than one of concentration.

Literature is the reflex expression and interpretation of social experience; hence it must follow upon and not precede such experience. It, therefore, cannot be made the basis, although it may be made the summary of unification.

Once more, history is of educative value insofar as it presents phases of social life and growth. It must be controlled by reference to social life. When taken simply as history it is thrown into the distant past and becomes dead and inert. Taken as the record of man's social life and progress it becomes full of meaning. I believe, however, that it cannot be so taken excepting as the child is also introduced directly into social life.

The primary basis of education is in the child's powers at work along the same general constructive lines as those which have brought civilization into being.

The only way to make the child conscious of his social heritage is to enable him to perform those fundamental types of activity which make civilization what it is.

In the so-called expressive or constructive activities is the center of correlation.

This gives the standard for the place of cooking, sewing, manual training, etc., in the school.

They are not special studies which are to be introduced over and above a lot of others in the way of relaxation or relief, or as additional accomplishments. I believe rather that they represent, as types, fundamental forms of social activity; and that it is possible and desirable that the child's introduction into the more formal subjects of the curriculum be through the medium of these constructive activities.

The study of science is educational insofar as it brings out the materials and processes which make social life what it is.

One of the greatest difficulties in the present teaching of science is that the material is presented in purely objective form, or is treated as a new peculiar kind of experience which the child can add to that which he has already had. In reality, science is of value because it gives the ability to interpret and control the experience already had. It should be introduced, not as so much new subject matter, but as showing the factors already involved in previous experience and as furnishing tools by which that experience can be more easily and effectively regulated.

At present we lose much of the value of literature and language studies because of our elimination of the social element. Language is almost always treated in the books of pedagogy simply as the expression of thought. It is true that language is a logical instrument, but it is fundamentally and primarily a social instrument. Language is the device for communication; it is the tool through which one individual comes to share the ideas and feelings of others. When treated simply as a way of getting individual information, or as a means of showing off what one has learned, it loses its social motive and end.

There is, therefore, no succession of studies in the ideal school curriculum. If education is life, all life has, from the outset, a scientific aspect, an aspect of art and culture, and an aspect of communication. It cannot, therefore, be true that the proper studies for one grade are mere reading and writing, and that at a later grade, reading, or literature, or science, may be introduced. The progress is not in the succession of studies, but in the development of new attitudes towards, and new interests in, experience.

Education must be conceived as a continuing reconstruction of experience; the process and the goal of education are one and the same thing.

To set up any end outside of education, as furnishing its goal and standard, is to deprive the educational process of much of its meaning, and tends to make us rely upon false and external stimuli in dealing with the child.

Article Four—The Nature of Method

I believe that the question of method is ultimately reducible to the question of the order of development of the child's powers and interests. The law for presenting and treating material is the law implicit within the child's own nature. Because this is so I believe the following statements are of supreme importance as determining the spirit in which education is carried on.

The active side precedes the passive in the development of the child nature; expression comes before conscious impression; the muscular development precedes the sensory; movements come before conscious sensations; I believe that consciousness is essentially motor or impulsive; that consicous states tend to project themselves in action.

The neglect of this principle is the cause of a large part of the waste of time and strength in school work. The child is thrown into a passive, receptive, or absorbing attitude. The conditions are such that he is not permitted to follow the law of his nature; the result is friction and waste.

Ideas also result from action and devolve for the sake of the better control of action. What we term reason is primarily the law of order or effective action. To attempt to develop the reasoning powers, the powers of judgment, without reference to the selection and arrangement of means in action, is the fundamental fallacy in our present methods of dealing with this matter. As a result we present the child with arbitrary symbols. Symbols are a necessity in mental development, but they have their place as tools for economizing effort; presented by themselves they are a mass of meaningless and arbitrary ideas imposed from without.

The image is the great instrument of instruction. What a child gets out of any subject presented to him is simply the images which he himself forms with regard to it.

If nine-tenths of the energy at present directed towards making the child learn certain things were spent in seeing to it that the child was forming proper images, the work of instruction would be indefinitely facilitated.

Much of the time and attention now given to the preparation and presentation of lessons might be more wisely and profitably expended in training the child's power of imagery and in seeing to it that he was continually forming definite vivid and growing images of the various subjects with which he comes in contact in his experience.

Interests are the signs and symptoms of growing power. I believe that they represent dawning capacities. Accordingly the constant and careful observation of interests is of the utmost importance for the educator.

These interests are to be observed as showing the state of development which the child has reached.

They prophesy the stage upon which he is about to enter.

Only through the continual and sympathetic observation of childhood's interests can the adult enter into the child's life and see what it is ready for, and upon what material it could work most readily and fruitfully.

These interests are neither to be humored nor repressed. To repress interest is to substitute the adult for the child, and so to weaken intellectual curiosity and alertness, to suppress initiative, and to deaden interest. To humor the interests is to substitute the transient for the permanent. The interest is always the sign of some power below; the important thing is to discover this power. To humor the interest is to fail to penetrate below the surface, and its sure result is to substitute caprice and whim for genuine interest.

The emotions are the reflex of actions.

To endeavor to stimulate or arouse the emotions apart from their corresponding activities is to introduce an unhealthy and morbid state of mind.

If we can only secure right habits of action and thought, with reference to the good, the true, and the beautiful, the emotions will for the most part take care of themselves.

Next to deadness and dullness, formalism and routine, our education is threatened with no greater evil than sentimentalism.

This sentimentalism is the necessary result of the attempt to divorce feeling from action.

Article Five—The School and Social Progress

I believe that education is the fundamental method of social progress and reform.

All reforms which rest simply upon the enactment of law, or the threatening of certain penalties, or upon changes in mechanical or outward arrangements, are transitory and futile.

Education is a regulation of the process of coming to share in the social consciousness; and the adjustment of individual activity on the basis of this social consciousness is the only sure method of social reconstruction.

This conception has due regard for both the individualistic and socialistic ideals. It is duly individual because it recognizes the formation of a certain character as the only genuine basis of right living. It is socialistic because it recognizes that this right character is not to be formed by merely individual precept, example, or exhortation, but rather by the influence of a certain form of institutional or community life upon the individual, and that the social organism through the school, as its organ, may determine ethical results.

In the ideal school we have the reconciliation of the individualistic and the institutional ideals.

The community's duty to education is, therefore, its paramount moral duty. By law and punishment, by social agitation and discussion, society can regulate and form itself in a more or less haphazard and chance way. But through education society can formulate its own purposes, can organize its own means and resources, and thus shape itself with definiteness and economy in the direction in which it wishes to move.

When society once recognizes the possibilities in this direction, and the obligations which these possibilities impose, it is impossible to conceive of the resources of time, attention, and money which will be put at the disposal of the educator.

It is the business of everyone interested in education to insist upon the school as the primary and most effective interest of social progress and reform in order that society may be awakened to realize what the school stands for, and aroused to the necessity of endowing the educator with sufficient equipment properly to perform his task.

Education thus conceived marks the most perfect and intimate union of science and art conceivable in human experience.

The art of thus giving shape to human powers and adapting them to social service is the supreme art; one calling into its service the best of artists; no insight, sympathy, tact, executive power, is too great for such service.

With the growth of psychological service, giving added insight into individual structure and laws of growth; and with growth of social science, adding to our knowledge of the right organization of individuals, all scientific resources can be utilized for the purposes of education.

When science and art thus join hands the most commanding motive for human action will be reached, the most genuine springs of human conduct aroused, and the best service that human nature is capable of guaranteed.

The teacher is engaged, not simply in the training of individuals, but in the formation of the proper social life.

Every teacher should realize the dignity of his calling; he is a social servant set apart for the maintenance of proper social order and the securing of the right social growth.

In this way the teacher always is the prophet of the true God and the usherer in of the true kingdom of God.

Traditional vs. Progressive Education

Mankind likes to think in terms of extreme opposites. It is given to formulating its beliefs in terms of *Either-Ors*, between which it recognizes no intermediate possibilities. When forced to recognize that the extremes cannot be acted upon, it is still inclined to hold that they are all right in theory but that when it comes to practical matters circumstances compel us to compromise. Educational philosophy is no exception. The history of educational theory is marked by opposition between the idea that education is development from within and that it is formation from without; that it is based upon natural endowments and that education is a process of overcoming natural inclination and substituting in its place habits acquired under external pressure.

At present, the opposition, so far as practical affairs of the school are concerned, tends to take the form of contrast between traditional and progressive education. If the underlying ideas of the former are formulated broadly, without the qualifications required for accurate statement, they are found to be about as follows: The subject matter of education consists of bodies of information and of skills that have been worked out in the past; therefore, the chief business of the school is to transmit them to the new generation. In the past, there have also been developed standards and rules of conduct; moral training consists in forming habits of action in conformity with these rules and standards. Finally, the general pattern of school organization (by which I mean the relations of pupils to one another and to the teachers) constitutes the school a kind of institution sharply marked off from other social institutions. Call up in imagination the ordinary schoolroom, its time schedules, schemes of classification, of examination and promotion, of rules of order, and I think you will grasp what is meant by "patterns of organization." If then you contrast this scene with what goes on in the family, for example, you will appreciate what is meant by the school being a kind of institution sharply marked off from any other form of social organization.

The three characteristics just mentioned fix the aims and methods of instruction and discipline. The main purpose or objective is to prepare the young for future responsibilities and for success in life, by means of acquisition of the organized bodies of information and prepared forms of skill which comprehend the material of instruction. Since the subject matter as well as standards of proper conduct are handed down from the past, the attitude of pupils must, upon the whole, be one of docility, receptivity, and obedience. Books, especially textbooks, are the chief representatives of the lore and wisdom of the past, while teachers are the organs through which pupils are brought into effective connection with the material. Teachers are the agents through which knowledge and skills are communicated and rules of conduct enforced.

I have not made this brief summary for the purpose of criticizing the underlying philosophy. The rise of what is called new education and progressive schools is of itself a product of discontent with traditional education. In effect it is a criticism of the latter. When the implied criticism is made explicit it reads somewhat as follows: The traditional scheme is, in essence, one of imposition from above and from outside. It imposes adult standards, subject matter, and methods upon those who are only growing slowly towards maturity. The gap is so great that the required subject matter, the methods of learning and of behaving are foreign to the existing capacities of the young. They are beyond the reach of the experience the young learners already possess. Consequently, they must be imposed; even though good teachers will use devices of art to cover up the imposition so as to relieve it of obviously brutal features.

But the gulf between the mature or adult products and the experience and abilities of the young is so wide that the very situation forbids much active participation by pupils in the development of what is taught. Theirs is to do—and learn, as it was the part of the Six Hundred to do and die. Learning here means acquisition of what already is incorporated in books and in the heads of the elders. Moreover, that which is taught is thought of as essentially static. It is taught as a finished product, with little regard either to the ways in which it was originally built up or to changes that will surely occur in the future. It is to a large extent the cultural product of societies that assumed the future would be much like the past, and yet it is used as educational food in a society where change is the rule, not the exception.

If one attempts to formulate the philosophy of education implicit in the practices of the newer education, we may, I think, discover certain common principles amid the variety of progressive schools now existing. To imposition from above is opposed expression and cultivation of individuality; to external discipline is opposed free activity; to learning from texts and teachers, learning through experience; to acquisition of isolated skills and techniques by drill, is opposed acquisition of them as means of attaining ends which make direct vital appeal; to preparation for a more or less remote future is opposed making the most of the opportunities of present life; to static aims and materials is opposed acquaintance with a changing world.

Now, all principles by themselves are abstract. They become concrete only in the consequences which result from their application. Just because the principles set forth are so fundamental and far reaching, everything depends upon the interpretation given them as they are put into practice in the school and the home. It is at this point that the reference made earlier to either-or philosophies becomes peculiarly pertinent. The general philosophy of the new education may be sound, and yet the difference in abstract principles will not decide the way in which the moral and intellectual preference involved shall be worked out in practice. There is always the danger in a new movement that in rejecting the aims and methods of that which it would supplant, it may develop its principles negatively rather than positively and constructively. Then it takes its clue in practice from that which is rejected instead of from the constructive development of its own philosophy.

I take it that the fundamental unity of the newer philosophy is found in the idea that there is an intimate and necessary relation between the processes of actual experience and education. If this be true, then a positive and constructive development of its own basic idea depends upon having a correct idea of experience. Take, for example, the question of organized subject matter. The problem for progressive education is: What is the place and meaning of subject matter and of organization *within* experience? How does subject matter function? Is there anything inherent in experience which tends towards progressive organization of its contents? What results follow when the materials of experience are not progressively organized? A philosophy which proceeds on the basis of rejection, of sheer opposition, will neglect these questions. It will tend to suppose that because the old education was based on ready-made organization, therefore it suffices to reject the principle of organization *in toto*, instead of striving to discover what it means and how it is to be attained on the basis of experience. We might go through all the points of difference between the new and the old education and reach similar conclusions. When external control is rejected, the problem becomes that of finding the factors of control that are inherent within experience. When external authority is rejected, it does not follow that all authority should be rejected, but rather that there is need to search for a more effective source of authority. Because the older education imposed the knowledge, methods, and the rules of conduct of the mature person upon the young, it does not follow, except upon the basis of the extreme either-or philosophy, that the knowledge and skill of the mature person has no directive value for the experience of the immature. On the contrary, basing education upon personal experience may mean more multiplied and more intimate contacts between the mature and the immature than ever existed in the traditional school, and consequently more, rather than less, guidance by others. The problem, then, is: how these contacts can be established without violating the principle of learning through personal experience. The solution of this problem requires a well-thought-out philosophy of the social factors that operate in the constitution of individual experience.

What is indicated in the foregoing remarks is that the general principles of the new education do not of themselves solve any of the problems of the actual or practical conduct and management of progressive schools. Rather, they set new problems which have to be worked out on the basis of a new philosophy of experience. The problems are not even recognized, to say nothing of being solved, when it is assumed that it suffices to reject the ideas and practices of the old education and then go to the opposite extreme. Yet I am sure that you will appreciate what is meant when I say that many of the newer schools tend to make little or nothing of organized subject matter of study; to proceed as if any form of direction and guidance by adults were an invasion of individual freedom, and as if the idea that education should be concerned with the present and future meant that acquaintance with the past has little or no role to play in education. Without pressing these defects to the point of exaggeration, they at least illustrate what is meant by a theory and practice of education which proceeds negatively or by reaction against what has been current in education rather than by a positive and constructive development of purposes, methods, and subject matter on the foundation of a theory of experience and its educational potentialities.

It is not too much to say that an educational philosophy which professes to be based on the idea of freedom may become as dogmatic as ever was the traditional education which is reacted against. For any theory and set of practices is dogmatic which is not based upon critical examination of its own underlying principles. Let us say that the new education emphasizes the freedom of the learner. Very well. A problem is now set. What does freedom mean and what are the conditions under which it is capable of realization? Let us say that the kind of external imposition which was so common in the traditional school limited rather than promoted the intellectual and moral development of the young. Again, very well. Recognition of this serious defect sets a problem. Just what is the role of the teacher and of books in promoting the educational development of the immature? Admit that traditional education employed as the subject matter for study facts and ideas so bound up with the past as to give little help in dealing with the issues of the present and future. Very well. Now we have the problem of discovering the connection which actually exists *within* experience between the achievements of the past and the issues of the present. We have the problem of ascertaining how acquaintance with the past may be translated into a potent instrumentality for dealing effectively with the future. We may reject knowledge of the past as the *end* of education and thereby only emphasize its importance as a *means*. When we do that we have a problem that is new in the story of education: How shall the young become acquainted with the past in such a way that the acquaintance is a potent agent in appreciation of the living present?

The Seven Misconceptions of Modern Education

Jacques Maritain
(1882–   )

The most important contemporary educational theorists squarely face the fact that education is inextricably caught in the current philosophical upheaval of the Western world. John Dewey saw only two roads which could take education out of its aimless drifting: he chose the complete acceptance of science. The eminent Catholic philosopher Jacques Maritain, equally convinced that ultimately one must choose in education between the scientific and the philosophical-religious ideas of man, chooses the latter.

For Maritain, the adoption of the scientific attitude leaves education with a thoroughly efficient pedagogy but without any true purpose. He maintains that the assumptions of scientific educational research and of progressive pedagogic theory are not so much wrong as incomplete. Those assumptions must, he argues, be informed by the kind of respect and understanding of the human person which can only come from faith in man's supernatural essence and destiny.

Maritain takes this conclusion as self-evident, but it should be noted that champions of other educational philosophies flatly reject the idea. A pragmatist like Sidney Hook, for example, contends that the ends of education are to be sought as the "fruits of experience" in actual teaching and learning. By that very concreteness, Hook argues, they "recommend themselves to us more validly than any allegedly justifying metaphysical or theological principle."

Maritain's frank acknowledgment of his Christian premise is important. Other influential critics of progressive education, such as Robert Hutchins, base their attacks on the same assumption, but they do not state it so forthrightly.

As Sidney Hook has argued, their belief that the true and unchanging ends of education can be deduced from the unique and unchanging nature of man, is justified only if man embodies a supernatural soul independent of his interaction with the world. Maritain realizes that acknowledgment of his Christian premise supports rather than undermines his critique of progressivism. His essay illustrates how a clear hierarchy of values can provide a way of resolving concrete educational problems such as overspecialization, proliferation of courses, moral and religious instruction, social adjustment, and the place of "learning through conditioning" in education.

Jacques Maritain is one of the foremost Catholic philosophers of modern times. Born in Paris in 1882, he was educated at the Sorbonne. Maritain taught at several universities in Europe and the United States before he left academic life in 1945 to become French ambassador to the Vatican. In 1948 he resigned to teach philosophy at Princeton, from which he retired in 1952. Maritain's published works include contributions to the fields of metaphysics, aesthetics, and political philosophy. The following selection is from *Education at the Crossroads,* published in 1943.

Man is not merely an animal of nature, like a skylark or a bear. He is also an animal of culture, whose race can subsist only within the development of society and civilization, he is a *historical* animal: hence the multiplicity of cultural or ethico-historical patterns into which man is diversified; hence, too, the essential importance of education. Due to the very fact that he is endowed with a knowing power which is unlimited and which nonetheless only advances step by step, man cannot progress in his own specific life, both intellectually and morally, without being helped by collective experience previously accumulated and preserved, and by a regular transmission of acquired knowledge. In order to reach self-determination, for which he is made, he needs discipline and tradition, which will both weigh heavily on him and strengthen him so as to enable him to struggle against them—

which will enrich that very tradition—and the enriched tradition will make possible new struggles, and so forth.

The First Misconception: a Disregard of Ends

Education is an art, and an especially difficult one. Yet it belongs by its nature to the sphere of ethics and practical wisdom. Education is an *ethical* art (or rather a practical wisdom in which a determinate art is embodied). Now every art is a dynamic trend toward an object to be achieved, which is the aim of this art. There is no art without ends, art's very vitality is the energy with which it tends toward its end, without stopping at any intermediary step.

Here we see from the outset the two most general misconceptions against which education must guard itself. The first misconception is a lack or disregard of ends. If means are liked and cultivated for the sake of their own perfection, and not as means alone, to that very extent they cease to lead to the end, and art loses its practicality; its vital efficiency is replaced by a process of infinite multiplication, each means developing and spreading for its own sake. This supremacy of means over end and the consequent collapse of all sure purpose and real efficiency seem to be the main reproach to contemporary education. The means are not bad. On the contrary, they are generally much better than those of the old pedagogy. The misfortune is precisely that they are so good that we lose sight of the end. Hence the surprising weakness of education today, which proceeds from our attachment to the very perfection of our modern educational means and methods and our failure to bend them toward the end. The child is so well tested and observed, his needs so well detailed, his psychology so clearly cut out, the methods for making it easy for him everywhere so perfected, that the end of all these commendable improvements runs the risk of being forgotten or disregarded. Thus modern medicine is often hampered by the very excellence of its means: for instance, when a doctor makes the examination of the patient's reactions so perfectly and carefully in his laboratory that he forgets the cure; in the meantime the patient may die, for having been too well tended, or rather analyzed. The scientific improvement of the pedagogical means and methods is in itself outstanding progress. But the more it takes on importance, the more it requires a parallel strengthening of practical wisdom and of the dynamic trend toward the goal.

The Second Misconception: False Ideas Concerning the End

The second general error or misconception of education does not consist of an actual dearth of appreciation of the end but false or incomplete ideas concerning the nature of this end. The educational task is both greater and more mysterious and, in a sense, humbler than many imagine. If the aim of education is the helping and guiding of man toward his own human achievement, education cannot escape the problems and entanglements of philosophy, for it supposes by its very nature a philosophy of man, and from the outset it is obliged to anwer the question: "What is man?" which the philosophical sphinx is asking.

THE SCIENTIFIC AND THE PHILOSOPHICAL-RELIGIOUS IDEA OF MAN

I should like to observe at this point that, definitely speaking, there are only two classes or categories of notions concerning man which play fair, so to speak: the purely scientific idea of man and the philosophical-religious one. According to its genuine methodological type, the scientific idea of man, like every idea recast by strictly experimental science, gets rid as far as possible of any ontological content, so that it may be entirely verifiable in sense-experience. On this point the most recent theorists of science, the neopositivists of the school of Vienna, are quite right. The purely scientific idea of man tends only to link together measurable and observable data taken as such, and is determined from the very start not to consider anything like being or essence, not to answer any question like: Is there a soul or isn't there? Does the spirit exist or only matter? Is there freedom or determinism? Purpose or chance? Value or simple fact? For such questions are out of the realm of science. The purely scientific idea of man is, and must be, a phenomenalized idea without reference to ultimate reality.

The philosophical-religious idea of man, on the contrary, is an ontological idea. It is not entirely verifiable in sense-experience, though it possesses criteria and proofs of its own, and it deals with the essential and intrinsic, though not visible or tangible characters, and with the intelligible density of that being which we call man.

Now it is obvious that the purely scientific idea of man can provide us with invaluable and ever-growing information concerning the means and tools of education, but by itself it can neither primarily found nor primarily guide education, for education needs primarily to know what man *is*, what is the nature of man and the scale of values it essentially involves; and the purely scientific idea of man, because it ignores "being-as-such," does not know such things, but only what emerges from the human being in the realm of sense observation and measurement. Young Tom, Dick, or Harry, who are the subjects of education, are not only a set of physical, biological, and psychological phenomena, the knowledge of which is moreover thoroughly needed and necessary; they are the children of man—this very name "man" designating for the common sense of parents, educators, and society the same ontological mystery as is recognized in the rational knowledge of philosophers and theologians.

It should be pointed out that if we tried to build education on the single pattern of the scientific idea of man and carry it out accordingly, we could only do so by distorting or warping this idea: for we should have to ask what is the nature and destiny of man, and we should be pressing the only idea at our disposal, that is the scientific one, for an answer to our question. Then we would try, contrary to its type, to draw from it a kind of metaphysics. From the logical point of view, we would have a spurious metaphysics disguised as science and yet deprived of any really philosophical insight; and from the practical point of view, we would have a denial or misconception of those very realities and values without which education loses all human sense or becomes the training of an animal for the utility of the state.

Thus the fact remains that the complete and integral idea of man which is the prerequisite of education can only be a philosophical and religious idea of man. I say philosophical, because this idea pertains to the nature or essence of man; I say religious, because of the existential status of this human nature in relation to God and the special gifts and trials and vocation involved.

THE CHRISTIAN IDEA OF MAN

There are many forms of the philosophical and religious idea of man. When I state that the education of man, in order to be completely well grounded, must be based upon the Christian idea of man, it is because I think that this idea of man is the true one, not because I see our civilization actually permeated with this idea. Yet, for all that, the man of our civilization *is* the Christian man, more or less secularized. Consequently we may accept this idea as a common basis and imply that it is to be agreed upon by the common consciousness in our civilized countries, except among those who adhere to utterly opposite outlooks, like materialistic metaphysics, positivism, or skepticism—I am not speaking here of Fascist and racist creeds, which do not belong at all in the civilized world.

Now such a kind of agreement is all that any doctrine in moral philosophy can be expected to have, for none can pretend actually to obtain the literal universal assent of all minds—not because of any weakness in objective proof but because of the weakness inherent in human minds.

There does exist, indeed, among the diverse great metaphysical outlooks, if they recognize the dignity of the spirit, and among the diverse forms of Christian creeds, or even of religious creeds in general, if they recognize the divine destiny of man, a community of analogy as concerns practical attitudes and the realm of action, which makes possible a genuine human cooperation. In a Judeo-Greco-Christian civilization like ours, this community of analogy, which extends from the most orthodox religious forms of thought to the mere humanistic ones, makes it possible for a Christian philosophy of education, if it is well founded and rationally developed, to play an inspiring part in the concert, even for those who do not share in the creed of its supporters. Be it added, by the way, that the term concert, which I just used, seems rather euphemistic with regard to our "modern philosophies of education," whose discordant voices have been so valuably studied in Professor Brubacher's book.*

In answer to our question, then, "What is man?" we may give the Greek, Jewish, and Christian idea of man: man as an animal

* Cf. John S. Brubacher, *Modern Philosophies of Education* (New York and London, 1939).

endowed with reason, whose supreme dignity is in the intellect; and man as a free individual in personal relation with God, whose supreme righteousness consists in voluntarily obeying the law of God; and man as a sinful and wounded creature called to divine life and to the freedom of grace, whose supreme perfection consists of love.

HUMAN PERSONALITY

From the philosophical point of view alone the main concept to be stressed here is the concept of human personality. Man is a person, who holds himself in hand by his intelligence and his will. He does not merely exist as a physical being. There is in him a richer and nobler existence; he has spiritual superexistence through knowledge and love. He is thus, in some way, a whole, not merely a part; he is a universe unto himself, a microcosm in which the great universe in its entirety can be encompassed through knowledge. And through love he can give himself freely to beings who are to him, as it were, other selves; and for this relationship no equivalent can be found in the physical world.

If we seek the prime root of all this, we are led to the acknowledgment of the full philosophical reality of that concept of the soul, so variegated in its connotations, which Aristotle described as the first principle of life in any organism and viewed as endowed with supramaterial intellect in man, and which Christianity revealed as the dwelling place of God and as made for eternal life. In the flesh and bones of man there exists a soul which is a spirit and which has a greater value than the whole physical universe. Dependent though he may be upon the slightest accidents of matter, the human person exists by virtue of the existence of his soul, which dominates time and death. It is the spirit which is the root of personality.

The notion of personality thus involves that of wholeness and independence. To say that a man is a person is to say that in the depth of his being he is more a whole than a part and more independent than servile. It is this mystery of our nature which religious thought designates when it says that the person is the image of God. A person possesses absolute dignity because he is in direct relationship with the realm of being, truth, goodness, and beauty, and with God, and it is only with these that he can arrive at his complete fulfillment. His spiritual fatherland consists of the entire order of things which have absolute value, and which reflect, in some manner, a divine Absolute superior to the world and which have a power of attraction toward this Absolute.

PERSONALITY AND INDIVIDUALITY

Now it should be pointed out that personality is only one aspect or one pole of the human being. The other pole is—to speak the Aristotelian language—individuality, whose prime root is matter. The same man, the same entire man who is, in one sense, a person or a whole made independent by his spiritual soul, is also, in another sense, a material individual, a fragment of a species, a part of the physical universe, a single dot in the immense network of forces and influences, cosmic, ethnic, historic, whose laws we must obey. His very humanity is the humanity of an animal, living by sense and instinct as well as by reason. Thus man is "a horizon in which two worlds meet." Here we face that classical distinction between the *ego* and the *self* which both Hindu and Christian philosophies have emphasized, though with quite diverse connotations. I shall come back to this thought later on.

I should like to observe now that a kind of animal training, which deals with psychophysical habits, conditioned reflexes, sense-memorization, etc., undoubtedly plays its part in education: it refers to material individuality, or to what is not specifically human in man. But education is not animal training. The education of man is a human awakening.

Thus what is of most importance in educators themselves is a respect for the soul as well as for the body of the child, the sense of his innermost essence and his internal resources, and a sort of sacred and loving attention to his mysterious identity, which is a hidden thing that no techniques can reach. And what matters most in the educational enterprise is a perpetual appeal to intelligence and free will in the young. Such an appeal, fittingly proportioned to age and circumstances, can and should begin with the first educational steps. Each field of training, each school activity—physical training as well as elementary reading or the rudiments of childhood etiquette and morals—can be intrinsically improved and can outstrip its own immediate practical value through being *humanized* in this way by understanding. Nothing should be required of the child without an explanation and without making sure that the child has understood.

We may now define in a more precise manner the aim of education. It is to guide man in the evolving dynamism through which he shapes himself as a human person—armed with knowledge, strength of judgment, and moral virtues—while at the same time conveying to him the spiritual heritage of the nation and the civilization in which he is involved, and preserving in this way the century-old achievements of generations. The utilitarian aspect of education—which enables the youth to get a job and make a living—must surely not be disregarded, for the children of man are not made for aristocratic leisure. But this practical aim is best provided by the general human capacities developed. And the ulterior specialized training which may be required must never imperil the essential aim of education.

Now in order to get a complete idea of the aim of education, it is necessary to take into closer consideration the human person and his deep natural aspirations.

THE CONQUEST OF INTERNAL FREEDOM

The chief aspirations of a person are aspirations to freedom—I do not mean that freedom which is free will and which is a gift of nature in each of us, I mean that freedom which is spontaneity, expansion, or autonomy, and which we have to gain through constant effort and struggle. And what is the more profound and essential form of such a desire? It is the desire for inner and spiritual freedom. In this sense Greek philosophy, especially Aristotle, spoke of the independence which is granted to men by intellect and wisdom as the perfection of the human being. And the Gospel was to lift up human perfection to a higher level—a truly divine one—by stating that it consists of the perfection of love and, as St. Paul put it, of the freedom of those who are moved by the divine Spirit. In any case it is by the activities that the philosophers call "immanent"—because they perfect the very subject which exerts them, and are within it the supreme activities of internal achievement and superabundance—that the full freedom of independence is won. Thus the prime goal of education is the conquest of internal and spiritual freedom to be achieved by the individual person, or, in other words, his liberation through knowledge and wisdom, good will, and love.

At this point we must observe that the freedom of which we are speaking is not a mere unfolding of potentialities without any object to be grasped, or a mere movement for the sake of movement, without aim or objective to be attained. It is sheer nonsense to offer such a movement to man as constituting his glory. A movement without aim is just running around in circles and getting nowhere. The aim, here on earth, will always be grasped in a partial and imperfect manner, and in this sense, indeed, the movement is to be pursued without end. Yet the aim will somehow be grasped, even though partially. Moreover the spiritual activities of the human being are *intentional* activities, they tend by nature toward an object, an objective aim, which will measure and rule them, not materially and by means of bondage, but spiritually and by means of liberty, for the object of knowledge or of love is internalized by the activity itself of the intelligence and the will, and becomes within them the very fire of their perfect spontaneity. Truth—which does not depend on us but on *what is*—truth is not a set of ready-made formulas to be passively recorded, so as to have the mind closed and enclosed by them. Truth is an infinite realm—as infinite as being—whose wholeness transcends infinitely our powers of perception, and each fragment of which must be grasped through vital and purified internal activity. This conquest of being, this progressive attainment of new truths, or the progressive realization of the ever-growing and ever-renewed significance of truths already attained, opens and enlarges our mind and life, and really situates them in freedom and autonomy. And speaking of will and love rather than knowledge, no one is freer, or more independent, than the one who gives himself for a cause or a real being worthy of the gift.

The Third Misconception: Pragmatism

Here we find ourselves confronted with the inappropriateness of the pragmatic overemphasis in education—a third error or misconception that we meet on our path. Many things are excellent in the emphasis on action and "praxis," for life consists of action. But action and praxis aim at an object, a determining end without which they lose direction and vitality. And life exists, too, for an end which makes it worthy of being lived. Contemplation and self-perfection, in which human life aspires to flower forth, escape the purview of the pragmatic mind.

It is an unfortunate mistake to define human thought as an organ of response to the actual stimuli and situations of the environment, that is to say, to define it in terms of animal knowledge and reaction, for such a definition exactly covers the way of "thinking" proper only to animals without reason. On the contrary, it is because every human idea, to have a meaning, must attain in some measure (be it even in the symbols of a mathematical interpretation of phenomena), what things *are* or consist of unto themselves; it is because human thought is an instrument or rather a vital energy of knowledge or spiritual intuition (I don't mean "knowledge about," I mean "knowledge into"); it is because thinking begins, not only with difficulties but with *insights*, and ends up in insights which are made true by rational proving or experimental verifying, not by pragmatic sanction, that human thought is able to illumine experience, to realize desires which are human because they are rooted in the prime desire for unlimited good, and to dominate, control, and refashion the world. At the beginning of human action, insofar as it is human, there is truth, grasped or believed to be grasped for the sake of truth. Without trust in truth, there is no human effectiveness. Such is, to my mind, the chief criticism to be made of the pragmatic and instrumentalist theory of knowledge.

In the field of education, this pragmatic theory of knowledge, passing from philosophy to upbringing, can hardly produce in the youth anything but a scholarly skepticism equipped with the best techniques of mental training and the best scientific methods, which will be unnaturally used against the very grain of intelligence, so as to cause minds to distrust the very idea of truth and wisdom, and to give up any hope of inner dynamic unity. Moreover, by dint of insisting that in order to teach John mathematics it is more important to know John than to know mathematics—which is true enough in one sense—the teacher will so perfectly succeed in knowing John that John will never succeed in knowing mathematics. Modern pedagogy has made invaluable progress in stressing the necessity of carefully analyzing and fixing its gaze on the human subject. The wrong begins when *the object to be taught* and *the primacy of the object* are forgotten, and when the cult of the means—not to an end, but without an end—only ends up in a psychological worship of the subject.

THE SOCIAL POTENTIALITIES OF THE PERSON

I have spoken of the aspiration of the human person to freedom, and, first of all, to inner and spiritual freedom. The second essential form of this desire is the desire for freedom externally manifested, and this freedom is linked to social life and lies at its very root. For society is "natural" to man in terms not only of animal or instinctive nature but of human nature, that is, of reason and freedom. If man is a naturally political animal, this is so in the sense that society, required by nature, is achieved through free consent, and because the human person demands the communications of social life through the openness and generosity proper to intelligence and love as well as through the needs of a human individual born naked and destitute. Thus it is that social life tends to emancipate man from the bondage of material nature. It subordinates the individual to the common good, but always in order that the common good flow back upon the individuals, and that they enjoy that freedom of expansion or independence which is insured by the economic guarantees of labor and ownership, political rights, civil virtues, and the cultivation of the mind.

As a result, it is obvious that man's education must be concerned with the social group and prepare him to play his part in it. Shaping man to lead a normal, useful and co-operative life in the community, or guiding the development of the human person in the social sphere, awakening and strengthening both his sense of freedom and his sense of obligation and responsibility, is an essential aim. But it is not the primary, it is the secondary essential aim. The ultimate end of education concerns the human person in his personal life and spiritual progress, not in his relationship to the social environment. Moreover, with regard to the secondary aim itself of which I am speaking, we must never forget that personal freedom itself is at the core of social life, and that a human society is veritably a group of human freedoms which accept obedience and self-sacrifice and a common law for the general welfare, in order to enable each of these freedoms to reach in everyone a truly human fulfillment. The man and the group are intermingled with each other and they surpass each other in different respects. Man finds himself by subordinating himself to the group, and the group attains its goal only by serving man and by realizing that man has secrets which escape the group and a vocation which is not included in the group.

The Fourth Misconception: Sociologism

Here we are confronted with a fourth error of misconception akin to the third one, which derives the supreme rule and standard of education from social conditioning. The essence of education does not consist in adapting a potential citizen to the conditions and interactions of social life, but first in *making a man,* and by this very fact in preparing a citizen. Not only is it nonsense to oppose education for the person and education for the commonwealth, but the latter supposes the former as a prerequisite, and in return the former is impossible without the latter, for one does not make a man except in the bosom of social ties where there is an awakening of civic understanding and civic virtues.

The old education is to be reproached for its abstract and bookish individualism. To have made education more experiential, closer to concrete life and permeated with social concerns from the very start is an achievement of which modern education is justly proud. Yet in order to reach completion such a necessary reform must understand, too, that to be a good citizen and a man of civilization what matters above all is the inner center, the living source of personal conscience in which originate idealism and generosity, the sense of law and the sense of friendship, respect for others, but at the same time deep-rooted independence with regard to common opinion. We must also understand that without abstract insight and intellectual enlightenment the more striking experiences are of no use to man, like beautiful colors in darkness; that the best way not to be bookish is to avoid textbooks as a plague, even textbooks in experientialism, but to read books, I mean to read them avidly; and to understand also that, in a more general way, the pursuit of concrete life becomes a decoy if it scatters the attention of man or child among practical trifles, psychotechnical recipes, and the infinity of utilitarian activities, while disregarding the genuine concrete life of the intellect and the soul. The sense of concrete reality is made blunt by utilitarianism; it develops and flowers forth through those activities which are all the more needed by human life since they are not at the service of any practical utility, because they are in themselves, freedom, fruit, and joy. Unfortunate is a youth who does not know the pleasure of the spirit and is not exalted in the joy of knowing and the joy of beauty, and enthusiasm for ideas, and quickening experience in the first love, delight, and luxury of wisdom and poetry. Boredom and weariness with human affairs will come early enough indeed; to deal with them is the job of the grownup.

To discuss the matter in a more specific manner, I should like to make the following observations: that conception which makes education itself a constantly renewed experiment, starting from the pupil's present purposes and developing in one way or another according to the success of his problem-solving activity with regard to these purposes and to new purposes arising from broadened experience in unforeseen directions, such a pragmatist conception has its own merits when it comes to the necessity of adapting educational methods to the natural interests of the pupil. But what are the standards for judging the purposes and values thus successively emerging in the pupil's mind? If the teacher himself has no general aim, nor final values to which all this process is related; if education itself is to grow "in whatever direction a novelly emerging future renders most feasible";* in other words, if the pragmatist theory requires a perpetual experimental reconstruction of the ends of the educator himself (and not only of the experience of the pupil), then it teaches educational recipes but gets away from any real art of education: for an education which does not have any goal of its own and tends only to growth itself without "end beyond further growth"† is no more an art than an art of architecture which would not have any idea of what is to be built, and would only tend to the growth of the construction in whatever direction a new addition of materials is feasible. In nature itself, biological growth is nothing but a morphological process, or the progressive acquisition of a definite form. And finally the pragmatist theory can only subordinate and enslave education to the trends which may develop in collective life and society, for in the last analysis the aims newly arising in

* Brubacher, *op. cit.*, p. 329.

† *Ibid.*

such a "reconstruction of ends" will only be determined by the precarious factors of the environment to be controlled and the values made at each moment predominant by given social conditions or tendencies or by the state.

The element of truth which must be preserved in the conception I have just discussed, is the fact that the final end of education—the fulfillment of man as a human person—is infinitely higher and broader than the aim of architectural art or even the aim of medical art, for it deals with our very freedom and spirit, whose boundless potentialities can be led to full human stature only by means of constant creative renewal. As a result, the vital spontaneity of the one to be educated plays a major part in the progress toward this final end, as well as the steady widening of the pupil's experience; and the need for constantly renewed adaptation of methods, means, and approaches is much greater in educational art than in any art dealing only with some material achievement.

The Fifth Misconception: Intellectualism

With regard to the powers of the human soul I should like now to indicate as briefly as possible two other errors which oppose one another and which come from overemphasis: intellectualism, the fifth error or misconception on our list; the other, voluntarism.

Intellectualism takes on two principal forms: a certain form of intellectualism seeks the supreme achievements of education in sheer dialectical or rhetorical skill—such was the case of classical pedagogy, especially in the bourgeois era, in which education was a privilege of privileged classes.

Another form of intellectualism, a modern one, gives up universal values and insists upon the working and experiential functions of intelligence. It seeks the supreme achievements of education in scientific and technical specialization. Now specialization is more and more needed by the technical organization of modern life, yet it should be compensated for by a more vigorous general training, especially during youth. If we remember that the animal is a specialist, and a perfect one, all of its knowing-power being fixed upon a single task to be done, we ought to conclude that an educational program which would only aim at forming specialists ever more perfect in ever more specialized fields, and unable to pass judgment on any matter that goes beyond their specialized competence, would lead indeed to a progressive animalization of the human mind and life. Finally, as the life of bees consists of producing honey, the real life of man would consist of producing in a perfectly pigeonholed manner economic values and scientific discoveries, while some cheap pleasure or social entertainment would occupy leisure time, and a vague religious feeling, without any content of thought and reality, would make existence a little less flat, perhaps a little more dramatic and stimulating, like a happy dream. The overwhelming cult of specialization dehumanizes man's life.

Fortunately, nowhere in the world has any educational system been set up solely on this basis. Yet there exists everywhere a trend toward such a conception of education, following a more or less conscious materialistic philosophy of life. This represents a great peril for the democracies, because the democratic ideal more than any other requires faith in and the development of spiritual energies—a field which is over and above any specialization—and because a complete division of the human mind and activities into specialized compartments would make impossible the very "government of the people, by the people, and for the people." How could the common man be capable of judging about the good of the people if he felt able to pass judgment only in the field of his own specialized vocational competence? Political activity and political judgment would become the exclusive job of specialized experts in the matter—a kind of state technocracy which does not open particularly felicitous perspectives either for the good of the people or for liberty. As for education—complemented by some imperative vocational guidance—it would become the regular process of differentiation of the bees in the human beehive. In reality, the democratic way of life demands primarily liberal education for all and a general humanistic development throughout society. Even as to industrial achievements, man's free ingenuity strengthened by an education which liberates and broadens the mind is of as great import as technical specialization, for out of these free resources of human intelligence there arises, in managers and workers, the power of adapting themselves to new circumstances and mastering them.

The Sixth Misconception: Voluntarism

Voluntarism, also, has two principal forms. In reaction against the first form of intellectualism, a voluntarist trend, developed since the time of Schopenhauer, has contributed to upset the internal order of human nature, by making intelligence subservient to the will and by appealing to the virtue of irrational forces. Accordingly, education was intended to concentrate either on the will which was to be disciplined according to some national pattern or on the free expansion of nature and natural potentialities. The merit of the best and wisest forms of voluntarism in the educational field* has been to call attention again to the essential importance of the voluntary functions, disregarded by intellectualist pedagogy, and to the primacy of morality, virtue, and generosity in the upbringing of man. For the main point is surely to be a good man rather than to be a learned man. As Rabelais put it, science without conscience is the ruin of the soul. Such was the ideal but in actual fact the pedagogic achievements of voluntarism have been strangely disappointing, at least from the point of view of the good. From the point of view of evil, they have had plenty of success—I mean in the effectiveness of Nazi training, schools, and youth organizations, in smashing all sense of truth in human minds and in perverting the very function of language and morally devastating the youth and making the intellect only an organ of the technical equipment of the state.

For the voluntarist trend in education combines very well with technical training. We find such a combination not only in the totalitarian corruption of education but elsewhere also, and there to some good purpose. As we see it in democratic countries, this peculiar form of educational voluntarism may be described as an effort to compensate for the inconveniences of the second form of intellectualism—overspecialized technical training—by what is known as education of will, education of feeling, formation of character, etc. Yet the misfortune is that this commendable effort has yielded, as a rule, the same disappointing result of which I spoke a moment ago.† Character is something easily warped or

* I am thinking for instance of the work of F. W. Foerster, whose influence has been great in many European pedagogical circles.

† Voluntarism does not succeed in forming and strengthening the will, but

debased, difficult to shape. All the pedagogical hammering of nails into the shoe doesn't make the shoe more comfortable to the foot. The methods which change the school into a hospital for refitting and vitalizing the wills, suggesting altruistic behavior or infusing good citizenship, may be well conceived and psychologically suitable, but they are for the most part dishearteningly ineffective.

We believe that intelligence is in and by itself nobler than the will of man, for its activity is more immaterial and universal. But we believe also that, in regard to the things or the very objects on which this activity bears, it is better to will and love the good than simply to know it. Moreover it is through man's will, when it is good, not through his intelligence, be it ever so perfect, that man is made good and right. A similar intermingling of roles is to be found in education, taken in its broadest sense. The upbringing of the human being must lead both intelligence and will toward achievement, and the shaping of the will is throughout more important to man than the shaping of the intellect. Yet, whereas the educational system of schools and colleges succeeds as a rule in equipping man's intellect for knowledge, it seems to be missing its main achievement, the equipping of man's will. What an infelicity!

The Seventh Misconception: Everything Can Be Learned

We are here confronted with some paradoxical aspects of education. The main paradox can be formulated as follows: what is most important in education is not the job of education, and still less that of learning. Here we face an error terribly current in the modern world—the seventh error or misconception on our list—which boils down to the belief that everything can be learned.

---

it succeeds in deforming and weakening the intellect, by the very fact that it exaggerates the province of the will in thought itself, so as to make everything a matter of one's will to believe. It has been pointed out in this connection that "just as in the realm of politics, the primacy of will identifies authority with force, so in the realm of thought the primacy of will reduces everything to arbitrary opinions or academic conventions. There are no first truths, but only postulates, demands of the will that something be taken for granted. In some sense, all knowledge rests on acts of faith, though the only principle of such faith is one's private predilections." Mortimer J. Adler, "Liberalism and Liberal Education," *The Educational Record*, July, 1939, pp. 435–436.

Greek sophists, too, believed that everything, even virtue, could be gotten by means of learning and discussing the matter. It is not true that everything can be learned, and that youth must earnestly expect from colleges not only courses in cooking, housekeeping, nursing, advertising, cosmetology,* money-making, and getting married, but also—why not?—courses on the scientific means of acquiring creative genius in art or science, or of consoling those who weep, or of being a man of generosity.

The teaching of morality, with regard to its intellectual bases, should occupy a great place in school and college education. Yet that right appreciation of practical cases which the ancients called *prudentia*, and which is an inner vital power of judgment developed in the mind and backed up by well-directed will, cannot be replaced by any learning whatsoever. Nor can experience, which is an incommunicable fruit of suffering and memory, and through which the shaping of man is achieved, be taught by any school or any courses. There are courses in philosophy, but no courses in wisdom; wisdom is gained through spiritual experience, and as for practical wisdom, as Aristotle put it, the experience of old men is both as undemonstrable and illuminating as the first principles of understanding. Moreover, is there anything of greater import in the education of man than that which is of the greatest import for man and human life? For man and human life there is indeed nothing greater than intuition and love. Not every love is right, nor every intuition well directed or conceptualized, yet if either intuition or love exists in any hidden corner, life and the flame of life are there, and a bit of heaven in a promise. Yet neither intuition nor love is a matter of training and learning, they are gift and freedom. In spite of all that, education should be primarily concerned with them. . . .†

* "I attacked vocationalism, and the University of California announced a course in cosmetology, saying 'The profession of beautician is the fastest growing in this state.' " Robert M. Hutchins, *Education for Freedom* (Louisiana State University Press, 1943), p. 19.

† "Education ought to teach us how to be in love always and what to be in love with. The great things of history have been done by the great lovers, by the saints and men of science and artists; and the problem of civilization is to give every man a chance of being a saint, a man of science, or an artist. But this problem cannot be attempted, much less solved, unless men desire to be saints, men of science, and artists, and if they are to desire that continuously and consciously, they must be taught what it means to be these

THE EDUCATIONAL AND EXTRA-EDUCATIONAL SPHERES

Another paradox deals with what may be called the educational and extra-educational spheres. By educational spheres I mean those collective entities which have always been recognized as especially committed to educational training: namely the family, the school, the state, and the Church. Here the surprising thing is that on the one hand the family, which is the first and fundamental educational sphere, grounded in nature, performs its educational task while not infrequently making the child a victim of psychological traumatisms, or of the bad example, ignorance, or prejudice of the adult; and that on the other hand the school, whose special and vocational function is education, performs its educational task while not infrequently making the youth a victim of stupefying overwork or disintegrating chaotic specialization, and often extinguishing the fire of natural gifts and defrauding the thirst of natural intelligence by dint of pseudoknowledge. The solution is surely not to get rid of the family or of the school, but to endeavor to make them more aware and more worthy of their call, to acknowledge not only the necessity of mutual help but also the inevitability of a reciprocal tension between the one and the other, and to recognize, too, that from the very start, I say from childhood on, man's condition is to suffer from and defend himself against the most worthy and indispensable supporters whom maternal nature has provided for his life, and thus to grow amidst and through conflict, if only energy, love, and good will quicken his heart.

Yet what is perhaps most paradoxical is that the extra-educational sphere—that is, the entire field of human activity, particularly everyday work and pain, hard experiences in friendship and love, social customs, law (which is a "pedagogue," according to St. Paul), the common wisdom embodied in the behavior of the people, the inspiring radiance of art and poetry, the penetrating influence of religious feasts and liturgy—all this extra-educational sphere exerts on man an action which is more important in the achievement of his education than education itself. Finally the

---

things." Sir Arthur Clutton-Brock, *The Ultimate Belief* (New York, 1916), p. 123. Quoted by John U. Nef, *The United States and Civilization* (Chicago, 1942), p. 265.

all-important factor is a transcendent one, that call of the hero which Henri Bergson so insistently emphasized, and which passes through the whole structure of social habits and moral regulations as a vitalizing aspiration toward the infinite Love which is the source of being. The saints and the martyrs are the true educators of mankind.

Dare the School Build a New Social Order?

George S. Counts
(1889–   )

The use of the schools to spearhead the reform of society is a perennial dream of Western educational thinkers. As Hannah Arendt has pointed out, many philosophers would like to prepare children to attain some ideal social framework which the adult world has failed to achieve. Dewey's *Pedagogic Creed*, published in 1897, made this idea part of the original progressive movement: "Education is the fundamental method of social progress and reform . . . the teacher is engaged, not simply in training individuals, but in the formation of the proper social life."

By the 1930s, however, progressive education had been institutionalized, professionalized, and emasculated. Gone were its bold reforming ideals. The Progressive Education Association, fearing to limit the movement by associating it with any one set of social ideas, refused to take a stand on the most vital issues of the day.

Such was the situation when George S. Counts addressed the Association's 1932 convention. In what was probably the most dramatic and controversial speech ever given at such a meeting, Counts tried to revive the social reform thrust of the early progressive movement. Acknowledging the achievements of progressivism in making instruction more humane and effective, Counts argued that this aim was not enough for the schools in the Depression-weary America of the early thirties. He accused the progressive movement of having surrendered itself into the hands of the upper middle class, avoiding a genuine confrontation with the problems of industrial democracy. Aware that he was advocating heresy, Counts urged that the teachers frankly announce that they were in business to formulate a rational (and radical) vision of society, and that they intended to use the schools to indoctrinate the next generation with this vision.

Counts' own image of the coming socialist society, and his detailed critique of progressive education as it existed in 1932, are of mainly historical interest to us today. But the principles by which he justified the use of the schools as the reforming agencies of society, and his argument that education must inevitably indoctrinate, purposively or not, are still relevant to any discussion of the proper role of the schools in society.

Perhaps it is too much to ask teachers to lead the way to Utopia, as Counts demanded, and it might even be dangerous if they tried. But a revolutionary critique may be useful even if it is never adopted, and it is certainly to be regretted that there is no one on the educational scene today who is keeping alive the vision of a truly radical educational philosophy.

George Sylvester Counts was born in Kansas in 1889. After earning LL.D. and Ph.D. degrees, he taught various aspects of professional education at Delaware College, Harris Teachers College, Washington University (Seattle), Yale, and Chicago. He moved to Teachers College, Columbia University, in 1927, and remained there until his retirement. He is currently Professor Emeritus. Extremely active in educational and other social affairs, Counts has published a number of important works on the sociological and political bases of American education. The following text is an abridged version of *Dare the School Build a New Social Order?*, published by The John Day Company in 1932.

That the existing school is leading the way to a better social order is a thesis which few informed persons would care to defend. Except as it is forced to fight for its own life during times of depression, its course is too serene and untroubled. Only in the rarest of instances does it wage war on behalf of principle or ideal. Almost everywhere it is in the grip of conservative forces and is serving the cause of perpetuating ideas and institutions suited to an age that is gone.

. . . .

This brings us to the most crucial issue in education—the question of the nature and extent of the influence which the school should exercise over the development of the child. The advocates of extreme freedom have been so successful in championing what they call the rights of the child that even the most skillful practitioners of the art of converting others to their opinions disclaim all intention of molding the learner. And when the word indoctrination is coupled with education there is scarcely one among us possessing the hardihood to refuse to be horrified. . . .

The issue is no doubt badly confused by historical causes. The champions of freedom are obviously the product of an age that has broken very fundamentally with the past and is equally uncertain about the future. In many cases they feel themselves victims of narrow orthodoxies which were imposed upon them during childhood and which have severely cramped their lives. At any suggestion that the child should be influenced by his elders they therefore envisage the establishment of a state church, the formulation of a body of sacred doctrine, and the teaching of this doctrine as fixed and final. If we are forced to choose between such an unenlightened form of pedagogical influence and a condition of complete freedom for the child, most of us would in all probability choose the latter as the lesser of two evils. But this is to create a wholly artificial situation: the choice should not be limited to these two extremes. Indeed today neither extreme is possible.

I believe firmly that a critical factor must play an important role in any adequate educational program, at least in any such program fashioned for the modern world. An education that does not strive to promote the fullest and most thorough understanding of the world is not worthy of the name. Also there must be no deliberate distortion or suppression of facts to support any theory or point of view. On the other hand, I am prepared to defend the thesis that all education contains a large element of imposition, that in the very nature of the case this is inevitable, that the existence and evolution of society depend upon it, that it is consequently eminently desirable, and that the frank acceptance of this fact by the educator is a major professional obligation. I even contend that failure to do this involves the clothing of one's own deepest prejudices in the garb of universal truth and the introduction into the theory and practice of education of an element of obscurantism. In the development of this thesis I shall examine a number of widespread fallacies which seem to me to underlie the theoretical opposition to all forms of imposition. Although certain of these fallacies are very closely related and to some extent even cover the same territory, their separate treatment will help to illuminate the problem.

There is the fallacy that man is born free. As a matter of fact, he is born helpless. He achieves freedom, as a race and as an individual, through the medium of culture. The most crucial of all circumstances conditioning human life is birth into a particular culture. By birth one becomes a Chinese, an Englishman, a Hottentot, a Sioux Indian, a Turk, or a one-hundred-percent American. Such a range of possibilities may appear too shocking to contemplate, but it is the price that one must pay in order to be born. Nevertheless, even if a given soul should happen by chance to choose a Hottentot for a mother, it should thank its lucky star that it was born into the Hottentot culture rather than entirely free. By being nurtured on a body of culture, however backward and limited it may be comparatively, the individual is at once imposed upon and liberated. The child is terribly imposed upon by being compelled through the accident of birth to learn one language rather than another, but without some language man would never become man. Any language, even the most poverty-stricken, is infinitely better than none at all. In the life cycle of the individual many choices must of necessity be made, and the most fundamental and decisive of these choices will always be made by the group. This is so obvious that it should require no elaboration. Yet this very obvious fact, with its implications, is commonly disregarded by those who are fearful of molding the child. One of the most important elements of any culture is a tradition of achievement along a particular line—a tradition which the group imposes upon the young and through which the powers of the young are focused, disciplined, and developed. One people will have a fine hunting tradition, another a maritime tradition, another a musical tradition, another a military tradition, another a scientific tradition, another a baseball tradition, another a business tradition, and another even a tradition of moral and religious prophecy. A particular society of the modern type commonly has a vast number of different traditions all of which may be bound together and integrated more or less by some broad and inclusive tradition. One might argue that the imposing of these traditions upon children involves a severe restriction upon their freedom. My thesis is that such imposition, provided the tradition is vital and suited to the times, releases the energies of the young, sets up standards of excellence, and makes possible really great achievement. The individual who fails to come under the influence of such a tradition may enjoy a certain kind of freedom, but it is scarcely a kind of freedom that anyone would covet for either himself or his children. It is the freedom of mediocrity, incompetence, and aimlessness.

There is the fallacy that the child is good by nature. The evidence from anthropology, as well as from common observation, shows that on entering the world the individual is neither good nor bad; he is merely a bundle of potentialities which may be developed in manifold directions. Guidance is, therefore, not to be found in child nature, but rather in the culture of the group and the purposes of living. There can be no good individual apart from some conception of the character of the *good* society; and the good society is not something that is given by nature: it must be fashioned by the hand and brain of man. This process of building a good society is to a very large degree an educational process. The nature of the child must of course be taken into account in the organization of any educational program, but it cannot furnish the materials and the guiding principles of that program. Squirm and wriggle as we may, we must admit that the bringing of materials and guiding principles from the outside involves the molding of the child.

There is the fallacy that the child lives in a separate world of his own. The advocates of freedom often speak of the adult as an alien influence in the life of the child. For an adult to intrude himself or his values into the domain of boys and girls is made to take on the appearance of an invasion by a foreign power. Such a dualism is almost wholly artificial. Whatever may be the view of the adult, the child knows but one society; and that is a society including persons of all ages. This does not mean that conflicts of interest may not occur or that on occasion adults may not abuse and exploit children. It does mean that in a proper kind of society the relationship is one of mutual benefit and regard in which the young repay in trust and emulation the protection and guidance provided by their elders. The child's conception of his position in society is well expressed in the words of Plentycoups, the famous Crow chieftain, who spoke thus of his boyhood: "We followed the buffalo herds over our beautiful plains, fighting a battle one day and sending out a war party against the enemy the next. My heart was afire. I wished so to help my people, to distinguish myself, so that I might wear an eagle's feather in my hair. How I worked to make my arms strong as a grizzly's, and how I practiced with my bow! A boy never wished to be a man more than I." Here is an emphatic and unequivocal answer to those who would raise a barrier between youth and age. Place the child in a world of his own and you take from him the most powerful incentives to growth and achievement. Perhaps one of the greatest tragedies of contemporary society lies in the fact that the child is becoming increasingly isolated from the serious activities of adults. Some would say that such isolation is an inevitable corollary of the growing complexity of the social order. In my opinion it is rather the product of a society that is moved by no great commanding ideals and is consequently victimized by the most terrible form of human madness—the struggle for private gain. As primitive peoples wisely protect their children from the dangers of actual warfare, so we guard ours from the acerbities of economic strife. Until school and society are bound together by common purposes the program of education will lack both meaning and vitality.

There is the fallacy that education is some pure and mystical essence that remains unchanged from everlasting to everlasting. According to this view, genuine education must be completely divorced from politics, live apart from the play of social forces, and pursue ends peculiar to itself. It thus becomes a method existing independently of the cultural milieu and equally beneficent at all times and in all places. This is one of the most dangerous of fallacies and is responsible for many sins committed in different countries by American educators traveling abroad. They have carried the same brand of education to backward and advanced races, to peoples living under relatively static conditions and to peoples passing through periods of rapid and fundamental transition. They have called it Education with a capital E, whereas in fact it has been American education with a capital A and a small e. Any defensible educational program must be adjusted to a particular time and place, and the degree and nature of the imposition must vary with the social situation. Under ordinary conditions the process of living suffices in itself to hold society together, but when the forces of disintegration become sufficiently powerful it may well be that a fairly large measure of deliberate control is desirable and even essential to social survival.

There is the fallacy that the school should be impartial in its emphases, that no bias should be given instruction. We have already observed how the individual is inevitably molded by the culture into which he is born. In the case of the school a similar process operates and presumably is subjected to a degree of conscious direction. My thesis is that complete impartiality is utterly impossible, that the school must shape attitudes, develop tastes, and even impose ideas. It is obvious that the whole of creation cannot be brought into the school. This means that some selection must be made of teachers, curricula, architecture, methods of teaching. And in the making of the selection the dice must always be weighted in favor of this or that. Here is a fundamental truth that cannot be brushed aside as irrelevant or unimportant; it constitutes the very essence of the matter under discussion. Nor can the reality be concealed beneath agreeable phrases. Professor Dewey states in his *Democracy and Education* that the school should provide a *purified* environment for the child. With this view I would certainly agree; probably no person reared in our society would favor the study of pornography in the schools. I am sure, however, that this means stacking the cards in favor of the particular systems of value which we may happen to possess. It is one of the truisms of the anthropologist that there are no maxims of purity on which all peoples would agree. Other vigorous opponents of imposition unblushingly advocate the "cultivation of democratic sentiments" in children or the promotion of child growth in the direction of "a better and richer life." The first represents definite acquiescence in imposition; the second, if it does not mean the same thing, means nothing. I believe firmly that democratic sentiments should be cultivated and that a better and richer life should be the outcome of education, but in neither case would I place responsibility on either God or the order of nature. I would merely contend that as educators we must make many choices involving the development of attitudes in boys and girls and that we should not be afraid to acknowledge the faith that is in us or mayhap the forces that compel us.

There is the fallacy that the great object of education is to produce the college professor, that is, the individual who adopts an agnostic attitude towards every important social issue, who can balance the pros against the cons with the skill of a juggler, who sees all sides of every question and never commits himself to any, who delays action until all the facts are in, who knows that all the facts will never come in, who consequently holds his judgment in a state of indefinite suspension, and who before the approach of middle age sees his powers of action atrophy and his social sympathies decay. With Peer Gynt he can exclaim:

Ay, think of it—wish it done—will it to boot,—
But do it—! No, that's past my understanding!

This type of mind also talks about waiting until the solutions of social problems are found, when as a matter of fact there are no solutions in any definite and final sense. For any complex social problem worthy of the name there are probably tens and even scores, if not hundreds, of "solutions," depending upon the premises from which one works. The meeting of a social situation involves the making of decisions and the working out of adjustments. Also it involves the selection and rejection of values. If we wait for a solution to appear like the bursting of the sun through the clouds or the resolving of the elements in an algebraic equation, we shall wait in vain. Although college professors, if not too numerous, perform a valuable social function, society requires great numbers of persons who, while capable of gathering and digesting facts, are at the same time able to think in terms of life, make decisions, and act. From such persons will come our real social leaders.

There is the closely related fallacy that education is primarily intellectualistic in its processes and goals. Quite as important is that ideal factor in culture which gives meaning, direction, and significance to life. I refer to the element of faith or purpose which lifts man out of himself and above the level of his more narrow personal interests. Here, in my judgment, is one of the great lacks in our schools and in our intellectual class today. We are able to contemplate the universe and find that all is vanity. Nothing really stirs us, unless it be that the bath water is cold, the toast burnt, or the elevator not running; or that perchance we miss the first section of a revolving door. Possibly this is the fundamental reason why we are so fearful of molding the child. We are moved by no great faiths; we are touched by no great passions. We can view a world order rushing rapidly towards collapse with no more concern than the outcome of a horse race; we can see injustice, crime and misery in their most terrible forms all about us and, if we are not directly affected, register the emotions of a scientist studying white rats in a laboratory. And in the name of freedom, objectivity, and the open mind, we would transmit this general attitude of futility to our children. In my opinion this is a confession of complete moral and spiritual bankruptcy. We cannot, by talk about the interests of children and the sacredness of personality, evade the responsibility of bringing to the younger generation a vision which will call forth their active loyalties and challenge them to creative and arduous labors. A generation without such a vision is destined, like ours, to a life of absorption in self, inferiority complexes, and frustration. The genuinely free man is not the person who spends the day contemplating his own navel, but rather the one who loses himself in a great cause or glorious adventure.

There is the fallacy that the school is an all-powerful educational agency. Every professional group tends to exaggerate its own importance in the scheme of things. To this general rule the teachers offer no exception. The leaders of progressive education in particular seem to have an overweening faith in the power of the school. On the one hand, they speak continually about reconstructing society through education; and on the other, they apparently live in a state of perpetual fear lest the school impose some one point of view upon all children and mold them all to a single pattern. A moment's reflection is sufficient to show that life in the modern world is far too complex to permit this: the school is but one formative agency among many, and certainly not the strongest at that. Our major concern consequently should be, not to keep the school from influencing the child in a positive direction, but rather to make certain that every progressive school will use whatever power it may possess in opposing and checking the forces of social conservatism and reaction. We know full well that, if the school should endeavor vigorously and consistently to win its pupils to the support of a given social program, unless it were supported by other agencies, it could act only as a mild counterpoise to restrain and challenge the might of less enlightened and more selfish purposes.

There is the fallacy that ignorance rather than knowledge is the way of wisdom. Many who would agree that imposition of some kind is inevitable seem to feel that there is something essentially profane in any effort to understand, plan, and control the process. They will admit that the child is molded by his environment, and then presumably contend that in the fashioning of this environment we should close our eyes to the consequences of our acts, or at least should not endeavor to control our acts in the light of definite knowledge of their consequences. To do the latter would involve an effort to influence deliberately the growth of the child in a particular direction—to cause him to form this habit rather than that, to develop one taste rather than another, to be sensitive to a given ideal rather than its rival. But this would be a violation of the "rights of the child," and therefore evil. Apparently his rights can be protected only if our influence upon him is thoroughly concealed under a heavy veil of ignorance. If the school can do no better than this, it has no reason for existence. If it is to be merely an arena for the blind play of psychological forces, it might better close its doors. Here is the doctrine of *laissez faire*, driven from the field of social and political theory, seeking refuge in the domain of pedagogy. Progressive education wishes to build a new world but refuses to be held accountable for the kind of world it builds. In my judgment, the school should know what it is doing, in so far as this is humanly possible, and accept full responsibility for its acts.

Finally, there is the fallacy that in a dynamic society like ours the major responsibility of education is to prepare the individual to adjust himself to social change. The argument in support of this view is fairly cogent. The world is changing with great rapidity; the rate of change is being accelerated constantly; the future is full of uncertainty. Consequently the individual who is to live and thrive in this world must possess an agile mind, be bound by no deep loyalties, hold all conclusions and values tentatively, and be ready on a moment's notice to make even fundamental shifts in outlook and philosophy. Like a lumberjack riding a raft of logs through the rapids, he must be able with lightning speed to jump from one insecure foundation to another, if he is not to be overwhelmed by the onward surge of the cultural stream. In a word, he must be as willing to adopt new ideas and values as to install the most up-to-the-minute labor-saving devices in his dwelling or to introduce the latest inventions into his factory. Under such a conception of life and society, education can only bow down before the gods of chance and reflect the drift of the social order. This conception is essentially anarchic in character, exalts the irrational above the rational forces of society, makes of security an individual rather than a social goal, drives every one of us into an insane competition with his neighbors, and assumes that man is incapable of controlling in the common interest the creatures of his brain. Here we have imposition with a vengeance, but not the imposition of the teacher or the school. Nor is it an enlightened form of imposition. Rather is it the imposition of the chaos and cruelty and ugliness produced by the brutish struggle for existence and advantage. Far more terrifying than any indoctrination in which the school might indulge is the prospect of our becoming completely victimized and molded by the mechanics of industrialism. The control of the machine requires a society which is dominated less by the ideal of individual advancement and more by certain far-reaching purposes and plans for social construction. In such a society, instead of the nimble mind responsive to every eddy in the social current, a firmer and more steadfast mentality would be preferable.

If we may now assume that the child will be imposed upon in some fashion by the various elements in his environment, the real question is not whether imposition will take place, but rather from what source it will come. If we were to answer this question in terms of the past, there could, I think, be but one answer: on all genuinely crucial matters the school follows the wishes of the groups or classes that actually rule society; on minor matters the school is sometimes allowed a certain measure of freedom. But the future may be unlike the past. Or perhaps I should say that teachers, if they could increase sufficiently their stock of courage, intelligence, and vision, might become a social force of some magnitude. About this eventuality I am not over sanguine, but a society lacking leadership as ours does, might even accept the guidance of teachers. Through powerful organizations they might at least reach the public conscience and come to exercise a larger measure of control over the schools than hitherto. They would then have to assume some responsibility for the more fundamental forms of imposition which, according to my argument, cannot be avoided.

That the teachers should deliberately reach for power and then make the most of their conquest is my firm conviction. To the extent that they are permitted to fashion the curriculum and the procedures of the school they will definitely and positively influence the social attitudes, ideals, and behavior of the coming generation. In doing this they should resort to no subterfuge or false modesty. They should say neither that they are merely teaching the truth nor that they are unwilling to wield power in their own right. The first position is false and the second is a confession of incompetence. It is my observation that the men and women who have affected the course of human events are those who have not hesitated to use the power that has come to them. Representing as they do, not the interests of the moment or of any special class, but rather the common and abiding interests of the people, teachers are under heavy social obligation to protect and further those interests. In this they occupy a relatively unique position in society. Also since the profession should embrace scientists and scholars of the highest rank, as well as teachers working at all levels of the educational system, it has at its disposal, as no other group, the knowledge and wisdom of the ages. It is scarcely thinkable that these men and women would ever act as selfishly or bungle as badly as have the so-called practical men of our generation—the politicians, the financiers, the industrialists. If all of these facts are taken into account, instead of shunning power, the profession should rather seek power and then strive to use that power fully and wisely and in the interests of the great masses of the people.

The point should be emphasized that teachers possess no magic secret to power. While their work should give them a certain moral advantage, they must expect to encounter the usual obstacles blocking the road to leadership. They should not be deceived by the pious humbug with which public men commonly flatter the members of the profession. To expect ruling groups or classes to give precedence to teachers on important matters, because of age or sex or sentiment, is to refuse to face realities. It was one of the proverbs of the agrarian order that a spring never rises higher than its source. So the power that teachers exercise in the schools can be no greater than the power they wield in society. Moreover, while organization is necessary, teachers should not think of their problem primarily in terms of organizing and presenting a united front to the world, the flesh, and the devil. In order to be effective they must throw off completely the slave psychology that has dominated the mind of the pedagogue more or less since the days of ancient Greece. They must be prepared to stand on their own feet and win for their ideas the support of the masses of the people. Education as a force for social regeneration must march hand in hand with the living and creative forces of the social order. In their own lives teachers must bridge the gap between school and society and play some part in the fashioning of those great common purposes which should bind the two together.

This brings us to the question of the kind of imposition in which teachers should engage, if they had the power. Our obligations, I think, grow out of the social situation. We live in troublous times; we live in an age of profound change; we live in an age of revolution. Indeed it is highly doubtful whether man ever lived in a more eventful period than the present. In order to match our epoch we would probably have to go back to the fall of the ancient empires or even to that unrecorded age when men first abandoned the natural arts of hunting and fishing and trapping and began to experiment with agriculture and the settled life. Today we are witnessing the rise of a civilization quite without precedent in human history—a civilization founded on science, technology, and machinery, possessing the most extraordinary power, and rapidly making of the entire world a single great society. Because of forces already released, whether in the field of economics, politics, morals, religion, or art, the old molds are being broken. And the peoples of the earth are everywhere seething with strange ideas and passions. If life were peaceful and quiet and undisturbed by great issues, we might with some show of wisdom center our attention on the nature of the child. But with the world as it is, we cannot afford for a single instant to remove our eyes from the social scene or shift our attention from the peculiar needs of the age.

In this new world that is forming, there is one set of issues which is peculiarly fundamental and which is certain to be the center of bitter and prolonged struggle. I refer to those issues which may be styled economic. President Butler has well stated the case: "For a generation and more past," he says, "the center of human interest has been moving from the point which it occupied for some four hundred years to a new point which it bids fair to occupy for a time equally long. The shift in the position of the center of gravity in human interest has been from politics to economics; from considerations that had to do with forms of government, with the establishment and protection of individual liberty, to considerations that have to do with the production, distribution, and consumption of wealth."

. . . The age is pregnant with possibilities. There lies within our grasp the most humane, the most beautiful, the most majestic civilization ever fashioned by any people. This much at least we know today. We shall probably know more tomorrow. At last men have achieved such a mastery over the forces of nature that wage slavery can follow chattel slavery and take its place among the relics of the past. No longer are there grounds for the contention that the finer fruits of human culture must be nurtured upon the toil and watered by the tears of the masses. The limits to achievement set by nature have been so extended that we are today bound merely by our ideals, by our power of self-discipline, by our ability to devise social arrangements suited to an industrial age. If we are to place any credence whatsoever in the word of our engineers, the full utilization of modern technology at its present level of development should enable us to produce several times as much goods as were ever produced at the very peak of prosperity, and with the working day, the working year, and the working life reduced by half. We hold within our hands the power to usher in an age of plenty, to make secure the lives of all, and to banish poverty forever from the land. The only cause for doubt or pessimism lies in the question of our ability to rise to the stature of the times in which we live.

Our generation has the good or the ill fortune to live in an age when great decisions must be made. The American people, like most of the other peoples of the earth, have come to the parting of the ways; they can no longer trust entirely the inspiration which came to them when the Republic was young; they must decide afresh what they are to do with their talents. Favored above all other nations with the resources of nature and the material instrumentalities of civilization, they stand confused and irresolute before the future. They seem to lack the moral quality necessary to quicken, discipline, and give direction to their matchless energies. In a recent paper Professor Dewey has, in my judgment, correctly diagnosed our troubles: "The schools, like the nation," he says, "are in need of a central purpose which will create new enthusiasm and devotion, and which will unify and guide all intellectual plans."

This suggests, as we have already observed, that the educational problem is not wholly intellectual in nature. Our progressive schools therefore cannot rest content with giving children an opportunity to study contemporary society in all of its aspects. This of course must be done, but I am convinced that they should go much farther. If the schools are to be really effective, they must become centers for the building, and not merely for the contemplation, of our civilization. This does not mean that we should endeavor to promote particular reforms through the educational system. We should, however, give to our children a vision of the possibilities which lie ahead and endeavor to enlist their loyalties and enthusiasms in the realization of the vision. Also our social institutions and practices, all of them, should be critically examined in the light of such a vision.

. . . .

Such a vision of what America might become in the industrial age I would introduce into our schools as the supreme imposition, but one to which our children are entitled—a priceless legacy which it should be the first concern of our profession to fashion and bequeath. The objection will of course be raised that this is asking teachers to assume unprecedented social responsibilities. But we live in difficult and dangerous times—times when precedents lose their significance. If we are content to remain where all is safe and quiet and serene, we shall dedicate ourselves, as teachers have commonly done in the past, to a role of futility, if not of positive social reaction. Neutrality with respect to the great issues that agitate society, while perhaps theoretically possible, is practically tantamount to giving support to the forces of conservatism. As Justice Holmes has candidly said in his essay on Natural Law, "we all, whether we know it or not, are fighting to make the kind of world that we should like." If neutrality is impossible even in the dispensation of justice, whose emblem is the blindfolded goddess, how is it to be achieved in education? To ask the question is to answer it.

To refuse to face the task of creating a vision of a future America immeasurably more just and noble and beautiful than the America of today is to evade the most crucial, difficult, and important educational task. Until we have assumed this responsibility we are scarcely justified in opposing and mocking the efforts of so-called patriotic societies to introduce into the schools a tradition which, though narrow and unenlightened, nevertheless represents an honest attempt to meet a profound social and educational need. Only when we have fashioned a finer and more authentic vision than they, will we be fully justified in our opposition to their efforts. Only then will we have discharged the age-long obligation which the older generation owes to the younger and which no amount of sophistry can obscure. Only through such a legacy of spiritual values will our children be enabled to find their place in the world, be lifted out of the present morass of moral indifference, be liberated from the senseless struggle for material success, and be challenged to high endeavor and achievement. And only thus will we as a people put ourselves on the road to the expression of our peculiar genius and to the making of our special contribution to the cultural heritage of the race.

The Distinctive Function of the Schools

Arthur Bestor

(1908–)

In July, 1955, the Progressive Education Association quietly disbanded. Two months later Arthur Bestor, Professor of History at the University of Illinois, published a book called *The Restoration of Learning.* The two events indicate the tenor of American educational debate in the mid-fifties: the progressives were under fire (as they had been ever since the 1920s), and the proponents of more traditional ideals were ready with remedies. The program put forward by Bestor brings us full circle in some respects from the post-Renaissance tradition culminating in John Dewey. It urges the reinstatement of intellectual discipline as the distinctive function of the schools, the elimination of the social, vocational, and psychological concerns which the reformers had found more important than just book learning, and the contraction of the school's aspirations, which had been expanded by progressives like George Counts to encompass the complete reformation of society. Lawrence Cremin, in his definitive history of the progressive movement in American education (*The Transformation of the School*), wrote that Bestor's writings "constituted by far the most serious, searching, and influential criticisms of progressive education to appear during the fifties."

Bestor began his educational writing with scathing attacks on the "life-adjustment" movement, accusing the professional educators and professors of education of a take-over of the schools. Soon, however, his criticism moved into a more constructive phase.

In Bestor's view, the schools have a unique *raison d'être* which the progressive reformers of American education had forgotten. That function is intellectual training: "the deliberate cultivation of the ability to think." In a democracy the schools must offer training in the basic academic subjects to all the students, because as adults they will all be called upon to exercise the responsibilities of self-direction and citizenship.

Bestor's argument is logically convincing. But educators today often face situations where the family, the church, and the community have failed in their responsibilities to children. In such cases teachers frequently must postpone their distinctive intellectual function and devote themselves, out of simple humanity, to meeting the more immediate needs of their pupils for discipline, vocational training, and guidance in solving their psychological problems. Bestor argues that such things *should* be taken care of by other, more appropriate agencies. He is right, but what are educators to do when the other agencies fail? The school is the one place to which all the youth of the community are legally compelled to come.

Arthur Bestor was born in New York State and educated at Yale, where he taught for several years and received his Ph.D. in history in 1936. He was later associated with Teachers College, Columbia University, and with Stanford and the University of Wisconsin. Since 1947 he has been on the faculty of the University of Illinois. His books include *Educational Wastelands, Backwoods Utopias, Education and Reform at New Harmony,* and *The Restoration of Learning,* his major work on education. The following essay first appeared in *Daedalus* magazine and was later reprinted in *Education in the Age of Science,* published by Basic Books in 1959.

"In its education," Admiral Rickover has said, paraphrasing Lord Haldane, "the soul of a people mirrors itself." A mirror, one must remember, is undiscriminating. It reflects the good and the bad, the beautiful and the ugly, with crystalline impartiality. Education is such a mirror. Defects in our educational system are reflections of weaknesses and shortcomings in our national life. This is a hard truth to accept, but a truth nonetheless. The danger lies in confusing explanation with justification. Because racial discrimination can be explained historically is no reason for viewing it in any other light than as an abomination. So with defects and weaknesses in American education. To explain them is not to condone them.

Fatalistic acceptance of weaknesses in education is equally unwarranted. The educational system is influenced, but not determined, by social forces. Of all the institutions of society (except possibly religion), education enjoys the greatest measure of autonomy. This is a precious autonomy, to be defended with unremitting tenacity, to be enlarged whenever and wherever the opportunity offers. The independence of education from social pressures must be defended not merely for the sake of education but primarily for the sake of society. Education is almost the only force *within* society that is capable, in some measure, of *altering* society. Its power in this respect can easily be exaggerated, and can even be crippled by such exaggeration. Professor George S. Counts's famous question, *Dare the School Build a New Social Order?* is as absurd as would be the question, "Dare Archimedes move the earth?" Neither is a matter of daring. The question is whether one can find a fulcrum outside society on which to rest the lever that might move society. Education has no such fulcrum. On the other hand, it is not absurd to suppose that education, working within society but retaining its power to discriminate among the purposes that society presses upon it, can bring about changes not only within the schoolroom but also, gradually and cumulatively, throughout society itself.

Education, if we would be realistic, is a minority force among the forces of society. Peculiarly applicable to education, therefore, is a pregnant sentence of Thoreau's: "A minority is powerless while it conforms to the majority; it is not even a minority then; but it is irresistible when it clogs by its whole weight." The school and the college have an obligation—*to society*—to clog by the friction of their resistance those movements in society that tend toward intellectual and cultural degradation. This requires not daring but will, a less spectacular virtue but one that is perhaps more truly heroic.

American education has been shaped to its present form by the forces in American society, forces which have been largely unresisted or even perversely reinforced. It can be reshaped by sternly resisting certain of these forces and by deliberately enhancing the strength of others. American education must be so reshaped if the United States is not to follow the path of degeneration blazed by other nations that in the past have complacently cherished their vices equally with their virtues, from a cozy feeling that both were their very own. The duty of American educators is to make the discriminations that are necessary if social forces are to be so directed as to revitalize American education, and, through education, American society.

The Three Areas of Concern

Schooling is part of the process by which infants eventually become adult members of society. It is an important part of the process, but only a part. Other agencies of society are also engaged in deliberately shaping the future of young persons. The task of the school can be defined only with reference to these other agencies, each with its particular sphere of competence and hence of responsibility.

In the last analysis, there are three areas of such great concern that every organized community provides some form of deliberate training for them. First of all, in even the most primitive society there is training for the practical tasks on which the livelihood of all depends. In the second place, every society provides elaborate means for indoctrinating its young members in the mores of the society, for transmitting its cultural traits and its ethical system. In the third place (though perhaps only in societies that we can call civilized), deliberate training is provided in the use of the intellectual tools that the civilization has developed: reading, writing, and arithmetic, at the lowest level; logic, history, mathematics, and science, or their equivalents, at higher levels. Until recent times, such training, in contradistinction to training of the first two kinds, has been provided only for a minority. Today universal literacy, the simplest index to the prevalence of at least rudimentary intellectual training, has become the accepted ideal of virtually every society and the actual achievement of many.

Each of these three kinds of training is closely related to a particular institution or group of institutions in society.

Training in practical skills is obviously related to the system of production. This functional relationship takes its most natural form in apprenticeship, a program, most literally, of "learning by doing." Apprenticeship, whether called by that name or not, can extend, and does extend, from the level of unskilled labor to the most complex professions. The physician's internship in a hospital is perhaps the best example of the latter, and is a proof that the essential principle is neither obsolete nor likely ever to become so. Where the problem is one of applying specific techniques in definite practical situations, the skill involved can be learned in no better place than on the job. To try to teach "know-how" in a schoolroom is to substitute a woefully inefficient and unrealistic procedure for an efficient and realistic one. As occupations and professions become increasingly complex, of course, more and more of the things that must be learned are transferred to the classroom. But the training that is so transferred is not—or should not be—training in "know-how," but training in the *intellectual components* of the profession, that is to say, the scholarly and scientific disciplines underlying it.

The second form of deliberate training undertaken by every society—indoctrination in the attitudes, customs, and standards of the culture—is associated, functionally as well as traditionally, with the family in the first instance, with religion in the second, with the institutions and ceremonies of the organized state in the third. This great category of training includes instruction and exhortation on such diverse matters as loyalty, the relations of the sexes, the norms of personality, morality in all its varied significances, acceptable conduct within a group and among groups, customary procedures and ceremonies, hierarchies of value—the list could be endless. Powerful group emotions are associated with all these things, powerful taboos exist, powerful forces can be unleashed against those guilty of deviation or even of criticism. Lapses in social conditioning can occur, of course, and even occasional breakdowns of social control. But it is naïve in the extreme to imagine that the agencies of society that operate in this realm are weak, helpless, or ineffectual. In fact, they marshal the most powerful forces that can operate upon the mind and spirit of man.

The third form of education is what we may call *liberal* education, or training in the scholarly and scientific disciplines basic to intellectual life. That there is such a thing as intellectual training, that it is distinguishable from job training and social conditioning —these are propositions which I find it necessary to defend in certain circles. Allow me to assume that I need not argue them here, but that I may proceed at once to examine the provision society makes for intellectual training.

The Distinctive Function of the School

The school, the college, and the university were created to perform a specific and recognized function. Their facilities and techniques—classrooms, libraries, laboratories, recitations, lectures, seminars, and examinations—were designed and developed for the particular purpose of intellectual training. To enable the school to carry out any other function, it must be altered and adapted, and its performance in the new role is usually haphazard, fumbling, and defective. Moreover, if intellectual training is pushed aside or neglected by schools and colleges, society is thereby impoverished of intellectual training, because it possesses no other resources, no other agencies, no other techniques for making up the loss. That the primary function of the educational system is to furnish intellectual training is as completely self-evident as any statement that can possibly be made about the function of a social institution, whether one approaches the matter from the point of view of logic or history or sociology.

The distribution of functions that I have described is never more than approximate, of course. Most institutions perform, in an incidental and indirect way, functions that belong primarily to institutions of another sort. Thus business and industry, not only in the "breaking in" of employees but also in advertising, attempt a good deal of social indoctrination, particularly in what are held to be the "economic virtues." The home carries on a good deal of vocational instruction and also a good deal of intellectual training. The school, even in its strictly academic work, maintains, and therefore helps to inculcate, the ethical standards of the surrounding culture, whenever issues involving these standards—for example, the matter of honesty in examinations—arise in the classroom. In providing the intellectual foundations for professional work, moreover, the school at times cannot avoid crossing the line that theoretically separates intellectual training from apprenticeship. A blurring of lines, in the degree which these examples represent, is both natural and inescapable, and it raises no question worth discussing.

Problems of tremendous magnitude, however, are created by any wholesale transfer of functions from one group of social institutions to another. The problems are particularly acute when one specialized agency suddenly projects its power over areas formerly the responsibility of other agencies. Such a situation is characteristically a revolutionary one, as when the church in effect takes over the state to create a theocracy, or when the state absorbs into itself the psychic potencies of the church to create an integral religion of nationalism, or when the business community captures the instruments of government to create an oligarchy, or when government seizes control over industry to create a communistic regime. These are extreme historical instances, no doubt, but they are suggestive. At the very least, they raise the question whether the wholesale transfer of social functions, in any given instance, is in fact necessary, justifiable, and beneficent. The mere fact that such a transfer results from—can only result from—insistent social pressures does not prove the inevitability of the development, and certainly furnishes no answer whatever to the question whether the change represents progress or degeneration.

Expansion of the Functions of the School

That American public schools have enormously expanded their functions is so obvious a fact that I do not suppose the point calls for elaboration or demonstration. Those who most vigorously oppose the point of view I take on educational policy do not deny this expansion of scope; indeed they acknowledge it and take pride in it. One of the most influential statements of the function of the public school, *Planning for American Youth,* a program published by the National Association of Secondary-School Principals, says: "Youth have specific needs they recognize; society makes certain requirements of all youth; together these form a pattern of common educational needs. . . . It is the Job of the School to Meet the Common and the Specific Individual Needs of Youth."

The "needs" that are particularized (in the ten points that make up the body of the statement) include those forms of training that I have described as job training and social conditioning. The responsibility of the school, in other words, is supposed to extend to all the areas in which society has customarily furnished some form of deliberate training.

This concept of the school as possessing a comprehensive and virtually unlimited social responsibility is itself a social concept, the product of social forces which can be traced historically. To trace them, however, is not the primary task, because explanation is not justification. There is no reason to believe that the social forces that produced this concept of the school were irresistible forces. The development of education in other countries seems to show that forces working in this particular direction can be resisted, if one wishes to resist them. And those who defend the American concept of an indefinitely extended responsibility for the school do not argue that the United States was *obliged* to accept this view of the school, but that the nation was *wise* to accept it.

Is it really necessary or desirable for the school to expand its responsibility to this extent? In fact, is the school capable of discharging such extended responsibility? Can it perform the tasks involved without fatally neglecting its primary social obligation—that of providing intellectual training?

The questions I am asking have reference to the *curriculum* of the school—the organized course of study conducted in the classroom and directed by the teacher. Young people are under the supervision of the school for certain hours in addition to those for which classroom work is scheduled. During these hours, many kinds of activities can be carried on and, if necessary, can be required: athletics, debate, shopwork, cooking, driver training, and so on. These are extracurricular activities. They are highly desirable, and in planning them the distinctions I have made between job training, social conditioning, and intellectual training have no particular relevance. In its *extracurricular* activities, the school may properly cater to any of the "felt needs" of young people. It may consciously undertake to foster and advance social purposes broader than those of intellectual training. Through its extracurricular activities, indeed, the school can often be extremely effective in redirecting the energies of young people, which otherwise may take an erratic course. The most traditionally minded educators have always recognized the importance of extracurricular activities in shaping the characters of young men and women. "The Battle of Waterloo," Wellington is supposed to have said, "was won on the playing fields of Eton"—the playing fields, be it noted, not the classrooms. Other kinds of battles, perhaps more important, were won in the latter. No one, I believe, has ever suggested that Eton should shut up its classrooms and turn the whole day over to sports.

The dominant educational philosophy in the United States today, however, repudiates this distinction between curricular and extracurricular activities. Its spokesmen are not saying, as I have just said, that the school can assume responsibility for vocational training and social conditioning in such hours of a student's time as the school may happen to control outside the regularly scheduled classroom periods. They are saying that the school *as part of the curriculum* should undertake to accomplish wide-ranging social objectives in addition to intellectual training. For great masses of students, this philosophy asserts, the pursuit of such other objectives may properly *replace* intellectual training.

This philosophy closes its eyes to the fact that the American public school is a *day school.* Students are under the supervision of the school for no more than half (and usually much less than half) of each waking day, for only five days out of each week's seven. During the greater part of his conscious life, a student is within the sphere of control of other institutions of society, upon which responsibility also rests. There must be a distribution of function among the agencies of society because there is a distribution of time among them. The school has responsibility for part of a child's upbringing because it controls, by law, part of his time. *Which* part of the child's upbringing, given this distribution of function, is the peculiar and inescapable responsibility of the school?

This question does not arise in a residential or boarding school, of which Eton is an example. Here the school is responsible for the entire life of the young person in its charge. The school stands *in loco parentis,* exercising the authority and assuming the responsibility of the home. It usually sponsors religious services and provides for religious guidance, thus making itself the channel through which the church performs its functions. In such a situation, the influence of every social agency except the school is suspended, and the school not only can but must assume responsibility for every variety of deliberate training that is provided. Significantly, schools of this kind invariably preserve inviolate the distinction between curricular and extracurricular activities, a distinction that is theoretically far less necessary for them than for day schools. That such schools believe no good purpose would be served by abandoning the distinction is a telling argument against permitting the distinction to be broken down in day schools, public or private.

The point is so simple that it can be stated in quantitative terms. The hours that a day pupil spends in school are roughly equal in number to the hours that a residential school sets aside for formal classroom instruction. Extracurricular activities are scheduled by the residential school in other hours than these. A student in a public day school can expect to receive an education of equal depth and intensity only if classroom periods are preserved inviolate for serious intellectual labor and only if homework is required in an amount equivalent to that which a residential school expects from scheduled study periods. A day school that permits extracurricular activities to intrude upon the hours of classroom instruction is giving its students an inferior education.

If the day school—specifically the American public school—is to undertake vast programs of social conditioning, it should demand from society the additional allotments of student time, as well as the additional allotments of money, necessary to carry out such programs. If the school is to take over the responsibilities of the home, for instance, it must take time away from the home life of the student and must be vested with the disciplinary authority of the home. A strong argument could be made for creating in the United States a large number of full-time residential schools, in which public funds would provide both subsistence and tuition for the students enrolled. Such schools would be capable of assuming the responsibilities that American educationists are talking about. But educationists are not urging the creation of such schools. They are asking the public day schools to assume these wide-ranging responsibilities without providing the appropriate means and the indispensable time for doing so. Their proposals involve not the expansion of extracurricular activities to embrace most of the rest of a student's day and most of his evening and week-end hours, but the replacement of much of the academic curriculum by activities of another sort.

Is the All-Purpose School a Necessity?

Do the societal needs of the present day call for an indefinite extension of the functions and responsibilities of the school—an extension that would involve remaking the curriculum? One cannot answer by pointing to the many problems of society that are not being adequately met. The adequacy with which social problems are handled by any society depends largely upon the appropriateness of the agencies that are developed to meet them, the exactitude with which the means devised are adapted to the ends in view.

To take a simple illustration, the discontent engendered by maldistribution of wealth can be met in several different ways: by increasing the police force of the state to repress disorders; by altering the social order through revolution; by strengthening the otherworldly emphasis of organized religion to produce greater psychological contentment ("You'll get pie in the sky when you die," sneered the old Wobbly song); by increasing productivity through technological change; by altering the incidence of taxation; by enacting minimum-wage laws and other welfare legislation; by developing the agencies of collective bargaining, especially trade unions. Each of these methods is obviously capable of producing some change in the given societal situation. In terms of desirability and long-run effectiveness, however, there are obviously marked differences between the various possible programs of action.

Some proposals represent the creation of appropriate agencies, some merely the seizure of power by existing but inappropriate ones. This latter point is important. A struggle for power is always involved, however concealed by professions of altruistic benevolence. Those who aspire to direct the process of social adjustment —whether government officials or members of the clergy or union leaders or school authorities—are rival parties in interest. Each is predisposed, consciously or unconsciously, to interpret the existence of social problems as a call to enlarge the functions of the institution with which he is immediately concerned. Skepticism with respect to these conflicting claims is the only safe attitude for an independent citizen.

The argument that the public day school in twentieth-century America must assume responsibility over wide-ranging areas of social concern apart from intellectual training is, at bottom, an argument that other agencies of society are not capable of, and cannot be made capable of, dealing with the problems involved. This argument I find completely unconvincing.

Job Training No Business of the Schools

So far as job training is concerned the argument verges on the preposterous. Never before has industry itself provided such comprehensive programs of on-the-job instruction at every level from the most elementary manual skills to the most complex technological and managerial ones. The Armed Forces do the same. On the other hand, never before has the high school been less fitted to provide such skills. In the first place, extreme specialization has created a diversity of occupations impossible for any school curriculum to encompass. In the second place, the mechanical equipment and the technical processes connected with the modern assembly line are far too complex and costly for any school to reproduce even in miniature; hence the instruction given on the simple and outmoded equipment of even the best-equipped high-school shop is pathetically unrelated to the "real-life" situations presented by an up-to-date factory.

Roughly the same situation obtains in matters connected with the home. Manufacturers of household appliances provide elaborate instructions for their use, and some (such as sewing-machine companies) offer extended courses of personal instruction. Most make some provision for installation and service. Popular magazines provide detailed recipes and instructions in the use of prepared foodstuffs and in the elegancies of home entertainment. It is true that the modern home offers less instruction than the home of a few generations ago in spinning, weaving, sewing, baking bread, laundering, and ironing. Few youngsters know how to harness a horse or milk a cow. This proves that household activities have changed, not that the home has lost the art of imparting practical skills to the young. The home has never been perfectly successful in passing on the household arts, of course; but the assumption that it has become or is becoming less effective in passing on the arts that are actually used is unsupported by any substantial evidence.

Automation in industry and the mechanization of the home have made the school an obsolescent instrument for *vocational* instruction. At the same time, the rising technological level of actual industrial operations, and even of actual household processes, has created a sharply increasing demand for precisely those *intellectual* skills that the school is particularly designed to impart: reading, mathematics, scientific understanding, and the rest. The English classroom, the chemistry laboratory, and the blackboard covered with mathematical symbols are the "functional" parts of a school today, not the woodworking shop and the homemaking room. These latter, quaint survivals from a simpler age, have considerable extracurricular value, but that they are necessary to sustain a modern technological economy is sheer fantasy.

The Perils of Social Conditioning

The wholesale extension of the public schools' responsibility into the realm of "social conditioning" is fraught with even graver dangers and is based upon equally dubious premises. Particularly dubious is the assumption that the forces that operate to produce social cohesion, conformity to the mores, and loyalty to accepted institutions have been all but fatally weakened in our society. Because of this collapse, the argument runs, the school must step into the breach by offering comprehensive programs of "life-adjustment" education.

This represents, in my judgment, a completely unrealistic appraisal of the strength of the forces that operate in this realm. Not only are they powerful to begin with, but their pressure is being constantly augmented as the new devices of mass communication are pressed into service. The possible omnipotence of the forces devoted to social conditioning ought to concern thoughtful men and women, most of all those engaged in education. In the nature of things, training in this realm is basically training in conformity. Law and order rather than devotion to principle, frictionless personal relationships rather than rationality, acceptance of group decisions rather than basic integrity of mind—these are the effects sought after (perhaps the only ones that can be sought after) by impersonal agencies of social control. No leaven of criticism lightens this heavy mass; creativity of mind is not an asset but an annoyance; dissent is not a virtue but a stumbling block.

The glowing spark of intellectual independence, which social conditioning is most apt to quench, can be kept alive in the school if the development of critical intelligence remains its overriding objective. Freedom to think—which means nothing unless it means freedom to think differently—can be society's most precious gift to itself. The first duty of a school is to defend and cherish it. This means resistance to the pressures for social and cultural conformity wherever they may arise. Church and state are less menacing to intellectual freedom in America today than are the anonymous forces in the community that insist on like-mindedness, on "belongingness" and "togetherness," on the kind of "other-direction" that Riesman has described.

Social conditioning, "life-adjustment," can only mean reinforcement of these pressures when undertaken by a public day school. Quite different is the situation in a residential school, which stands, as it were, between the student and the immediate pressures of the community. The latter can be fended off, and the school can discriminate deliberately between the ideals it will foster and those it will repudiate as unworthy. The social conditioning that such a school undertakes will be partly nonconformist; it will give its students some powers of "inner-direction" (to borrow Riesman's distinction again), some ability to resist the seductions of "other-direction." The public day school—supported by taxes derived from the community, subject to immediate community pressure, recognizably an agent of local government and of the state—lacks any such power to resist conformism, unless it takes the high ground that its proper task is to develop critical, independent, well-informed judgment by means of disciplined intellectual training. Not the indiscriminate molding of attitudes desired by the community, but the deliberate molding of a specifically *intellectual* attitude, is the function and the responsibility of a publicly supported school in a society that wishes to preserve its vital freedoms.

The adjustment to life that we must strive for through the school is the kind of adjustment that results from applying the varied resources and the developed powers of a mature and disciplined intellect to each successive problem as it arises. Adjustment in this highest sense *is* an outcome of education. It is not an outcome that can be reached by short cuts, by a miscellany of experiences, by playroom imitations of the mere externals of adult activity. "There is no 'royal road' to geometry," said Euclid to his sovereign, Ptolemy I. "There is no royal road to intelligent citizenship" is the message that educators should deliver to the sovereign people of today. Serious, sustained, systematic labor, in libraries, laboratories, and classrooms, is the only way of producing educated men and women in the twentieth century, as in every preceding century.

A Requirement of Democracy

Serious, sustained, systematic study is the one way in a democracy, as it is the one way under a monarchy or an aristocracy. The crucial difference is that in a genuine democracy the school system provides this kind of intellectual training for all its citizens instead of for a selected few. If a nation permits something else to be substituted for intellectual training in the upbringing of substantial groups of its citizens, then it is no more democratic in its educational system than any other country that relegates part of its population to inferior status by furnishing that part with inferior education. Intellectual training for some of the people, vocational training and life-adjustment for the rest, is the epitome of a class-structured educational philosophy. Those who preach it in the United States are simply repeating the arguments that have been used by opponents of democratic education in every age and in every country. These opponents have always asserted, as frightening numbers of American educationists today assert, that the majority of men either have no need for serious intellectual training or are incapable of receiving it, and that for them mere training for the job or for adjustment to life will suffice.

How has it happened that a democratic society like the United States, committed to the democratization of education, has produced in the twentieth century an educational theory that is patently antidemocratic in its fundamental assumptions and its practical proposals? This is one of those historical developments, like the emergence of dictatorship out of a basically egalitarian revolution, that appear at first glance paradoxical but are nevertheless susceptible of historical explanation.

A diffused anti-intellectualism is characteristic of any group and any society that is largely uneducated. Anti-intellectualism is a social force to be reckoned with in any historical period; it is a force of critical importance in any period of educational expansion or democratization. How it is dealt with by those responsible for education determines the success or the failure of their efforts to develop an effective school system.

The anti-intellectualism of which I speak is not necessarily a virulent hatred of intellectual values; it is more often a mere indifference to them. It ordinarily does not imply opposition to schooling as such; rather it involves contempt for the outcome of schooling. Though jealousy and class antagonism have something to do with anti-intellectual attitudes, the fundamental cause is ignorance itself. Uneducated men and women not only do not know, they do not know what it is they do not know. The outward results of possessing education, measurable in terms of wealth and prestige, are observed by them, but not its inner characteristics. In this view from the bottom, intellectual training often appears to be simply a particular form of job training, that is to say, training for well-paid and respectable jobs. It may even appear to be training in an arbitrary set of subjects to which completely artificial distinctions have been attached—a kind of protective tariff imposed by the privileged classes to keep out possible competitors.

The problem of extending education to groups and classes that have hitherto been deprived of it is, therefore, a twofold problem. It is not enough simply to provide schools. It is essential also to make perfectly clear the precise purpose that schools are to serve. If fundamental purposes are not defined and adhered to, anti-intellectualism may rush in to fill the vacuum, with the result that schools may become allies of the very thing that they were designed to eradicate, namely ignorance.

Where Educational Responsibility Lies

The responsibility for defining the primary purpose of any institution is a professional responsibility devolving upon those who already understand the matters with which the institution is to deal. Similar is the responsibility of the medical profession to define the purpose of a hospital, prescribing what it should do and what it must never consent to do, no matter what public pressure is put upon it. This is in no sense an attempt to dictate to the public; the latter can decide whether they wish to support schools or hospitals or not. The question is whether a professional man may permit the perversion to different purposes of an institution he is charged with defending. He has a professional obligation to combat every such destructive trend and to resign if he is defeated.

The central problem is to make use of social forces in such

a way as to build up an institution, instead of permitting such forces to tear it down. Take, for example, the powerful motive of economic striving. Properly utilized, it can contribute immensely to the raising of the school's standards of intellectual competence. Improperly utilized, it can so warp the school program in the direction of narrow vocationalism as to destroy its integrity and all but destroy its usefulness.

Horace Mann, to take one notable educational statesman, recognized the distinction. He appealed frankly to economic motives in rallying support for public-school improvement, but he did not surrender the intellectual purpose of the school in so doing. In his Twelfth Annual Report he wrote: "For the creation of wealth, then—for the existence of a wealthy people and a wealthy nation—intelligence is the grand condition. The number of improvers will increase, as the intellectual constituency, if I may so call it, increases. . . . The greater the proportion of minds in any community which are educated, and the more thorough and complete the education which is given them, the more rapidly . . . will that community advance in all the means of enjoyment and elevation."

Until the beginning of the twentieth century and somewhat beyond, social forces in the United States were effectively harnessed to the task of educational expansion and improvement because educational leaders translated the demands of society into terms appropriate to the school. Educational advancement ceased when educationists deserted the ideal of disciplined intelligence and accepted the fallacious notion that the character and content of school programs should be determined by the "felt needs"—that is, the immediate uncriticized, shortsighted demands—of those in society who had least comprehension of what education was for and how it accomplished its ends. No wonder health departed, once medicines began to be prescribed not by the physician out of his knowledge but by the patient out of his ignorance.

Educational statesmanship consists in directing the insistent demands of society into such channels that the intellectual needs of society, felt or unfelt, will be effectively met. By adhering firmly to the distinctions that educated men know to exist, by uniting the learned world in defense of standards, by giving academic recognition only to those who demonstrate intellectual achievement, educators can use the vague and heedless desires of the ignorant themselves as the motive power of a system that will dispel ignorance. The secret is to love the sinner but not his sin.

The Negative Theory of Education

Bertrand Russell

(1872-   )

In education, the best questions are the most basic. Thus "should we teach mathematics?" is better than "how should we teach mathematics?" Better still is "should we teach?" This last is the question to which the British philosopher Bertrand Russell applies himself in this essay.

As Russell notes, the "negative theory of education" was the latest of the great educational philosophies to be formulated. We have seen its original expression by Rousseau. As a contemporary viewpoint it reflects a number of post-enlightenment influences. For example, the negative theory of education springs in part from the Western tradition of social and political liberalism, though it is not the system of schooling promulgated by liberal movements.

Given this and other paradoxes within its formulations, the negative theory is less impressive as an ideological position than as the considered judgment of an important minority of teachers, radical social critics, and psychiatrists, who dissent from the widespread modern belief that formal education is an unmitigated blessing. Yet the theory must be weighed against the demands of our highly complex technical society for mass education. Can we escape the dilemma of having to choose between dooming children to the sometimes Procrustean rigors of formal schooling, and dooming them to incompetence as undisciplined and untrained adults? In this essay Bertrand Russell analyzes the advantages and limitations of the negative theory of education.

Bertrand Russell was born in Wales, and educated at home and at Trinity College, Cambridge. During the First World War he served four months in prison as a pacifist, where he wrote *Introduction to Mathematical Philosophy*. His work in mathematics climaxed with the publication, beginning in 1910, of the monumental *Principia Mathematica*, with Alfred North Whitehead. From 1927 to 1932 Bertrand Russell ran a progressive school in Sussex. Coming to the United States, he taught at the University of Chicago, the University of California at Los Angeles, Harvard, and the City College of New York. Russell has published numerous books of philosophy and social criticism. Most recently he has been active in the British antinuclear-testing movement. The following selection is from *Education and the Modern World*, published in 1932.

Three divergent theories of education all have their advocates in the present day. Of these the first considers that the sole purpose of education is to provide opportunities of growth and to remove hampering influences. The second holds that the purpose of education is to give culture to the individual and to develop his capacities to the utmost. The third holds that education is to be considered rather in relation to the community than in relation to the individual, and that its business is to train useful citizens. Of these theories the first is the newest while the third is the oldest. The second and third theories have in common the view that education can give something positive, while the first regards its function as purely negative. No actual education proceeds wholly and completely on any one of the three theories. All three in varying proportions are found in every system that actually exists. It is, I think, fairly clear that no one of the three is adequate by itself, and that the choice of a right system of education depends in great measure upon the adoption of a due proportion between the three theories. For my part, while I think that there is more truth in the first theory, which we may call the negative view of education, I do not think that it contains by any means the whole truth. The negative view has dominated much progressive thinking on education. It is part of the general creed of liberty which has inspired liberal thought since the time of Rousseau.

Oddly enough, political liberalism has been connected with the belief in compulsory education, while the belief in freedom in education exists in great measure among Socialists, and even Communists. Nevertheless, this belief is ideologically connected with liberalism, and has the same degree of truth and falsehood that belongs to the conception of liberty in other spheres.

Until very recent times hardly anybody questioned the view that it is the business of education to train the child in the way he should go. He was to be taught moral maxims, habits of industry, and a stock of knowledge proportional to his social station. The methods by which this was to be achieved were rough and ready, in fact not unlike those employed in the training of horses. What the whip was to do to the horse the rod was to do to the child. It cannot be denied that this system, for all its crudity, produced on the whole the results at which it aimed. It was only a minority that suffered education, but in that minority certain habits had been formed, habits of self-discipline and social conformity, of capacity for command, and of harshness that took no account of human needs. Men trained under Dr. Keate and similar pedagogues made our England what it is, and extended the blessings of our civilization to the benighted heathen in India and Africa. I do not wish to belittle this achievement, and I am not sure that it would have been possible by any other method with the same economy of effort. Its products, owing to a certain Spartan toughness and to a complete incapacity for intellectual doubt, acquired the qualities needed by an imperial race among backward peoples. They were able to pass on the stern rule to which they had been subjected in youth, and to avoid the realization that what they supposed to be their education had starved the intelligence and the emotions in order to strengthen the will. In America a similar result was achieved by Puritanism while it remained vigorous.

The Romantic Movement was essentially a protest in the name of the emotions against the previous undue emphasis upon the will. The Romantic Movement achieved something as regards the treatment of very young children, but in the main the educational authorities were too firmly entrenched and too much habituated to command to be appreciably affected by the softer ideals of the Romantics. It is only in our own day that their general outlook upon life has begun to produce any really widespread effect upon educational theory, but just as *laissez faire* in economics has had to give way to new forms of ordered planning, so in education *laissez faire*, while it is a necessary stage, is not, I think, the last word. I propose in this essay to state the case in its favor, and then to examine its limitations.

The case for the greatest possible freedom in education is a very strong one. To begin with, absence of freedom involves conflicts with adults, which frequently have a much more profound psychological effect than was realized until very recently. The child who is in any way coerced tends to respond with hatred, and if, as is usual, he is not able to give free vent to his hatred, it festers inwardly, and may sink into the unconscious with all kinds of strange consequences throughout the rest of life. The father as the object of hatred may come to be replaced by the State, the Church, or a foreign nation, thus leading a man to become an anarchist, an atheist, or a militarist as the case may be. Or again, hatred of the authorities who oppress the child may become transferred into a desire to inflict equal oppression later on upon the next generation. Or there may be merely a general moroseness, making pleasant social and personal relations impossible. I found one day in school a boy of medium size ill-treating a smaller boy. I expostulated, but he replied: "The bigs hit me, so I hit the babies; that's fair." In these words he epitomized the history of the human race.

Another effect of compulsion in education is that it destroys originality and intellectual interest. Desire for knowledge, at any rate for a good deal of knowledge, is natural to the young, but is generally destroyed by the fact that they are given more than they desire or can assimilate. Children who are forced to eat acquire a loathing for food, and children who are forced to learn acquire a loathing for knowledge. When they think, they do not think spontaneously in the way in which they run or jump or shout: they think with a view to pleasing some adult, and therefore with an attempt at correctness rather than from natural curiosity. The killing of spontaneity is especially disastrous in artistic directions. Children who are taught literature or painting or music to excess, or with a view to correctness rather than to self-expression, become progressively less interested in the aesthetic side of life. Even a boy's interest in mechanical devices can be killed by too much instruction. If you teach a boy the principle of the common pump in lesson time, he will try to avoid acquiring the knowledge you are trying to impart, whereas if you have a pump in your back yard and forbid him to touch it he will spend all his leisure studying it. A great many of these troubles are avoided by making lessons voluntary. There is no longer friction between teacher and pupil, and in a fairly large proportion of cases the pupils consider the knowledge imparted by the teacher worth having. Their initiative is not destroyed, because it is by their own choice that they learn, and they do not accumulate masses of undigested hate to lie festering in the unconscious throughout the rest of life. The arguments for free speech, for freedom from politeness, and for freedom in regard to sex knowledge are even stronger.

For all these reasons, reforming educators tend, and I think tend rightly, towards greater freedom in the school. I do not think, however, that freedom in school can be erected into an absolute principle. It has its limitations, and it is important to realize what they are.

As one of the most obvious examples we may take cleanliness. I should like to say to begin with that most children of well-to-do parents are kept a great deal too clean. Parents excuse their behavior on the ground that cleanliness is hygienic, but the motive for making it excessive is one of snobbery. If you see two children, one of whom is clean and the other is dirty, you tend to suppose that the clean one's parents have a larger income than the parents of the dirty one. Consequently snobs try to keep their children very clean. This is an abominable tyranny which interferes with the children doing a great many of the things they had better be doing. From the point of view of health it is well that the children should be clean twice a day, when they get up in the morning and when they go to bed at night. Between these two painful moments they should be grubbing about exploring the world, especially its grimier portions, ruining their clothes and wiping muddy hands on their faces. To deprive children of these pleasures is to lessen their initiative, their impulse towards exploration, and their acquisition of useful muscular habits. But although dirt is such an admirable thing, cleanliness also has its place in the morning and evening, as we said before, and even this limited place it will not secure in a child's life except through a good deal of coercion. If we wore no clothes and lived in a hot climate, we should get all the cleanliness that would be necessary through splashing in the water to keep cool. No doubt *pithecanthropus erectus* managed in this way, but we who wear clothes and live in temperate climates have not as much instinct towards cleanliness as health requires, and we therefore have to be taught to wash. The same thing applies to brushing teeth. If we ate our food raw like our remote ancestors, we should not need to brush our teeth, but so long as we retain the unnatural habit of cooking we have to balance it by another unnatural habit, namely the toothbrush. The "back-to-nature" cult, if it is to be compatible with health, must be thorough-going, and must involve the abandonment of clothes and cooking. If we are not prepared to go to these lengths we must teach our children certain habits which they will not acquire for themselves. In the matter of cleanliness and hygiene, therefore, although present conventional education involves much too great a limitation of freedom, yet some limitation is necessary in the interests of health.

Another rather humble virtue which is not likely to be produced by a wholly free education is punctuality. Punctuality is a quality the need of which is bound up with social co-operation. It has nothing to do with the relation of the soul to God, or with mystic insight, or with any of the matters with which the more elevated and spiritual moralists are concerned. One would be surprised to find a saint getting drunk, but one would not be surprised to find him late for an engagement. And yet in the ordinary business of life punctuality is absolutely necessary. It would not do for the engineer or the postman to wait till the spirit moved him to drive his locomotive or collect the letters. All economic organizations of any complexity would become unworkable if those concerned were often late. But habits of punctuality are hardly likely to be learned in a free atmosphere. They cannot exist in a man who allows his moods to dominate him. For this reason they are perhaps incompatible with the highest forms of achievement. Newton, as we know, was so unpunctual at his meals that his dog ate them without Newton's ever finding it out. The highest achievement in most directions demands capacity for absorption in a mood, but those whose work is less skilled, from royalty downward, do much harm if they are habitually unpunctual. It seems unavoidable, therefore, that young people should be subjected to the necessity of doing certain things at certain times if they are to be fitted to take any ordinary part in modern life. Those who show extraordinary talent, as poets or composers or pure mathematicians, may be exempted, but ninety-nine per cent of mankind need a discipline in observing time which is quite impossible if they are allowed to grow freely as their natural impulses dictate. The noble savage, one presumes, went hunting when he was hungry, and not at 8.53 A.M. like his descendant in the suburbs. The education of the noble savage, therefore, does not supply all that the dweller in the suburbs requires.

A rather more serious matter, to which similar considerations apply, is honesty. I do not mean this term in any fancy sense; I mean merely respect for the property of others. This is not a natural characteristic of human beings. The undisciplined human being appropriates the property of others whenever he considers it safe to do so. Perhaps even the disciplined human being does this not infrequently, but discipline has taught him that theft is often not safe when at first sight it seems so. There is, I think, in the minds of some humane moderns a certain confusion of thought on this subject. Having discovered that there is such a thing as kleptomania, they are inclined to regard all thieving as kleptomania. But this is quite a mistake. Kleptomania consists of stealing things, which often the thief does not really want, in circumstances where he is pretty sure to be caught. It has as a rule some psychological source: the kleptomaniac, unconsciously to himself, is stealing love, or objects having some sexual significance. Kleptomania cannot be dealt with by punishment, but only by psychological understanding. Ordinary thieving, however, is by no means irrational, and just because it is rational it can be prevented by being made contrary to self-interest through social penalties. In a community of children whom their elders leave free, the thief, unless he is the biggest of the group, will be severely punished by the others. The elders may wash their hands of the punishment and say that in their system there is no penal code, but in this they are guilty of self-deception. The chances are that the penal code spontaneously created by a group of children will be more severe and more unreliable than one invented by adults. For the sake of the thief himself, therefore, it is on the whole wise that adults should take cognizance of acts of theft, and deal with them in a manner which prevents the other children from wreaking vengeance on their own account. An adequate respect for the property of others is hardly possible except through the creation of a conditioned reflex. Under the influence of temptation the chance of detection always appears less than it is, and the person to whom thieving is an active possibility is hardly likely to go through life without yielding to the temptation sufficiently often to be caught in the end.

Another respect in which, to my mind, many apostles of freedom go astray, is that they fail to recognize sufficiently the importance of routine in the life of the young. I do not mean that a routine should be rigid and absolute: there should be days when it is varied, such as Christmas Day and holidays. But even these variations should, on the whole, be expected by the child. A life of uncertainty is nervously exhausting at all times, but especially in youth. The child derives a sense of security from knowing more or less what is going to happen day by day. He wishes his world to be safe, and subject to the reign of law. Our belief in the uniformity of nature is largely the projection upon the cosmos of the child's desire for routine in the nursery. Adventurousness and courage are highly desirable qualities, but they are most easily developed against a background of fundamental security.

A further point in favor of a large element of routine is that children find it both tiring and boring to have to choose their own occupation at all odd times. They prefer that at many times the initiative should not be theirs, and that their own choice should be confined within a framework imposed by friendly adults. Children, like grownups, enjoy the sense of achievement derived from mastering a difficulty, but this requires a consistency of effort of which few are capable without some outside encouragement. The capacity for consistent self-direction is one of the most valuable that a human being can possess. It is practically unknown in young children, and is never developed either by a very rigid discipline or by complete freedom. Very rigid discipline, such as that of soldiers in wartime, makes a man incapable of acting without the goad of external command. On the other hand, complete freedom throughout childhood does not teach him to resist the solicitations of a momentary impulse: he does not acquire the capacity of concentrating upon one matter when he is interested in another, or of resisting pleasures because they will cause fatigue that will interfere with subsequent work. The strengthening of the will demands, therefore, a somewhat subtle mixture of freedom and discipline, and is destroyed by an excess of either.

What is important as imposing limitations upon the desirable amount of discipline is that all training should have the co-operation of the child's will, though not of every passing impulse. Every child who is surrounded by friendly adults is conscious at bottom that he himself is rather foolish, and is grateful for a fair amount of guidance from those whom he can trust to be really concerned with his good, and not only with their own convenience or power. Athletes submit themselves to discipline as a matter of course, and young people whose desire for intellectual achievement is as great as the athlete's desire for success in his field will be equally ready to submit themselves to the necessary discipline. But in an atmosphere where all discipline is thought evil, it will not occur to young people that voluntary submission of this sort is an essential of almost every kind of success. Difficult success as an ideal should be present in the mind of the young if they are not to become wayward and futile. But there are few to whom it will occur in an environment where freedom is absolute.

The use of authority as opposed to persuasion can be reduced almost to nothing where the right sort of adult is in charge of not too large a number of children. Take, for example, such a matter as kindliness. I do not think that precept or punishment can do anything to produce a kindly disposition, though it can restrain overt acts of cruelty. A kindly disposition requires, on the one hand, instinctive happiness, and on the other hand the example of kindly behavior on the part of adults. The mere teaching of kindliness as a moral principle is, to my mind, almost useless.

It is of the highest importance that whatever discipline may exist should not involve more than a minimum of emotional restraint, for a child who feels himself thwarted in any important way is liable to develop various undesirable characteristics, the nature of which will depend upon his strength of character. If he is strong, he will become an angry rebel, while if he is weak he will become a whining hypocrite. Discipline, therefore, while it cannot be entirely absent, should be reduced as much as is compatible with the training of decent and competent human beings.

The matter of instruction is the crux of the whole question. Experience has persuaded me, somewhat to my surprise, that it is possible to give adequate instruction, and to produce highly educated human beings, without imposing any obligation to be present at lessons. To do this requires a combination of circumstances which is not at present possible on a large scale. It requires among adults a genuine and spontaneous interest in intellectual pursuits. It requires small classes. It requires sympathy and tact and skill in the teacher. And it requires an environment in which it is possible to turn a child out of a class and tell him to go and play, if he wishes to be in class solely for the purpose of creating a disturbance. It will be a long time before these conditions can be realized in ordinary schools, and therefore, for the present, compulsory attendance in class is likely to be necessary in the great majority of cases.

There are some who argue that if a child is left alone he will teach himself to read and write and so forth from a wish not to be inferior to his neighbors, and that therefore absence of compulsion causes at most a delay of a year or two in the acquisition of knowledge. I think that this position is unconsciously parasitic. In a world where every other child learns to read and write, it is probable that any given child will in time wish to escape the sense of inferiority which would be produced by ignorance. But in a world where all children escaped compulsion, there would soon be no occasion for this sense of inferiority, and each generation would be somewhat more ignorant than its predecessor. Very few children have a spontaneous impulse to learn the multiplication table. While their neighbors are compelled to learn it, they may, for very shame, feel that they ought to learn it too, but in a community where no child was obliged to learn it there would, before long, be only a few erudite pedants who would know what six times nine is.

The acquisition of concrete knowledge is pleasant to most children: if they live on a farm, they will watch the farmer's operations and get to know all about them. But abstract knowledge is loved by very few, and yet it is abstract knowledge that makes a civilized community possible. Preservation of a civilized community demands, therefore, some method of causing children to behave in a manner which is not natural to them. It may be possible to substitute coaxing for compulsion, but it is not possible to leave the matter to the unaided operation of nature. The idea of education as merely affording opportunities for natural growth is not, I think, one which can be upheld by a person who realizes the complexity of modern societies. It is, of course, possible to say that this complexity is regrettable, and that it would be better to return to a simpler way of life, but unfortunately the process of so returning would involve the death by starvation of a very large percentage of the population. This alternative is so horrible that we are practically committed to the whole complex apparatus of the modern industrial world, and being so committed, we are also bound to fit our children to take their part in carrying it on. The negative theory of education, therefore, while it has many important elements of truth, and is largely valid so far as the emotions are concerned, cannot be accepted in its entirety as regards intellectual and technical training. Where these are concerned, something more positive is required.

The Rhythm of Education

Alfred North Whitehead

(1861–1957)

As modern psychology developed into a coherent discipline, it took over certain areas of educational philosophy in much the same way that the physical sciences were usurping some of the provinces of traditional natural philosophy. The classical educational theorists—Quintilian, Vives, Montaigne, Comenius, Rousseau, Pestalozzi—all have one characteristic which differentiates them from most current writers in the field: they speculate on the psychology of learning. Our twentieth-century educational philosophers, whatever their stature, and however much they consider the great forces of science, democracy, nationalism, and industrialism which shape contemporary schools and colleges, frequently forego discussion of the ultimate target of all our educational efforts: the mind of the individual student. They leave such discussion to the technical psychologists.

This essay—one of the most vivid descriptions ever written of how human beings "get education"—provides a contrast to the prevalent neglect of the psychological principles of learning by educational philosophers. Whitehead's essay is in the tradition of the modern educational reformers from Comenius to Dewey. His emphasis on the importance of exploiting the present moment and state of development; his interest in the first, "natural" cycle of education; his insistence that education must engender intellectual power, not merely inculcate knowledge; and his attention to the learning process of the individual pupil—all align him with the most radical of the educational reformers. "We must garner our crops each in its due season," writes the English mathematician and philosopher, but the principle could have come quite as naturally from Rousseau or even Comenius.

Whitehead's paradigm of learning, with its three stages of Romance, Precision, and Generalization, may not be verifiable by empirical psychology. But it describes a universal pattern which every teacher and learner will recognize. At the least, Whitehead's comprehensive plan for education from infancy to adulthood is a coherent program based on clearly defined principles. It thus contrasts strikingly with our current American system of schooling, a patchwork of historical accident and educational expediency.

Alfred North Whitehead was born in Ramsgate, England. After graduation from Trinity College, Cambridge, in 1884, he lectured in mathematics there until 1911, and at the University of London from 1911 to 1924. At the age of 63 he came to Harvard as professor of philosophy. Among his important works in mathematics are *Principia Mathematica* (with Bertrand Russell), *The Concept of Nature, Process and Reality,* and *Science and the Modern World.* The following essay is a chapter from *The Aims of Education,* published as a separate pamphlet in 1922.

By the Rhythm of Education I denote a certain principle which in its practical application is well known to everyone with educational experience. I do think, however, that the principle has not been subjected to an adequate discussion taking account of all the factors which should guide its application.

I first seek for the baldest statement of what I mean by the Rhythm of Education, a statement so bald as to exhibit the point in its utter obviousness. The principle is merely this—that different subjects and modes of study should be undertaken by pupils at fitting times when they have reached the proper stage of mental development. You will agree with me that this is a truism, never doubted and known to all. I am really anxious to emphasize the obvious character of the foundational idea for one reason, because this audience will certainly find it out for itself. But the other reason, the reason I choose this subject for discourse, is that I do not think that this obvious truth has been handled in educational practice with due attention to the psychology of the pupils.

The Tasks of Infancy

I commence by challenging the adequacy of some principles by which the subjects for study are often classified in order. By this I mean that these principles can only be accepted as correct if they are so explained as to be explained away. Consider first the criterion of difficulty. It is not true that the easier subjects should precede the harder. On the contrary, some of the hardest must come first because nature so dictates, and because they are essential to life. The first intellectual task which confronts an infant is the acquirement of spoken language. What an appalling task, the correlation of meanings with sounds! It requires an analysis of ideas and an analysis of sounds. We all know that the infant does it, and that the miracle of his achievement is explicable. But so are all miracles, and yet to the wise they remain miracles. All I ask is that with this example staring us in the face we should cease talking nonsense about postponing the harder subjects.

What is the next subject in the education of the infant minds? The acquirement of written language; that is to say, the correlation of sounds with shapes. Great heavens! Have our educationists gone mad? They are setting babbling mites of six years old to tasks which might daunt a sage after lifelong toil. Again, the hardest task in mathematics is the study of the elements of algebra, and yet this stage must precede the comparative simplicity of the differential calculus.

I will not elaborate my point further; I merely restate it in the form, that the postponement of difficulty is no safe clue for the maze of educational practice.

The alternative principle of order among subjects is that of necessary antecedence. There we are obviously on firmer ground. It is impossible to read *Hamlet* until you can read; and the study of the integers must precede the study of fractions. And yet even this firm principle dissolves under scrutiny. It is certainly true, but it is only true if you give an artificial limitation to the concept of a subject for study. The danger of the principle is that it is accepted in one sense, for which it is almost a necessary truth, and that it is applied in another sense for which it is false. You cannot read Homer before you can read; but many a child, and in ages past many a man, has sailed with Odysseus over the seas of Romance by the help of the spoken word of a mother, or of some wandering bard. The uncritical application of the principle of the necessary antecedence of some subjects to others has, in the hands of dull people with a turn for organization, produced in education the dryness of the Sahara.

Stages of Mental Growth

The reason for the title which I have chosen for this essay, the Rhythm of Education, is derived from yet another criticism of current ideas. The pupil's progress is often conceived as a uniform steady advance undifferentiated by change of type or alteration in pace; for example, a boy may be conceived as starting Latin at ten years of age and by a uniform progression steadily developing into a classical scholar at the age of eighteen or twenty. I hold that this conception of education is based upon a false psychology of the process of mental development which has gravely hindered the effectiveness of our methods. Life is essentially periodic. It comprises daily periods, with their alternations of work and play, of activity and of sleep, and seasonal periods, which dictate our terms and our holidays; and also it is composed of well-marked yearly periods. These are the gross obvious periods which no one can overlook. There are also subtler periods of mental growth, with their cyclic recurrences, yet always different as we pass from cycle to cycle, though the subordinate stages are reproduced in each cycle. That is why I have chosen the term "rhythmic," as meaning essentially the conveyance of difference within a framework of repetition. Lack of attention to the rhythm and character of mental growth is a main source of wooden futility in education. I think that Hegel was right when he analyzed progress into three stages, which he called Thesis, Antithesis, and Synthesis; though for the purpose of the application of his idea to educational theory I do not think that the names he gave are very happily suggestive. In relation to intellectual progress I would term them, the stage of romance, the stage of precision, and the stage of generalization.

THE STAGE OF ROMANCE

The stage of romance is the stage of first apprehension. The subject matter has the vividness of novelty; it holds within itself unexplored connections with possibilities half-disclosed by glimpses and half-concealed by the wealth of material. In this stage knowledge is not dominated by systematic procedure. Such system as there must be is created piecemeal *ad hoc*. We are in the presence of immediate cognizance of fact, only intermittently subjecting fact to systematic dissection. Romantic emotion is essentially the excitement consequent on the transition from the bare facts to the first realizations of the import of their unexplored relationships. For example, Crusoe was a mere man, the sand was mere sand, the footprint was a mere footprint, and the island a mere island, and Europe was the busy world of men. But the sudden perception of the half-disclosed and half-hidden possibilities relating Crusoe and the sand and the footprint and the lonely island secluded from Europe constitutes romance. I have had to take an extreme case for illustration in order to make my meaning perfectly plain. But construe it as an allegory representing the first stage in a cycle of progress. Education must essentially be a setting in order of a ferment already stirring in the mind: you cannot educate mind in *vacuo*. In our conception of education we tend to confine it to the second stage of the cycle; namely, to the stage of precision. But we cannot so limit our task without misconceiving the whole problem. We are concerned alike with the ferment, with the acquirement of precision, and with the subsequent fruition.

THE STAGE OF PRECISION

The stage of precision also represents an addition to knowledge. In this stage, width of relationship is subordinate to exactness of formulation. It is the stage of grammar, the grammar of language and the grammar of science. It proceeds by forcing on the students' acceptance a given way of analyzing the facts, bit by bit. New facts are added, but they are the facts which fit into the analysis.

It is evident that a stage of precision is barren without a previous stage of romance: unless there are facts which have already been vaguely apprehended in their broad generality, the previous analysis is an analysis of nothing. It is simply a series of meaningless statements about bare facts, produced artificially and without any further relevance. I repeat that in this stage we do not merely remain within the circle of the facts elicited in the romantic epoch. The facts of romance have disclosed ideas with possibilities of wide significance, and in the stage of precise progress we acquire other facts in a systematic order, which thereby form both a disclosure and an analysis of the general subject matter of the romance.

THE STAGE OF GENERALIZATION

The final stage of generalization is Hegel's synthesis. It is a return to romanticism with added advantage of classified ideas and relevant technique. It is the fruition which has been the goal of the precise training. It is the final success. I am afraid that I have had to give a dry analysis of somewhat obvious ideas. It has been necessary to do so because my subsequent remarks presuppose that we have clearly in our minds the essential character of this threefold cycle.

The Cyclic Processes

Education should consist in a continual repetition of such cycles. Each lesson in its minor way should form an eddy cycle issuing in its own subordinate process. Longer periods should issue in definite attainments, which then form the starting grounds for fresh cycles. We should banish the idea of a mythical, far-off end of education. The pupils must be continually enjoying some fruition and starting afresh—if the teacher is stimulating in exact proportion to his success in satisfying the rhythmic cravings of his pupils.

An infant's first romance is its awakening to the apprehension of objects and to the appreciation of their connections. Its growth in mentality takes the exterior form of occupying itself in the co-ordination of its perceptions with its bodily activities. Its first stage of precision is mastering spoken language as an instrument for classifying its contemplation of objects and for strengthening its apprehension of emotional relations with other beings. Its first stage of generalization is the use of language for a classified and enlarged enjoyment of objects.

This first cycle of intellectual progress from the achievement of perception to the acquirement of language, and from the acquirement of language to classified thought and keener perception, will bear more careful study. It is the only cycle of progress which we can observe in its purely natural state. The later cycles are necessarily tinged by the procedure of the current mode of education. There is a characteristic of it which is often sadly lacking in subsequent education; I mean, that it achieves complete success. At the end of it the child *can* speak, its ideas *are* classified, and its perceptions *are* sharpened. The cycle achieves its object. This is a great deal more than can be said for most systems of education as applied to most pupils. But why should this be so? Certainly, a newborn baby looks a most unpromising subject for intellectual progress when we remember the difficulty of the task before it. I suppose it is because nature, in the form of surrounding circumstances, sets it a task for which the normal development of its brain is exactly fitted. I do not think that there is any particular mystery about the fact of a child learning to speak and in consequence thinking all the better; but it does offer food for reflection.

In the subsequent education we have not sought for cyclic processes which in a finite time run their course and within their own limited sphere achieve a complete success. This completion is one outstanding character in the natural cycle for infants. Later on we start a child on some subject, say Latin, at the age of ten, and hope by a uniform system of formal training to achieve success at the age of twenty. The natural result is failure, both in interest and in acquirement. When I speak of failure, I am comparing our results with the brilliant success of the first natural cycle. I do not think that it is because our tasks are intrinsically too hard, when I remember that the infant's cycle is the hardest of all. It is because our tasks are set in an unnatural way, without rhythm and without the stimulus of intermediate successes and without concentration.

I have not yet spoken of this character of concentration which so conspicuously attaches to the infant's progress. The whole being of the infant is absorbed in the practice of its cycle. It has nothing else to divert its mental development. In this respect there is a striking difference between this natural cycle and the subsequent history of the student's development. It is perfectly obvious that life is very various and that the mind and brain naturally develop so as to adapt themselves to the many-hued world in which their lot is cast. Still, after making allowance for this consideration, we will be wise to preserve some measure of concentration for each of the subsequent cycles. In particular, we should avoid a competition of diverse subjects in the same stage of their cycles. The fault of the older education was unrhythmic concentration on a single undifferentiated subject. Our modern system, with its insistence on a preliminary general education, and with its easy toleration of the analysis of knowledge into distinct subjects, is an equally unrhythmic collection of distracting scraps. I am pleading that we shall endeavor to weave in the learner's mind a harmony of patterns, by co-ordinating the various elements of instruction into subordinate cycles each of intrinsic worth for the immediate apprehension of the pupil. We must garner our crops each in its due season.

The Romance of Adolescence

We will now pass to some concrete applications of the ideas which have been developed.

The first cycle of infancy is succeeded by the cycle of adolescence, which opens with by far the greatest stage of romance which we ever experience. It is in this stage that the lines of character are graven. How the child emerges from the romantic stage of adolescence is how the subsequent life will be moulded by ideals and colored by imagination. It rapidly follows on the generalization of capacity produced by the acquirement of spoken language and of reading. The stage of generalization belonging to the infantile cycle is comparatively short because the romantic material of infancy is so scanty. The initial knowledge of the world in any developed sense of the word "knowledge" really commences after the achievement of the first cycle, and thus issues in the tremendous age of romance. Ideas, facts, relationships, stories, histories, possibilities, artistry in words, in sounds, in form and in color, crowd into the child's life, stir his feelings, excite his appreciation, and incite his impulses to kindred activities. It is a saddening thought that on this golden age there falls so often the shadow of the crammer. I am thinking of a period of about four years of the child's life, roughly, in ordinary cases, falling between the age of eight and twelve or thirteen. It is the first great period of the utilization of the native language, and of developed powers of observation and of manipulation. The infant cannot manipulate, the child can; the infant cannot observe, the child can; the infant cannot retain thoughts by the recollection of words, the child can. The child thus enters upon a new world.

Of course, the stage of precision prolongs itself as recurring in minor cycles which form eddies in the great romance. The perfecting of writing, of spelling, of the elements of arithmetic, and of lists of simple facts, such as the Kings of England, are all elements of precision, very necessary both as training in concentration and as useful acquirements. However, these are essentially fragmentary in character, whereas the great romance is the flood which bears on the child towards the life of the spirit.

The success of the Montessori system is due to its recognition of the dominance of romance at this period of growth. If this be the explanation, it also points to the limitations in the usefulness of that method. It is the system which in some measure is essential for every romantic stage. Its essence is browsing and the encouragement of vivid freshness. But it lacks the restraint which is necessary for the great stages of precision.

The Mastery of Language

As he nears the end of the great romance the cyclic course of growth is swinging the child over towards an aptitude for exact knowledge. Language is now the natural subject matter for concentrated attack. It is the mode of expression with which he is thoroughly familiar. He is acquainted with stories, histories, and poems illustrating the lives of other people and of other civilizations. Accordingly, from the age of eleven onwards there is wanted a gradually increasing concentration towards precise knowledge of language. Finally, the three years from twelve to fifteen should be dominated by a mass attack upon language, so planned that a definite result, in itself worth having, is thereby achieved. I should guess that within these limits of time, and given adequate concentration, we might ask that at the end of that period the children should have command of English, should be able to read fluently fairly simple French, and should have completed the elementary stage of Latin; I mean, a precise knowledge of the more straightforward parts of Latin grammar, the knowledge of the construction of Latin sentences, and the reading of some parts of appropriate Latin authors, perhaps simplified and largely supplemented by the aid of the best literary translations so that their reading of the orginal, plus translation, gives them a grip of the book as a literary whole. I conceive that such a measure of attainment in these three languages is well within the reach of the ordinary child, provided that he has not been distracted by the effort at precision in a multiplicity of other subjects. Also some more gifted children could go further. The Latin would come to them easily, so that it would be possible to start Greek before the end of the period, always provided that their bent is literary and that they mean later to pursue that study at least for some years. Other subjects will occupy a subordinate place in the timetable and will be undertaken in a different spirit. In the first place, it must be remembered that the semiliterary subjects, such as history, will largely have been provided in the study of the languages. It will be hardly possible to read some English, French, and Latin literature without imparting some knowledge of European history. I do not mean that all special history teaching should be abandoned. I do, however, suggest that the subject should be exhibited in what I have termed the romantic spirit, and that the pupils should not be subjected to the test of precise recollection of details on any large systematic scale.

At this period of growth science should be in its stage of romance. The pupils should see for themselves, and experiment for themselves, with only fragmentary precision of thought. The essence of the importance of science, both for interest in theory or for technological purposes, lies in its application to concrete detail, and every such application evokes a novel problem for research. Accordingly, all training in science should begin as well as end in research, and in getting hold of the subject matter as it occurs in nature. The exact form of guidance suitable to this age and the exact limitations of experiment are matters depending on experience. But I plead that this period is the true age for the romance of science.

Concentration on Science

Towards the age of fifteen the age of precision in language and of romance in science draws to its close, to be succeeded by a period of generalization in language and of precision in science. This should be a short period, but one of vital importance. I am thinking of about one year's work, and I suggest that it would be well decisively to alter the balance of the preceding curriculum. There should be a concentration on science and a decided diminution of the linguistic work. A year's work on science, coming on the top of the previous romantic study, should make everyone understand the main principles which govern the development of mechanics, physics, chemistry, algebra, and geometry. Understand that they are not beginning these subjects, but they are putting together a previous discursive study by an exact formulation of their main ideas. For example, take algebra and geometry, which I single out as being subjects with which I have some slight familiarity. In the previous three years there has been work on the applications of the simplest algebraic formulas and geometrical propositions to problems of surveying, or of some other scientific work involving calculations. In this way arithmetic has been carefully strengthened by the insistence on definite numerical results, and familiarity with the ideas of literal formulas and of geometrical properties has been gained; also some minor methods of manipulation have been inculcated. There is thus no long time to be wasted in getting used to the ideas of the sciences. The pupils are ready for the small body of algebraic and geometrical truths which they ought to know thoroughly. Furthermore, in the previous period some boys will have shown an aptitude for mathematics and will have pushed on a little more, besides in the final year somewhat emphasizing their mathematics at the expense of some of the other subjects. I am simply taking mathematics as an illustration.

Meanwhile, the cycle of language is in its stage of generalization. In this stage the precise study of grammar and composition is discontinued, and the language study is confined to reading the literature with emphasized attention to its ideas and to the general history in which it is embedded; also the time allotted to history will pass into the precise study of a short definite period, chosen to illustrate exactly what does happen at an important epoch and also to show how to pass the simpler types of judgments on men and policies.

I have now sketched in outline the course of education from babyhood to about sixteen and a half, arranged with some attention to the rhythmic pulses of life. In some such way a general education is possible in which the pupil throughout has the advantage of concentration and of freshness. Thus precision will always illustrate subject matter already apprehended and crying out for drastic treatment. Every pupil will have concentrated in turn on a variety of different subjects, and will know where his strong points lie. Finally—and this of all the objects to be attained is the most dear to my heart—the science students will have obtained both an invaluable literary education and also at the most impressionable age an early initiation into habits of thinking for themselves in the region of science.

After the age of sixteen new problems arise. For literary students science passes into the stage of generalization, largely in the form of lectures on its main results and general ideas. New cycles of linguistic, literary, and historical study commence. But further detail is now unnecessary. For the scientists the preceding stage of precision maintains itself to the close of the school period with an increasing apprehension of wider general ideas.

However, at this period of education the problem is too individual, or at least breaks up into too many cases, to be susceptible of broad general treatment. I do suggest, nevertheless, that all scientists should now keep up their French, and initiate the study of German if they have not already acquired it.

University Education

I should now like, if you will bear with me, to make some remarks respecting the import of these ideas for a university education.

The whole period of growth from infancy to manhood forms one grand cycle. Its stage of romance stretches across the first dozen years of its life, its stage of precision comprises the whole school period of secondary education, and its stage of generalization is the period of entrance into manhood. For those whose formal education is prolonged beyond the school age, the university course or its equivalent is the great period of generalization. The spirit of generalization should dominate a university. The lectures should be addressed to those to whom details and procedure are familiar; that is to say, familiar at least in the sense of being so congruous to pre-existing training as to be easily acquirable. During the school period the student has been mentally bending over his desk; at the university he should stand up and look around. For this reason it is fatal if the first year at the university be frittered away in going over the old work in the old spirit. At school the boy painfully rises from the particular towards glimpses at general ideas; at the university he should start from general ideas and study their applications to concrete cases. A well-planned university course is a study of the wide sweep of generality. I do not mean that it should be abstract in the sense of divorce from concrete fact, but that concrete fact should be studied as illustrating the scope of general ideas.

CULTIVATION OF MENTAL POWER

This is the aspect of university training in which theoretical interest and practical utility coincide. Whatever be the detail with which you cram your student, the chance of his meeting in afterlife exactly that detail is almost infinitesimal; and if he does meet it, he will probably have forgotten what you taught him about it. The really useful training yields a comprehension of a few general principles with a thorough grounding in the way they apply to a variety of concrete details. In subsequent practice the men will have forgotten your particular details; but they will remember by an unconscious common sense how to apply principles to immedate circumstances. Your learning is useless to you till you have lost your textbooks, burnt your lecture notes, and forgotten the minutiae which you learnt by heart for the examination. What, in the way of detail, you continually require will stick in your memory as obvious facts like the sun and moon; and what you casually require can be looked up in any work of reference. The function of a university is to enable you to shed details in favor of principles. When I speak of principles I am hardly even thinking of verbal formulations. A principle which has thoroughly soaked into you is rather a mental habit than a formal statement. It becomes the way the mind reacts to the appropriate stimulus in the form of illustrative circumstances. Nobody goes about with his knowledge clearly and consciously before him. Mental cultivation is nothing else than the satisfactory way in which the mind will function when it is poked up into activity. Learning is often spoken of as if we are watching the open pages of all the books which we have ever read, and then, when occasion arises, we select the right page to read aloud to the universe.

Luckily, the truth is far otherwise from this crude idea; and for this reason the antagonism between the claims of pure knowledge and professional acquirement should be much less acute than a faulty view of education would lead us to anticipate. I can put my point otherwise by saying that the ideal of a university is not so much knowledge, as power. Its business is to convert the knowledge of a boy into the power of a man.

The Rhythmic Character of Growth

I will conclude with two remarks which I wish to make by way of caution in the interpretation of my meaning . . . of the rhythmic character of growth. The interior spiritual life of man is a web of many strands. They do not all grow together by uniform extension. I have tried to illustrate this truth by considering the normal unfolding of the capacities of a child in somewhat favorable circumstances but otherwise with fair average capacities. Perhaps I have misconstrued the usual phenomena. It is very likely that I have so failed, for the evidence is complex and difficult. But do not let any failure in this respect prejudice the main point which I am here to enforce. It is that the development of mentality exhibits itself as a rhythm involving an interweaving of cycles, the whole process being dominated by a greater cycle of the same general character as its minor eddies. Furthermore, this rhythm exhibits certain ascertainable general laws which are valid for most pupils, and the quality of our teaching should be so adapted as to suit the stage in the rhythm to which our pupils have advanced. The problem of a curriculum is not so much the succession of subjects; for all subjects should in essence be begun with the dawn of mentality. The truly important order is the order of quality which the educational procedure should assume.

My second caution is to ask you not to exaggerate into sharpness the distinction between the three stages of a cycle. I strongly suspect that many of you, when you heard me detail the three stages in each cycle, said to yourselves—How like a mathematician to make such formal divisions! I assure you that it is not mathematics but literary incompetence that may have led me into the error against which I am warning you. Of course, I mean throughout a distinction of emphasis, of pervasive quality—romance, precision, generalization, are all present throughout. But there is an alternation of dominance, and it is this alternation which constitutes the cycles.

Free Schools for All

James Bryant Conant

(1893–)

The most distinctive feature of American education is still its unparalleled democracy. America led the way on the road to complete equality of educational opportunity, and it has carried this principle further than any other nation. No one is better qualified than James B. Conant—whose *American High School Today*, published in 1959, gained him public and professional recognition as the "Inspector General of the nation's schools"—to argue this principle for our time.

Ever since Jefferson demanded three years of schooling for every American child in 1814, the justification for extending universal education has been reinterpreted by each succeeding generation. Horace Mann spoke eloquently of the moral improvement and the political stability which public schools would create; advocates of free collegiate education in the mid-nineteenth century laid great stress on the upgrading of the rural population and the stimulation of cultural activities throughout the nation. Conant's restatement of this theme fits our mid-twentieth-century style of thinking: he justifies free schools for all on essentially sociological grounds. Public education, Conant argues, assures "a minimum of class distinction, the maximum of fluidity, the maximum of understanding between different vocational groups."

Conant sees private schools as inevitably divisive: "It is difficult [for private schools] to recruit students," he writes, "without undermining public confidence in tax-supported schools." But public confidence, we might reply, cannot be undermined if it is won through unquestioned excellence. Perhaps the private schools serve as an indispensable force to push the public schools to higher standards than the latter would readily achieve without such competition.

At any rate, Conant's essay provides a clear, comprehensive rationale for public education as it exists in America today, and a powerful plea for the expansion of its most novel element, the comprehensive high school.

James Bryant Conant was born in Massachusetts. He received his Ph.D. from Harvard University in 1916, afterwards teaching there and serving as president from 1933 to 1953. From 1953 to 1955 he was U.S. High Commissioner for Germany, and from 1955 to 1957, U.S. Ambassador to the Federal German Republic. For the past several years Conant has been conducting studies of American education under grants from the Carnegie Corporation of New York. These studies culminated in the books *The American High School Today, Education in the Junior High School Years,* and *Slums and Suburbs.* The following essay is from *Education and Liberty,* published by the Harvard University Press in 1953.

This American pattern of education is quite different from that which has evolved in the other English-speaking nations. We have already noted the high percentage of the youth attending school in this country on a full-time basis; in addition, our pattern is characterized by the small numbers attending private schools. The absence of tax-supported denominational schools is in contrast with England and Scotland. Is this American pattern now so widely accepted that one need not argue for its preservation? Twenty or thirty years ago I think the answer would have been in the affirmative. But not so today. Any frank discussion of the future of education in the United States must recognize the existence of many powerful church leaders who do not accept the present pattern as a permanent feature of American life. One must likewise realize that while only some 10 per cent of the youth of the country now in school attend private schools, in some cities the figure is as high as 40 per cent. Furthermore, the percentage of students attending private schools is increasing in certain sections of the country. Therefore I believe it of importance for all citizens to consider carefully the basic issue—the continuance of the American pattern.

I shall not detain the reader by reciting the attacks on the public schools that have taken place in the last few years (1949 to 1952). The formation in many localities of citizens' groups to defend the public schools is clear evidence of the devotion to them of a vast majority of the citizens of most towns and cities. Irresponsible attacks will certainly be warded off, and though some damage will be done, one need not fear the drastic alteration of the American pattern from violent, prejudiced criticism. But I am convinced that it is wise to discuss the fundamental criticisms of the American pattern of public education and to explore the alternative patterns which some critics favor. As a matter of convenience I shall call them the Australian and English patterns. In the one, a large proportion of the youth attending school at ages 15 to 17 is enrolled in church-connected private schools financed *without* tax support; in the other, the private school—church-connected or not—may receive tax money.

Public education, like all other education and all public institutions, needs critics. But critics who believe in the continuation of the American pattern and seek to improve the schools within this framework must be clearly distinguished from those who wish to bring about an educational revolution. Therefore I think it is only fair to insist that the critics of our public schools should make clear their stand on two important points. To each one who questions the performance of our public schools, I would ask the question: "Would you like to increase the number and scope of the private schools?" If the answer is in the affirmative, I would then ask a second question: "Do you look forward to the day when tax money will directly or indirectly assist these schools?" If the answer is again in the affirmative, the lines have been clearly drawn and a rational debate on a vital issue can proceed.

Needless to say, I would find myself on the opposite side from those who answer either or both of these questions in the affirmative. But what I am more concerned with in the year 1952 is that the critics of the public schools in the United States should show their colors. This is not an issue involving any single denomination. The proponents of the expansion of sectarian secondary schools are to be found in several Christian churches. One of the most vocal of the critics of public high schools is a Protestant clergyman who reveals himself when he writes: "The Communist is not, as a matter of fact, much of a revolutionist. The Communist would only substitute the logical secularism of Karl Marx for the pragmatic secularism of John Dewey." If this clergyman would start off all his attacks on modern education by stating that for him secularism and communism are equal dangers, the reader would be in a better position to evaluate what he was about to read.

There are many sincere Protestants, Jews, and Catholics who believe that secondary education divorced from a denominational religious core of instruction is highly unsatisfactory education. They assume—erroneously, I believe—that the tax-supported schools because they must be free of any denominational bias cannot be concerned with moral and spiritual values. . . . Such people, to my mind, are wrong in equating a religious outlook with a strictly denominational viewpoint, yet that they have a right to organize their own schools is beyond question. The United States Supreme Court settled the law on that point in the famous Oregon Case of 1925. But over and beyond the legal issue is the fundamental belief in tolerance of diversity so basic to our society. I know of no one today who wishes to suppress private schools. If there were anyone who had such a notion, the means of putting the idea into effect would involve such drastic state action as to be repugnant to our fundamental ideas of liberty.

But unwillingness even to consider advocating state or national action to suppress private schools is quite a different matter from being indifferent to their expansion. It is certainly a very different thing from acquiescing in the use of tax money directly or indirectly for the support of private schools.

Public funds are used to assist private schools including denominational schools in England and Scotland. No one can object to an open advocacy of the adoption of the English pattern here in the United States. Indeed, for those who believe that education divorced from denominational control is bad education, such an advocacy would seem highly logical. It is important for every American citizen to examine this issue as unemotionally as possible and see where he or she stands. For there is more than one way of changing a social pattern; we could easily drift by slow stages into a situation where in some states the adoption of the English pattern would be inevitable. If in a number of cities and towns the public high schools no longer received popular support, their successful rivals—the private schools—would be logical recipients of tax money. By one method or another the present constitutional barriers against the use of public funds for religious schools would be swept aside.

During the past seventy-five years all but a few per cent of the children in the United States have attended public schools. More than one foreign observer has remarked that without these schools we never could have assimilated so rapidly the different cultures which came to North America in the nineteenth century. Our schools have served all creeds and all economic groups within a given geographic area. I believe it to be of the utmost importance that this pattern be continued. To this end the comprehensive high school deserves the enthusiastic support of the American taxpayer. The greater the proportion of our youth who fail to attend our public schools and who receive their education elsewhere, the greater the threat to our democratic unity. To use taxpayers' money to assist private schools is to suggest that American society use its own hands to destroy itself. This is the answer I must give to those who would advocate the transformation of the American pattern into that of England.

What is the basic objection to the Australian or English pattern, you may ask. Or, to put it the other way around—what are the advantages of free schools for all? To ask these questions is almost to give the answers. If one accepts the ideal of a democratic, fluid society with a minimum of class distinction, the maximum of fluidity, the maximum of understanding between different vocational groups, then the ideal secondary school is a comprehensive public high school. Of this much there can be no doubt: If one wished generation after generation to perpetuate class distinction based on hereditary status in a given society, one would certainly demand a dual system of schools; this is the case in the Province of Quebec where a majority of the people wish to perpetuate two different cultural groups. A dual system serves and helps to maintain group cleavages, the absence of a dual system does the reverse. This is particularly true of the secondary schools. Indeed, I would plead with those who insist as a matter of conscience on sending their children to denominational schools that they might limit their insistence on this type of education to the elementary years.

In terms of numbers involved, the dual nature of our present pattern may seem slight—about 92 per cent of our secondary-school pupils are in public schools. In terms of a stratification of society on economic and religious lines, however, the duality is marked. In socio-economic terms we are not as far from the English "public-school" system as we sometimes like to think. Chancellor McConnell of the University of Buffalo, reporting on English education, notes the predominance of "public-school" graduates over grammar-school graduates in the entrants to Oxford in 1948. A half dozen of the best-known Eastern colleges in the United States would show a similar social phenomenon; they enroll something like half their students from private Protestant schools which encompass only a few per cent of an entire age group. But it is only fair to point out that these same colleges have been trying desperately hard in the last twenty-five years to attract a larger number of public high-school graduates. They aim to be national in terms of geography and representative of all income groups; that they have to some degree succeeded in moving nearer their goal is, to me, a hopeful sign.

I cannot help regretting that private schools have been established in the last twenty years in certain urban areas where a generation ago a public high school served all the youth of the town or city. In some of our Western cities in particular, the trend toward private education for the sons and daughters of the well-to-do has recently been pronounced, but there is no use for those of us who are committed to public high schools as schools for all to denounce or bemoan the growth of private secondary schools. The founding of a new independent school in a locality is a challenge to those connected with public education. Granted the "snob appeal" of some of these new independent schools, nevertheless I feel sure in many cases they would never have come into existence if the management of the local high school had been wiser. Education is a social process. This is a free country and people will not be pushed around by educators. What is required is for those concerned to improve the high schools; public-school administrators must recognize the validity of some of the criticisms now directed against them in terms of the failure of the high school to provide adequate education for the gifted. The problem is especially acute in metropolitan areas. The success of the private school in Australian cities should be a reminder of where we may be headed.

Private schools exist and will continue to exist in the United

States. Parents have the privilege of deciding whether to send their children to private or public schools. If they have doubts about the ability of secular schools to promote the growth of moral and spiritual values, then these doubts must be weighed against the advantages of a pupil's attending a free school for all denominations. Similarly, if a family questions the ability of the local high school to prepare a gifted boy or girl adequately for university work (and the question unfortunately must be raised in many communities today), the family will have to balance these misgivings against the advantage of mixing with all sorts of people while at school. It is hardly worth debating whether or not under ideal conditions in the United States all the public high schools would be so excellent that there would be no room for the private nonsectarian school. Many of those actively engaged in teaching in private schools hope that their efforts will so challenge the public schools that fewer and fewer parents will have to decide in favor of the private school for the gifted child.

Within limits, competition between private schools and public schools can be of advantage to the latter. I have used the phrase "competition within limits" advisedly, for it is difficult to run a private school without continuously recruiting students and it is difficult to recruit students without undermining public confidence in the tax-supported schools. Since the amount of money available for public education depends largely on the enthusiasm of the taxpayer, a chain reaction inimical to public education in a community may easily be started by zealous proponents of a private school. This is obvious in regard to a denominational school. If a religious group starts a school in a community, it is difficult for the promoters to avoid showing a derogatory attitude towards the rival public school. Thus even if the members of the denomination in question have no desire to receive tax money for their own private school, their criticism of the public schools may often tend to discourage the taxpayer. The same thing may happen as a result of schools that draw sons and daughters from well-to-do homes. That the growth of private schools, quite apart from the numbers enrolled, may endanger public education in a community is a fact often overlooked by those actively concerned with private education.

A comparable situation does not exist as between private colleges or universities on the one hand and state or municipal institutions on the other. There has been no such attack on state universities as the recent attacks on the public secondary schools. There is no movement, as far as I am aware, to have denominational colleges or universities supported by public funds. Universities and colleges serve only a small fraction of an age group; whether state or private, they cannot, by their nature, have the unifying influence of the comprehensive high school. Some proponents of an expansion of private secondary schools have attempted to win the allegiance of private colleges by equating the function and status of a school and a college. If a private college is worth supporting, why are not all private schools worthwhile, it is asked. This argument misses the point at issue: namely, the value to our society of a school enrolling essentially *all* the youth of a community.

A line of rational debate becomes possible if attention is centered on a community now served only by a comprehensive high school. The question is: "Would you favor the dispersion of a considerable proportion of the present student body into a group of parallel private schools, some free and church connected, some charging fees and nonsectarian?" If your answer is yes, then a subsidiary question is whether you advocate the present Australian pattern (no tax money for the private schools) or the English pattern. But the important question is the first, for it brings to a focus the issue of the American public school as an instrument for strengthening the spirit of national unity. If a given community does not now have a comprehensive high school, or has a very poor one, the question is: "Would you try to establish a first-rate public school or a group of private schools?" The basic issue is the same.

We Americans desire to provide through our schools unity in our national life. On the other hand, we seek the diversity that comes from freedom of action and expression for small groups of citizens. We look with disfavor on any monolithic type of educational structure; we shrink from any idea of regimentation, of uniformity as to the details of the many phases of secondary education. Unity we can achieve if our public schools remain the primary vehicle for the education of our youth, and if, as far as possible, all the youth of a community attend the same school irrespective of family fortune or cultural background. Diversity in experimentation we maintain by continued emphasis on the concept of local responsibility for our schools. Both these ideas are to a considerable degree novel in the development of civilization; a combination of them is to be found nowhere in the world outside of the United States.

By organizing our free schools on as comprehensive a basis as possible, we can continue to give our children an understanding of democracy. Religious tolerance, mutual respect between vocational groups, belief in the rights of the individual are among the virtues that the best of our high schools now foster. Any understanding of the political machinery of our federal union, of the significance of the Anglo-Saxon tradition of the common law, of the distinction between decisions arrived at by "due process" and those obtained by social pressures and by duress, all this is now being achieved to some degree in the free tax-supported schools of this country.

What the great "public schools" of England accomplished for the future governing class of that nation in the nineteenth century the American high school is now attempting to accomplish for those who govern the United States, namely, all the people. Free schools where the future doctor, lawyer, professor, politician, banker, industrial executive, labor leader, and manual worker have studied and played together from the age of 15 to 17 are a characteristic of large sections of the United States; they are an American invention. That such schools should be maintained and made even more democratic and comprehensive seems to me to be essential for the future of this republic.

Those who would grant all this but still question our free schools on religious grounds I would refer to a recent publication on "Moral and Spiritual Values in the Public Schools." There is set forth in strong terms the belief of many of us that in spite of their nondenominational character, our tax-supported schools have had as a great and continuing purpose the development of moral and spiritual values.

Diversity in American secondary education will be assured if we continue to insist on the doctrine of local control. We have few restrictions on the variety of approaches to secondary education presented by our thousands of local boards. Indeed, to an outsider I should think our diversity would look like educational chaos. But this is a characteristic of our flexible decentralized concept of democracy. The time may conceivably come when a state or the Federal Government may jeopardize this concept, but as far as secondary education is concerned, I do not detect any danger signals in that direction. The National Youth Administration threat, which was real in the 1930s, has almost been forgotten. In short, the answer to the question, "Can we achieve national unity through our public schools and still retain diversity?" is that we can if we so desire. My own personal answer would be that we must.

And now one final look ahead. In spite of the inadequacies of many of our high-school programs and the undeveloped nature of our two-year community colleges, we have made great progress in the last twenty-five years in our attempt to provide adequate schools for *all* American youth. For the future we must endeavor to combine the British concern for training the "natural aristocracy of talents" with the American insistence on general education for *all* future citizens. If we can do that, then our industrialized society will prosper and at the same time the necessary degree of instruction will be provided for all the people so that in their hands "our liberties will remain secure."

The Process of Education

Jerome S. Bruner
(1915–)

The controversy over American education in the 1950s produced varied results, from the trivial to the deeply significant. One of the most important single results was the re-entry of academic scholars and scientists into the field of education. Rightly or wrongly, these experts had felt exiled from the field of education. Consequently they had retreated to their studies, emerging from time to time only to issue diatribes against the academic flaccidity of the schools. With the Great Debate, however, they began to take a more constructive role in putting intellectual rigor back into our elementary and high-school classrooms. Joining forces with practicing teachers and educational researchers, they worked on major curriculum reforms in the scientific subjects. Leading physicists, mathematicians, biologists, and chemists turned out books, films, and teacher-training materials. At the same time, the experimental psychologists began to feel that the psychological study of teaching and learning should recover some of the ground it had lost since the days of James and Thorndike. Fortunately funds were available for both of these efforts from foundations, private and public.

A culmination of sorts came in 1960, with the publication of *The Process of Education* by Harvard psychologist Jerome S. Bruner. Based on a 1955 conference attended by the men who were making the new curriculums, this report attempted to synthesize two major patterns which figured importantly in that work: the developing structure of the child's mind, and the logical structure of the subject-matter disciplines themselves.

Bruner's principles were not all new. Many appear in the writings of the nineteenth-century educational reformers, particularly Pestalozzi and Herbart. Others were recognized by the pioneer of systematic educational theory, John Amos Comenius. Bruner's idea of a spiral curriculum—the bold hypothesis that "any subject can be taught effectively in some intellectually honest form to any child at any stage of development"— echoed Comenius' principle that throughout his schooling each student should be constantly dealing with the same basic subject matter but at different levels of profundity. While perhaps not entirely original, Bruner's synthesis was extraordinarily stimulating. It suggested the possibility of radical improvements in the way science and the humanities are taught in our schools.

Jerome S. Bruner received his Bachelor's Degree from Duke University and his Doctorate in Psychology from Harvard University. He has been on the faculties of Princeton University, the University of Cambridge, and Harvard University. Currently he is Professor of Psychology at Harvard University and Co-Director of the Center for Cognitive Studies at that institution. His most recent book is *On Knowing: Essays for the Left Hand.*

We begin with the hypothesis that any subject can be taught effectively in some intellectually honest form to any child at any stage of development. It is a bold hypothesis and an essential one in thinking about the nature of a curriculum. No evidence exists to contradict it; considerable evidence is being amassed that supports it.

To make clear what is implied, let us examine three general ideas. The first has to do with the process of intellectual development in children, the second with the act of learning, and the third with the notion of the "spiral curriculum."

Intellectual Development

Research on the intellectual development of the child highlights the fact that at each stage of development the child has a characteristic way of viewing the world and explaining it to himself. The task of teaching a subject to a child at any particular age is one of representing the structure of that subject in terms of the child's way of viewing things. The task can be thought of as one of translation. The general hypothesis that has just been stated is premised on the considered judgment that any idea can be represented honestly and usefully in the thought forms of children of school age, and that these first representations can later be made more powerful and precise the more easily by virtue of this early learning. To illustrate and support this view, we present here a somewhat detailed picture of the course of intellectual development, along with some suggestions about teaching at different stages of it.

The work of Piaget and others suggests that, roughly speaking, one may distinguish three stages in the intellectual development of the child. The first stage need not concern us in detail, for it is characteristic principally of the preschool child. In this stage, which ends (at least for Swiss school children) around the fifth or sixth year, the child's mental work consists principally in establishing relationships between experience and action; his concern is with manipulating the world through action. This stage corresponds roughly to the period from the first development of language to the point at which the child learns to manipulate symbols. In this so-called preoperational stage, the principal symbolic achievement is that the child learns how to represent the external world through symbols established by simple generalization; things are represented as equivalent in terms of sharing some common property. But the child's symbolic world does not make a clear separation between internal motives and feelings on the one hand and external reality on the other. The sun moves because God pushes it, and the stars, like himself, have to go to bed. The child is little able to separate his own goals from the means for achieving them, and when he has to make corrections in his activity after unsuccessful attempts at manipulating reality, he does so by what are called intuitive regulations rather than by symbolic operations, the former being of a crude trial-and-error nature rather than the result of taking thought.

What is principally lacking at this stage of development is what the Geneva school has called the concept of reversibility. When the shape of an object is changed, as when one changes the shape of a ball of plasticene, the preoperational child cannot grasp the idea that it can be brought back readily to its original state. Because of this fundamental lack the child cannot understand certain fundamental ideas that lie at the basis of mathematics and physics—the mathematical idea that one conserves quantity even when one partitions a set of things into subgroups, or the physical idea that one conserves mass and weight even though one transforms the shape of an object. It goes without saying that teachers are severely limited in transmitting concepts to a child at this stage, even in a highly intuitive manner.

The second stage of development—and now the child is in school—is called the stage of concrete operations. This stage is operational in contrast to the preceding stage, which is merely active. An operation is a type of action: it can be carried out rather directly by the manipulation of objects, or internally, as when one manipulates the symbols that represent things and relations in one's mind. Roughly, an operation is a means of getting data about the real world into the mind and there transforming them so that they can be organized and used selectively in the solution of problems. Assume a child is presented with a pinball machine which bounces a ball off a wall at an angle. Let us find out what he appreciates about the relation between the angle of incidence and the angle of reflection. The young child sees no problem: for him, the ball travels in an arc, touching the wall on the way. The somewhat older child, say age ten, sees the two angles as roughly related—as one changes so does the other. The still older child begins to grasp that there is a fixed relation between the two, and usually says it is a right angle. Finally, the thirteen- or fourteen-year-old, often by pointing the ejector directly at the wall and seeing the ball come back at the ejector, gets the idea that the two angles are equal. Each way of looking at the phenomenon represents the result of an operation in this sense, and the child's thinking is constrained by his way of pulling his observations together.

An operation differs from simple action or goal-directed behavior in that it is internalized and reversible. "Internalized" means that the child does not have to go about his problem-solving any longer by overt trial and error, but can actually carry out trial and error in his head. Reversibility is present because operations are seen as characterized where appropriate by what is called "complete compensation"; that is to say, an operation can be compensated for by an inverse operation. If marbles, for example, are divided into subgroups, the child can grasp intuitively that the original collection of marbles can be restored by being added back together again. The child tips a balance scale too far with a weight and then searches systematically for a lighter weight or for something with which to get the scale rebalanced. He may carry reversibility too far by assuming that a piece of paper, once burned, can also be restored.

With the advent of concrete operations, the child develops an internalized structure with which to operate. In the example of the balance scale, the structure is a serial order of weights that the child has in his mind. Such internal structures are of the essence. They are the internalized symbolic systems by which the child represents the world, as in the example of the pinball machine and the angles of incidence and reflection. It is into the language of these internal structures that one must translate ideas if the child is to grasp them.

But concrete operations, though they are guided by the logic of classes and the logic of relations, are means for structuring only immediately present reality. The child is able to give structure to the things he encounters, but he is not yet readily able to deal with possibilities not directly before him or not already experienced. This is not to say that children operating concretely are not able to anticipate things that are not present. Rather, it is that they do not command the operations for conjuring up systematically the full range of alternative possibilities that could exist at any given time. They cannot go systematically beyond the information given them to a description of what else might occur. Somewhere between ten and fourteen years of age the child passes into a third stage, which is called the stage of "formal operations" by the Geneva school.

Now the child's intellectual activity seems to be based upon an ability to operate on hypothetical propositions rather than being constrained to what he has experienced or what is before him. The child can now think of possible variables and even deduce potential relationships that can later be verified by experiment or observation. Intellectual operations now appear to be predicated upon the same kinds of logical operations that are the stock in trade of the logician, the scientist, or the abstract thinker. It is at this point that the child is able to give formal or axiomatic expression to the concrete ideas that before guided his problem-solving but could not be described or formally understood.

Earlier, while the child is in the stage of concrete operations, he is capable of grasping intuitively and concretely a great many of the basic ideas of mathematics, the sciences, the humanities, and the social sciences. But he can do so only in terms of concrete operations. It can be demonstrated that fifth-grade children can play mathematical games with rules modeled on highly advanced mathematics; indeed, they can arrive at these rules inductively and learn how to work with them. They will flounder, however, if one attempts to force upon them a formal mathematical description of what they have been doing, though they are perfectly capable of guiding their behavior by these rules. . . .

What is most important for teaching basic concepts is that the child be helped to pass progressively from concrete thinking to the utilization of more conceptually adequate modes of thought. But it is futile to attempt this by presenting formal explanations based on a logic that is distant from the child's manner of thinking and sterile in its implications for him. Much teaching in mathematics is of this sort. The child learns not to understand mathematical order but rather to apply certain devices or recipes without understanding their significance and connectedness. They are not translated into his way of thinking. Given this inappropriate start, he is easily led to believe that the important thing is for him to be "accurate"—though accuracy has less to do with mathematics than with computation. Perhaps the most striking example of this type of thing is to be found in the manner in which the high-school student meets Euclidian geometry for the first time, as a set of axioms and theorems, without having had some experience with simple geometric configurations and the intuitive means whereby one deals with them. If the child were earlier given the concepts and strategies in the form of intuitive geometry at a level that he could easily follow, he might be far better able to grasp deeply the meaning of the theorems and axioms to which he is exposed later.

But the intellectual development of the child is no clockwork sequence of events; it also responds to influences from the environment, notably the school environment. Thus instruction in scientific ideas, even at the elementary level, need not follow slavishly the natural course of cognitive development in the child. It can also lead intellectual development by providing challenging but usable opportunities for the child to forge ahead in his development. Experience has shown that it is worth the effort to provide the growing child with problems that tempt him into next stages of development. As David Page, one of the most experienced teachers of elementary mathematics, has commented: "In teaching from kindergarten to graduate school, I have been amazed at the intellectual similarity of human beings at all ages, although children are perhaps more spontaneous, creative, and energetic than adults. As far as I am concerned young children learn almost anything faster than adults do if it can be given to them in terms they understand. Giving the material to them in terms they understand, interestingly enough, turns out to involve knowing the mathematics oneself, and the better one knows it, the better it can be taught. It is appropriate that we warn ourselves to be careful of assigning an absolute level of difficulty to any particular topic. When I tell mathematicians that fourth-grade students can go a long way into 'set theory' a few of them reply: 'Of course.' Most of them are startled. The latter ones are completely wrong in assuming that 'set theory' is intrinsically difficult. Of course it may be that nothing is intrinsically difficult. We just have to wait until the proper point of view and corresponding language for presenting it are revealed. Given particular subject matter or a particular concept, it is easy to ask trivial questions or to lead the child to ask trivial questions. It is also easy to ask impossibly difficult questions. The trick is to find the medium questions that can be answered and that take you somewhere. This is the big job of teachers and textbooks." One leads the child by the well-wrought "medium questions" to move more rapidly through the stages of intellectual development, to a deeper understanding of mathematical, physical, and historical principles. We must know far more about the ways in which this can be done.

. . . .

A comparable approach can surely be taken to the teaching of social studies and literature. There has been little research done on the kinds of concepts that a child brings to these subjects, although there is a wealth of observation and anecdote. Can one teach the structure of literary forms by presenting the child with the first part of a story and then having him complete it in the form of a comedy, a tragedy, or a farce—without ever using such words? When, for example, does the idea of "historical trend" develop, and what are its precursors in the child? How does one make a child aware of literary style? Perhaps the child can discover the idea of style through the presentation of the same content written in drastically different styles, in the manner of Beerbohm's *Christmas Garland*. Again, there is no reason to believe that any subject cannot be taught to any child at virtually any age in some form.

Here one is immediately faced with the question of the economy of teaching. One can argue that it might be better to wait until the child is thirteen or fourteen before beginning geometry so that the projective and intuitive first steps can immediately be followed up by a full formal presentation of the subject. Is it worth while to train the young inductively so that they may discover the basic order of knowledge before they can appreciate its formalism? . . . There is evidence to indicate that such rigorous and relevant early training has the effect of making later learning easier. Indeed the experiments on "learning set" seem to indicate just that —that one not only learns specifics but in so doing learns how to learn. So important is training per se that monkeys who have been given extensive training in problem solving suffer considerably less loss and recover more quickly after induced brain damage than animals who had not been previously thus educated. But the danger of such early training may be that it has the effect of training out original but deviant ideas. There is no evidence available on the subject, and much is needed.

The Act of Learning

Learning a subject seems to involve three almost simultaneous processes. First there is *acquisition* of new information —often information that runs counter to or is a replacement for what the person has previously known implicitly or explicitly. At the very least it is a refinement of previous knowledge. Thus one teaches a student Newton's laws of motion, which violate the testimony of the senses. Or in teaching a student about wave mechanics, one violates the student's belief in mechanical impact as the sole source of real energy transfer. Or one bucks the language and its built-in way of thinking in terms of "wasting energy" by introducing the student to the conservation theorem in physics which asserts that no energy is lost. More often the situation is less drastic, as when one teaches the details of the circulatory system to a student who already knows vaguely or intuitively that blood circulates.

A second aspect of learning may be called *transformation*—the process of manipulating knowledge to make it fit new tasks. We learn to "unmask" or analyze information, to order it in a way that permits extrapolation or interpolation or conversion into another form. Transformation comprises the ways we deal with information in order to go beyond it.

A third aspect of learning is *evaluation:* checking whether the way we have manipulated information is adequate to the task. Is the generalization fitting, have we extrapolated appropriately, are we operating properly? Often a teacher is crucial in helping with evaluation, but much of it takes place by judgments of plausibility without our actually being able to check rigorously whether we are correct in our efforts.

In the learning of any subject matter, there is usually a series of episodes, each episode involving the three processes. Photosynthesis might reasonably comprise material for a learning episode in biology, fitted into a more comprehensive learning experience such as learning about the conversion of energy generally. At its best a learning episode reflects what has gone before it and permits one to generalize beyond it.

A learning episode can be brief or long, contain many ideas or a few. How sustained an episode a learner is willing to undergo depends upon what the person expects to get from his efforts, in the sense of such external things as grades but also in the sense of a gain in understanding.

We usually tailor material to the capacities and needs of students by manipulating learning episodes in several ways: by shortening or lengthening the episode, by piling on extrinsic rewards in the form of praise and gold stars, or by dramatizing the shock of recognition of what the material means when fully understood. The unit in a curriculum is meant to be a recognition of the importance of learning episodes, though many units drag on with no climax in understanding. There is a surprising lack of research on how one most wisely devises adequate learning episodes for children at different ages and in different subject matters. There are many questions that need answers based on careful research, and to some of these we turn now.

There is, to begin with, the question of the balance between extrinsic rewards and intrinsic ones. There has been much written on the role of reward and punishment in learning, but very little indeed on the role of interest and curiosity and the lure of discovery. If it is our intention as teachers to inure the child to longer and longer episodes of learning, it may well be that intrinsic rewards in the form of quickened awareness and understanding will have to be emphasized far more in the detailed design of curricula. One of the least discussed ways of carrying a student through a hard unit of material is to challenge him with a chance to exercise his full powers, so that he may discover the pleasure of full and effective functioning. Good teachers know the power of this lure. Students should know what it feels like to be completely absorbed in a problem. They seldom experience this feeling in school. Given enough absorption in class, some students may be able to carry over the feeling to work done on their own.

There is a range of problems that have to do with how much emphasis should be placed on acquisition, transformation, and evaluation in a learning episode—getting facts, manipulating them, and checking one's ideas. Is it the case, for example, that it is best to give the young child a minimum set of facts first and then encourage him to draw the fullest set of implications possible from this knowledge? In short, should an episode for a young child contain little new information but emphasize what can be done to go beyond that bit on one's own? One teacher of social studies has had great success with fourth-graders through this approach: he begins, for example, with the fact that civilizations have most often begun in fertile river valleys—the only "fact." The students are encouraged in class discussion to figure out why this is the case and why it would be less likely for civilizations to start in mountainous country. The effect of this approach, essentially the technique of discovery, is that the child generates information on his own, which he can then check or evaluate against the sources, getting more new information in the process. This obviously is one kind of learning episode, and doubtless it has limited applicability. What other kinds are there, and are some more appropriate to certain topics and ages than others? It is not the case that "to learn is to learn is to learn," yet in the research literature there appears to be little recognition of differences in learning episodes.

With respect to the optimum length of a learning episode, there are a few common-sense things one can say about it, and these are perhaps interesting enough to suggest fruitful research possibilities. It seems fairly obvious, for example, that the longer and more packed the episode, the greater the payoff must be in terms of increased power and understanding if the person is to be encouraged to move to a next episode with zest. Where grades are used as a substitute for the reward of understanding, it may well be that learning will cease as soon as grades are no longer given—at graduation.

It also seems reasonable that the more one has a sense of the structure of a subject, the more densely packed and longer a learning episode one can get through without fatigue. Indeed, the amount of new information in any learning episode is really the amount that we cannot quite fit into place at once. And there is a severe limit, as we have already noted, on how much of such unassimilated information we can keep in mind. The estimate is that adults can handle about seven independent items of information at a time. No norms are available for children—a deplorable lack.

There are many details one can discuss concerning the shaping of learning episodes for children, but the problems that have been mentioned will suffice to give their flavor. Inasmuch as the topic is central to an understanding of how one arranges a curriculum, it seems obvious that here is an area of research that is of the first importance.

The "Spiral Curriculum"

If one respects the ways of thought of the growing child, if one is courteous enough to translate material into his logical forms and challenging enough to tempt him to advance, then it is possible to introduce him at an early age to the ideas and styles that in later life make an educated man. We might ask, as a criterion for any subject taught in primary school, whether, when fully developed, it is worth an adult's knowing, and whether having known it as a child makes a person a better adult. If the answer to both questions is negative or ambiguous, then the material is cluttering the curriculum.

If the hypothesis with which this section was introduced is true —that any subject can be taught to any child in some honest form —then it should follow that a curriculum ought to be built around the great issues, principles, and values that a society deems worthy of the continual concern of its members. Consider two examples —the teaching of literature and of science. If it is granted, for example, that it is desirable to give children an awareness of the meaning of human tragedy and a sense of compassion for it, is it not possible at the earliest appropriate age to teach the literature of tragedy in a manner that illuminates but does not threaten? There are many possible ways to begin: through a retelling of the great myths, through the use of children's classics, through presentation of and commentary on selected films that have proved themselves. Precisely what kinds of materials should be used at what age with what effect is a subject for research—research of several kinds. We may ask first about the child's conception of the tragic, and here one might proceed in much the same way that Piaget and his colleagues have proceeded in studying the child's conception of physical causality, of morality, of number, and the rest. It is only when we are equipped with such knowledge that we will be in a position to know how the child will translate whatever we present to him into his own subjective terms. Nor need we wait for all the research findings to be in before proceeding, for a skillful teacher can also experiment by attempting to teach what seems to be intuitively right for children of different ages, correcting as he goes. In time, one goes beyond to more complex versions of the same kind of literature or simply revisits some of the same books used earlier. What matters is that later teaching build upon earlier reactions to literature, that it seek to create an ever more explicit and mature understanding of the literature of tragedy. Any of the great literary forms can be handled in the same way, or any of the great themes—be it the form of comedy or the theme of identity, personal loyalty, or what not.

So too in science. If the understanding of number, measure, and probability is judged crucial in the pursuit of science, then instruction in these subjects should begin as intellectually honestly and as early as possible in a manner consistent with the child's forms of thought. Let the topics be developed and redeveloped in later grades. Thus, if most children are to take a tenth-grade unit in biology, need they approach the subject cold? Is it not possible, with a minimum of formal laboratory work if necessary, to introduce them to some of the major biological ideas earlier, in a spirit perhaps less exact and more intuitive?

Many curricula are originally planned with a guiding idea much like the one set forth here. But as curricula are actually executed, as they grow and change, they often lose their original form and suffer a relapse into a certain shapelessness. It is not amiss to urge that actual curricula be reexamined with an eye to the issues of continuity and development referred to in the preceding pages. One cannot predict the exact forms that revision might take; indeed, it is plain that there is now available too little research to provide adequate answers. One can only propose that appropriate research be undertaken with the greatest vigor and as soon as possible.

Why Is Education Obsolescent?

Margaret Mead
(1901–   )

It is a familiar theme of current educational literature that our ideas about education, schooling, and the learning process are outmoded and unsuited to the realities of contemporary life. What does this really mean? Anthropologist Margaret Mead analyzes such charges in this essay.

The traditional conception of education as the transmission of culture is given a broader significance by modern anthropologists. For they conceive of culture as something encompassing much more than aesthetic attainments. Culture in the anthropological sense is the entire man-made part of the environment. It is this larger "culture," now changing so rapidly, which inspires the basic assumption of Margaret Mead's critique of contemporary education. Her basic principle is: "No one will live all his life in the world into which he was born, and no one will die in the world in which he worked in his maturity."

From this underlying fact of contemporary life Dr. Mead examines the contradictory array of demands which society makes on its schools and colleges, including the antedated assumption that someone can "complete his education." Her recommendations are designed to provide a fuller experience for "students" of all ages. For the young, she advocates the right to work, if for some that is the most promising road to maturity. For the mature, she insists on the right to learn—not as an extraordinary retreat back to the academy, but as an accepted way of keeping up with a changing world.

Margaret Mead was born in Philadelphia. She earned the M.A. and Ph.D. degrees at Columbia University. After finishing her university work she spent many years living among various South Sea peoples. One of her principal interests is studying contemporary cultures in the light of the perspective gained by a study of small, homogeneous, stable societies. Her published books include *Coming of Age in Samoa, Growing Up in New Guinea, Soviet Attitudes Toward Authority,* and *New Lives for Old.* She has lectured at numerous universities in the United States, and is currently Associate Curator of Ethnology at the American Museum of Natural History in New York. The following essay first appeared in the *Harvard Business Review,* November–December, 1958.

When we look realistically at the world in which we are living today and become aware of what the actual problems of learning are, our conception of education changes radically. Although the educational system remains basically unchanged, we are no longer dealing primarily with the *vertical* transmission of the tried and true by the old, mature, and experienced teacher to the young, immature, and inexperienced pupil. This was the system of education developed in a stable, slowly changing culture. In a world of rapid change, vertical transmission of knowledge alone no longer serves the purposes of education.

What is needed and what we are already moving toward is the inclusion of another whole dimension of learning: the *lateral* transmission, to every sentient member of society, of what has just been discovered, invented, created, manufactured, or marketed. This need for lateral transmission exists no less in the physics or genetics laboratory than it does on the assembly line with its working force of experienced and raw workmen. The man who teaches another individual the new mathematics or the use of a newly invented tool is not sharing knowledge he acquired years ago. He learned what was new yesterday, and his pupil must learn it today.

The whole teaching-and-learning continuum, which once was tied in an orderly and productive way to the passing of generations and the growth of the child into a man—this whole process has exploded in our faces. Yet even as we try to catch hold of and patch up the pieces, we fail to recognize what has happened. . . .

In order to understand the issues, let us begin by looking at some of the features and underlying assumptions of our American educational system as it is today. Even a brief examination of the picture we carry in our minds of "education" and of "students" will indicate the state of confusion at which we have arrived and the immediate need for creative leadership in working out a more realistic system of education.

We have moved into a period in which the break with the past provides an opportunity for creating a new framework for activity in almost every field—but in each field the fact that there has been a break must be rediscovered. In education there has been up to now no real recognition of the extent to which our present system is outmoded. Meanwhile, as the turmoil over our educational system grows, the various responsible groups in the United States are jockeying for position. But some of them, particularly those representing industry, have as yet hardly entered the field.

Historians point sagely to the last two educational crises—the first of which ended with the establishment of the universal elementary school and the second with the establishment of the universal high school—and with remarkable logic and lack of imagination they predict that the present crisis will follow the same pattern. (And what is history for if not to tell us exactly how to make the same mistakes as in the past!) According to such present predictions, the crisis will last until 1970, when it will end with the establishment of universal college education, accessible in principle to all young Americans.

Implicit in this prediction is a series of other ideas, such as: (1) The assumption that our educational system has fallen behind in something (though it is not now clear what the "something" is—the work training of German apprentices, or the technical training of young Soviets, or the linguistic mastery of Netherlands students), and that it should therefore arrange to catch up. (2) The explanation that our difficulties are due to the "bulge"—the host of babies that tricked the statisticians peacefully extrapolating their population curves and bedeviled a people who had decided that orphan asylums could slowly be turned into homes for the aged and elementary schools into high schools as a population with a falling birth rate aged into maturity. (Only a few people followed out the simile to senility!) (3) The thinking of the people who are sure that the pendulum is swinging back to sense—to discipline and dunce caps, switches and multiplication tables, and the highly satisfactory forms of torture which somebody (they themselves or at least their grandfathers) once suffered in the cause of learning.

But in the midst of the incessant discussion and the search for scapegoats to take the blame for what everyone admits is a parlous state, extraordinarily little attention is paid to any basic issues. Everyone simply wants more of what we already have: more children in more schools for more hours studying more of something. The scientists want more students to be taught more mathematics, while the liberal-arts advocates want more of their subject matter included in the curriculum. The planners want more school buildings built, and the educators want more teachers trained who have studied more hours and who will get more pay. Meanwhile, the child-labor committees want more inspection and more attention to migratory children, and the youth boards want more social workers and more special schools and more clinics provided.

Likewise, extraordinarily little attention is paid to the fact that two great new educational agencies—the armed services and industry—have entered the field, and there is little awareness of the ways in which operations in these institutions are altering traditional education. Recruitment programs of the armed services now include explicit statements of their role as educational institutions. . . .

But most important, the pattern itself is hardly questioned. For we *think* we know what education is and what a good education ought to be; and however deficient we may be as a people, as taxpayers, or as educators, we may be actualizing our ideals. An occasional iconoclast can ask wistfully: "Wouldn't it be fine if we could scrap our whole school system and start anew?" But he gets no hearing because everyone knows that what he is saying is nonsense. Wishful dreams about starting all anew are obviously impractical, but this does not mean that someone should not ask these crucial questions:

Is our present historic idea of education suitable for people in the mid-twentieth century, who have a life expectancy of 70 years, and who live in a world of automation and global communication, ready to begin space exploration and aware of the possibility that we can bring about the suicide of the entire human species?

As all these present and pressing concerns of the human race are new, is it not possible that a system of education may be out of date which was designed for small societies that were connected by horse-drawn coaches and sailing ships, and where any war could threaten only small sections of the human species at any one time?

Is it not possible that the problem of the educational system's obsolescence goes beyond such issues as methods of teaching reading or physics, or the most desirable age for leaving school, or the payment of teachers, or the length of summer holidays, or the number of years best devoted to college, or even the comparative advantages of working while going to high school or college?

Is not the break between past and present—and so the whole problem of outdating in our educational system—related to a change in the rate of change? For change has become so rapid that adjustment cannot be left to the next generation; adults must—not once, but continually—take in, adjust to, use, and make innovations in a steady stream of discovery and new conditions.

Our educational system, besides being the oldest system of universal free primary education in the world, bears the marks of its long history. But is it not possible to think that an educational system that was designed to teach what was known to little children and to a selected few young men (after which they could be regarded as "educated") may not fit a world in which the most important factors in everyone's life are those things that are not yet, but soon will be, known?

Is it not equally possible that our present definition of a pupil or a student is out of date when we define the learner as a child (or at best an immature person) who is entitled to those things to which a child is entitled—moral protection and a meager subsistence in a dependency position—and who is denied those things which are denied to a child—moral autonomy, sex and parenthood, alcoholic beverages, and exposure to hazards?

In the picture which we have of the student, we have muddled together *both* a conception of the young child who is unable to fend for himself or to protect himself against moral and physical hazards, and who is entitled to be fed and sheltered *and* our own historical conception of the scholar's role as one in which some few men could claim lifelong support provided they themselves accepted an economic dependency that was demeaning to other men and a type of life in which they were subject to supervision (and, until recently in Christian history, gave up sex and parenthood). This composite picture is one into which we can fit the scholarly monk, the Cambridge don who was not permitted to marry, and the student who lives in college and whose degree depends on his sleeping there (a touchingly infantile method of attaining a degree). All of these match our conception of the learner as a dependent who is subject to the supervision appropriate to a child and who must pay for his learning by abnegating some of the rewards of maturity.

Yet the combined ideas of the child and the monk do not complete our picture of the student; we have added still other things to it. With the industrial revolution there came new possibilities of exploiting human labor. Work, which through long ages had often been disliked by members of the upper classes and had been delegated to women, slaves, or serfs, became something different —more hazardous, more menacing. In this situation children were the most identifiable victims, and their fate was dramatized as a conflict between their right to an education and their subjection to dangerous and ruthless exploitation in the mines, in the factories, in dives, and in the street trades. The common school, born at a period in the United States when we were particularly concerned with extending the rights of the common man, was sponsored and fought for by labor groups. In this way the common school became doubly identified as the means of making all children literate and as the official enemy of child labor. A vote to raise the school-leaving age was a vote against child labor, and, like sin or cancer, child labor became something no one could be in favor of, officially.

So, as inevitably happens when different institutions in a culture become intertwined, raising the school-leaving age came to stand for several things: it was, on the one hand, a way of increasing the privileges of every child born in the United States and, on the other hand, a way of protecting children against the hazards of work to their health and morals.

That our picture of harmful labor is itself very complex can be seen even from a cursory examination of federal and state child-labor laws. Looking at these we find that work outdoors is better than work indoors, that work in small cities is better than work in large cities, that work in summer and during vacations is less harmful than work in winter or during school terms, that work done for parents does not count as work, and that there is one form of work in which all the rules can be broken about age, hours, places, hazards from the weather, weight of objects dealt with, being on the streets, going to strange places, and so forth, —which, characteristically and in the best spirit of Horatio Alger, is delivering newspapers.

This one exception to our children's right to protection highlights the whole picture. In the American myth, men rise to success and greatness by working hard as children, and as we have progressively forbidden them this traditional preparation for greatness, we have left them the one symbolic activity of delivering newspapers. (Nowadays, however, it may be the father—bank president or chief justice—who actually delivers the papers because the son is in bed with a cold under the care of an expensive pediatrician.)

Slowly, as a society, we have codified the rights and the disabilities of minors and also the conditions under which a minor may take on the privileges appropriate to adults because they require maturity. These are problems which are dealt with in the most primitive societies, though the way in which they are thought of may contrast with ours. What has happened in our contemporary society is that the codified rules, each intended to serve some specific need, fail to fit the contemporary situation—and the result is confusion.

The state of confusion that characterizes our attitudes toward maturity in students shows up in a variety of ways. For instance: School regulations may forbid a married student to attend high school even though he or she may be below the age and the grade when it is legal to leave high school. Even more quaintly, in one large city the schoolgirl who has an illegitimate child may go back to school after the child has been born, but the married girl who becomes a mother may not return. In some school systems, not only expectant mothers but also expectant *fathers* are barred from the daytime high school.

The complexity of the total picture and the confusion about the relationship of being a child, a minor, a student, and a morally incapable individual are further increased when we include, as nowadays we must, the armed services. For in different degrees the armed services permit a boy to enlist who is too young to marry, to leave school, to buy cigarettes or to drink beer, to vote, to make a legal contract, to bequeath property, to change his citizenship, to work in a hazardous occupation or in other occupations between the hours of seven and seven, or to have contact with dangerous machinery. Yet by enlisting he is enabled to operate the complex instruments of death and to die for his country.

So, when we think about education and try to identify the student, we have in our minds—whether or not we are aware of it—an exceedingly complex picture, the elements of which are compounded and confused in their historic connections. Yet we must identify what they are if we are to remodel our educational system so that it is devoted to the kind of teaching and learning that is appropriate to the United States today. For this purpose a look at education in other societies will be helpful.

Education which is limited to small children is appropriate in a very primitive society like that of the Eskimo. The nine-year-old Eskimo child has learned, from father or from mother, the basic skills of a spoken language, the handling of tools and equipment, knowledge of the weather, relevant personal relations, and religious taboos. He must wait until he is physically mature before he can marry; as he grows older he will gain proficiency in hunting, in religious practices, in his knowledge of time, the seasons, and the landscape; and he may come to exercise leadership. But his education, in the sense of learning whatever adults could teach him directly, was over long before.

In other societies that are more complex, education may not be completed before adolescence, when some young people may elect, or may be chosen, to learn more complicated skills and may memorize the classics, master complex weaving skills, or become skilled craftsmen or leaders of ritual activities.

After the invention of writing and the development of mathematics and medicine, these did not become part of the whole tradition which had to be imparted to everyone. Like techniques of gold working or a knowledge of magical charms, they were taught by a few to a few in a long continuum of teaching-and-learning, in which the teacher responded as much to the pupil as the pupil did to the demands of the teacher, and both attempted not so much to add to the sum total of knowledge as to increase the skill of its manipulation. Under these circumstances, new knowledge was added so gradually that the slow web of transmission of ancient skills was not torn.

Parallel to these developments was the special education given by specially chosen tutors and teachers to the children of the aristocracy; such an education was designed to ground the pupils well in many arts and graces and in a scholarship which they would not practice but would wear as an adornment or use for wise government.

In a country governed by a conqueror or in a country to which large numbers of immigrants come, there are special problems of education as the government becomes responsible for people who speak a different language and have different customs. For, in these situations, the function—or at least one function—of the educational system is not the transmission to the next generation of something that all adults or that specialized groups of adults know, but rather the transmission of something the parents' generation does *not* know to children whom the authorities wish to have educated.

So, looking at our educational system today, we can see that in various ways it combines these different functions: (1) The protection of the child against exploitation and the protection of society against precocity and inexperience. (2) The maintenance of learners in a state of moral and economic dependency. (3) Giving to all children the special, wider education once reserved for the children of privileged groups, in an attempt to form the citizen of a democracy as once the son of a noble house was formed. (4) The teaching of complex and specialized skills which, under our complex system of division of labor, is too difficult and time-consuming for each set of parents to master or to hand on to their own children. (5) The transmission of something which the parents' generation does *not* know (in the case of immigrants with varied cultural and linguistic backgrounds) to children whom the authorities or the parents wish to have educated.

To these multiple functions of an educational system, which, in a slowly changing society, were variously performed, we have added slowly and reluctantly a quite new function: *education for rapid and self-conscious adaptation to a changing world*. Yet we hardly recognize how new this function of our educational system is. It is implicit in the demands of educators that schools develop flexibility, open-mindedness, and creativity; but such demands might equally well have been made 200 years ago, well before the rhythm of change had radically altered.

That we have as yet failed to recognize the new character of change is apparent in a thousand ways. Despite the fact that a subject taught to college freshmen may have altered basically by the time the same students are seniors, it is still said that colleges are able to give students "a good education"—finished, wrapped up, and sealed with a degree.

A student who is still in college can "go on" to a higher degree because he has not as yet "completed" his education, i.e., the lump of the known which he has decided to bite off. But a student who has once let a year go by after he is "out of school" does not "go *on*," but rather "goes *back*" to school. And as we treat education as the right of a minor who has not yet completed high school (for the position of a boy who has completed high school at the age of 14 is a different and anomalous one, in which he is exempt from most of the forms of protection accorded minors because a high-school diploma is equated with physiological maturity, the capacity for parenthood, and the ability to resist the seductions of hostel and bowling-alley life), just so we equate marriage and parenthood with getting a diploma; both indicate that one's education is "finished."

Consistent with these ideas and with our conception of what a student is, our educational institutions are places where we keep "children" for a shorter or longer period. The length of time depends in part on their intelligence and motivation and in part on their parents' incomes and the immediately recognized national needs for particular skills or types of training—and as long as they are there, we treat them as minors.

Once they have left, we regard them as in some sense finished, neither capable of nor in need of further "education," for we still believe that education should come all in one piece, or rather, in a series of connected pieces, each presented as a whole at the elementary school, the high-school, and the college level. All other behaviors are aberrant. So we speak of "interrupted" education—that is, education which has been broken into by sickness, delinquency, or military service—and we attempt to find means of repairing this interruption. Indeed, the whole GI bill, which in a magnificent way gave millions of young men a chance for a different kind of education than they would otherwise have got was conceived of primarily as a means of compensating young men for an unsought but unavoidable interruption.

Thus we avoid facing the most vivid truth of the new age: *no one will live all his life in the world into which he was born, and no one will die in the world in which he worked in his maturity.*

For those who work on the growing edge of science, technology, or the arts, contemporary life changes at even shorter intervals. Often, only a few months may elapse before something which previously was easily taken for granted must be unlearned or transformed to fit the new state of knowledge or practice.

In this world, no one can "complete an education." The students we need are not just children who are learning to walk and talk and to read and write plus older students, conceived of as minors, who are either "going on" with or "going back" to specialized education. Rather, we need children *and* adolescents *and* young *and* mature *and* "senior" adults, each of whom is learning at the appropriate pace and with all the special advantages and disadvantages of experience peculiar to his own age.

If we are to incorporate fully each new advance, we need simultaneously: (1) The wide-eyed freshness of the inquiring child. (2) The puzzlement of the near-dunce who, if the system is to work, must still be part of it. (3) The developing capacities of the adolescent for abstract thinking. (4) The interest of the young adult whose motives have been forged in the responsibilities of parenthood and first contacts with a job. (5) The special awareness of the mature man who has tempered experience, skepticism, and the power to implement whatever changes he regards as valuable. (6) The balance of the older man who has lived through cycles of change and can use this wisdom to place what is new.

Each and every one of these is a learner, not of something old and tried—the alphabet or multiplication tables or Latin declensions or French irregular verbs or the rules of rhetoric or the binomial theorem, all the paraphernalia of learning which children with different levels of aspiration must acquire—but of new, hardly tried theories and methods: pattern analysis, general system theory, space lattices, cybernetics, and so on.

Learning of this kind must go on not only at special times and in special places, but all through production and consumption—from the technician who must handle a new machine to the factory supervisor who must introduce its use, the union representative who must interpret it to the men, the foreman who must keep the men working, the salesman who must service a new device or find markets for it, the housewife who must understand how to care for a new material, the mother who must answer the questions of an observant four-year-old.

In this world the age of the teacher is no longer necessarily relevant. For instance, children teach grandparents how to manage TV, young expediters come into the factory along with the new equipment, and young men invent automatic programing for computers over which their seniors struggle because they, too, need it for their research.

This, then, is what we call the *lateral transmission* of knowledge. It is not an outpouring of knowledge from the "wise old teacher" into the minds of young pupils, as in vertical transmission. Rather, it is a sharing of knowledge by the informed with the uninformed, whatever their ages. The primary prerequisite is the desire to know.

Given this situation, which of the institutions that are concerned with the revision of our educational system is to take the initiative: the educational world, the government, the armed services, citizens' voluntary organizations, churches, or industry? Each has a stake in the outcome; each has power to influence what happens; each has its own peculiar strengths and weaknesses.

Industry, however, has the peculiar advantage of understanding the major evil from which our whole educational system is suffering—*obsolescence*. Modern ideas of obsolescence have come out of studies of industrial processes, and industrialists have made these ideas so much a part of their thinking that making allowance for the costs of obsolescence and supporting continuing research on problems of obsolescence are a normal part of their professional behavior. In any major effort to modernize our educational system, of course, it would be appropriate for all the institutions to have a voice. It would be well, for example: for educators to watch out so that all they know would not be lost in the shuffle; for government to guard the needs of the nation; for church and synagogue to protect the religious values of the past;

for the armed services to concentrate on our defense needs; for citizens to organize means of protecting the health, safety, and welfare (present and future) of their own and the community's children.

In these circumstances, would it not be most appropriate for industry to take the lead in highlighting the obsolescence of our present educational system? In the United States, in 1958, approximately 67 per cent of the civilian labor force was engaged in some kind of work in industry. Of the advances which account for obsolescence, a very large proportion have come out of industry. But, at the same time, much of the thinking that is holding up a real revision of our school system is based on an outmoded public image of industry as a monstrous and wicked institution which, if not restrained, would permit little boys to be sent down into coal mines or to work in conditions in which their lungs would be filled with powdered silicon.

In fact, industry has already taken the lead—within its own walls—in developing a new type of education that includes all levels of competence and training and that freely faces the need for education at the senior levels of management. . . . The thinking that has gone into this contribution, however, has not yet become an articulate, leading part of our rethinking of the educational system as a whole. But if industry, as represented by individual leaders from management and labor in many parts of the country, would come forward with plans which dramatized our dilemma, such plans would be heard.

What might these plans be? First, in regard to work performed by young people, industry could say to all those who believe that children should be kept in school primarily so that they will not be on the streets or at work under bad conditions: "We will agree that young people need more supervision than older workers—that someone should know where they are each day, that their health should be protected and checked, and that they should be protected from organized attempts to deprave them. We will undertake to train and supervise the young people who *at this time* cannot gain anything by remaining in school."

But this would not be enough. This offer would need to be accompanied by a second one: "As soon as *any* worker—of any age, at any level—in our plant, office, or laboratory is ready to study again, we will facilitate his, or her, doing so."

This is, admittedly, a large order. But we cannot have one without the other. For as long as we continue to think that free and, when necessary, subsidized education is appropriate *only* when it is *preliminary* to work (though, exceptionally, it may be continued after some inevitable "interruption"), just so long the guardians of character, of political literacy, and of our store of talent that comes from all classes and in many cases shows itself only very slowly, will argue for—and will get—longer and longer years of compulsory education and longer and longer years of free education.

Under these circumstances, the meaning of education and the purpose of schools—especially for young people between the ages of 14 and 20—will only become more confused. On the one hand, the education that is absolutely necessary for those who, at an early age, are ready to go on to become scientists, statesmen, philosophers, and poets will be hamstrung by the presence of those others who, at the same age, do not want schooling; and on the other hand, the lives and characters of the temporary nonlearners will be ruined, and they will be incapacitated as potential later learners.

What we need to do, instead, is to separate primary and secondary education—in an entirely new way:

By *primary education* we would mean the stage of education in which all children are taught what they need to know in order to be fully human in the world in which they are growing up—including the basic skills of reading and writing and a basic knowledge of numbers, money, geography, transportation and communication, the law, and the nations of the world.

By *secondary education* we would mean an education that is based on primary education and that can be obtained *in any amount* and *at any period* during the individual's whole lifetime.

By so doing, we could begin to deal effectively with the vast new demands that are being made on us. The high schools would be relieved of the nonlearners, among whom are found a large number of delinquents. But, more important, men and women, instead of preparing for a single career to which—for lack of any alternative—they must stick during their entire active lives, would realize that they might learn something else. The very knowledge that this was so would relieve much of the rigidity that now bedevils management. Women, after their children became older, could be educated for particular new tasks—instead of facing the rejection that today is related to fears about new learning that is acquired in middle age.

Whatever their age, those who were obtaining a secondary education at any level (high school, college, or even beyond) would be in school because they *wanted* to learn and *wanted* to be there —*then.* A comparison of GI and non-GI students has shown how great have been the achievements of students who have chosen to go to school. Furthermore, the student—of whatever age—who was obtaining a secondary education would no longer be defined as someone without adult rights who must accept dependency and meager stipends and have a dedicated delight in poverty.

In an educational system of this kind we could give primary education and protection to actual children as well as protection and sensitive supervision to adolescents. We could back up to the hilt the potentiality of every human being—of whatever age—to learn at any level. And we could do this proudly.

The kind and amount of leadership that industry can best take in making individual plans for sending workers—*on pay*—to get more education, and the kind and amount of leadership that can best come from tax-supported activities is a problem that will have to be threshed out. In the United States, we usually depend upon private initiative to make the first experiments before tax-supported agencies pick up the check. So, too, we shall have to work out the problem of providing special work situations for adolescents and on this basis make our decisions as to whether tax-supported institutions—rather than individual industries—should become chiefly responsible for the employment of adolescents.

But we also need to recognize articulately that there are other routes to competence than the one route provided by the conventional school. Experimental co-operative-work plans in the public schools need to be supplemented by experiments in industry. . . .

The right to obtain a secondary education when and where the individual could use it would include not only the right of access to existing conventional types of schools but also the right of access to types of work training not yet or only now being developed—new kinds of apprenticeship and also new kinds of work teams.

In thinking about an effective educational system we should recognize that the adolescent's need and right to work is as great as (perhaps greater than) his immediate need and right to study. And we must recognize that the adult's need and right to study more is as great as (perhaps greater than) his need and right to hold the same job until he is 65 years old.

Among the nations whose industrial capacities make them our competitors, the United States has a comparatively small total population. The more completely we are able to educate each individual man and woman, the greater will be our productive capacity. But we cannot accomplish the essential educational task merely by keeping children and young adults—whom we treat like children—in school longer. We can do it by creating an educational system in which all individuals will be assured of the secondary and higher education they want and can use any time throughout their lives.

The School of Tomorrow

J. Lloyd Trump and Dorsey Baynham

(1908–) (1909–)

In 1915 John Dewey and his daughter Evelyn published *Schools of To-Morrow*, describing the experiments of the progressive pioneers in American education. In 1961 educator J. Lloyd Trump (assisted by journalist Dorsey Baynham) published *Focus on Change: Guide to Better Schools*, a survey of current experimentation in the nation's schools. The contrast between the two books reflects the extraordinary change in the very conception of educational experimentation which had come about in roughly half a century.

The Deweys' book had described schools based on radically new ideas about the role of education, the nature of the child, and the place of culture in a democratic society. Most of the schools had been built from the ground up on fresh principles. In contrast, Trump's book described experiments in well-established schools with fairly conventional philosophies. Their innovations were not based on radical new theories about the role of education. They focused rather on practical methods of achieving the traditional end of schooling—the development of the intellect—in schools strained by burgeoning enrollments and shortages of first-rate teachers. The experiments included "team teaching," the use of new tools of instruction, and emphasis on independent study for students of all levels of ability. They were for the most part ingenious new techniques for solving some of the persistent problems of mass education.

Trump's essay, less theoretical and more detailed than the other selections in this volume, is a reminder that educational theory only improves our schools to the extent that it is tested in experiments like those on which his plan for the school of tomorrow is based. As Immanuel Kant wrote:

One fancies, indeed, that experiments in education would not be necessary; and that we might judge by the understanding whether any plan would turn out well or ill. But this is a great mistake. Experience shows that often in our experiments we get quite opposite results from what we had anticipated. We see, too, that since experiments are necessary, it is not in the power of one generation to form a complete plan of Education.

Moreover, the experiments Trump writes about were not mere expedient attempts to improve school practices. Behind them existed a comprehensive vision of a school which would differ from the conventional one quite as much as did the ideal progressive classrooms described by the Deweys. In Trump's school of tomorrow teaching will no longer be conducted in isolated, uniform classrooms with fixed numbers of students; teachers, freed from nonprofessional clerical chores and routine presentations of factual information, will function exclusively as the planners and guides of students' learning; and students will spend almost half of their time studying by themselves, but with instant access to new learning resources such as magnetic-tape language laboratories and teaching machines. Comenius, who called for "less teaching and more learning," would have applauded Trump's vision of a school in which students are freed from the inflexible routines which currently clamp restrictions upon self-initiated learning.

Lloyd Trump is Associate Director of a commission appointed by the National Association of Secondary-School Principals. From 1956 to 1961 this commission supported experiments in nearly 100 junior and senior high schools across the United States. Based on the reports of these projects, this essay envisions the school of the future.

The world faces a simple fact: It may not long survive as we know it.

That fact is a complex of problems which have never been experienced, collectively, before. No nation and no aspect of life can escape their pressure. The problems fall under six broad headings: the expansion of population, the burst of technology, the discovery of new forms of energy, the extension of knowledge, the rise of new nations, and the worldwide rivalry of ideologies.

The complexity of the problems demands unprecedented, many-sided solutions. The problems will not yield to the specialists, who are today the major products of our schools. They will yield only to specialists plus. Tomorrow's leaders must be able to relate the past to the future, the specific with the general. Tomorrow's problem solvers may be physicists who share with world statesmen the responsibility of charting disarmament. They may be businessmen who function in the governments of undeveloped countries. They may be teachers who knock down the barriers of ignorance and misunderstanding between nations. Events in our classrooms today will prompt world events tomorrow.

The practical question is: Are the schools ready for the job? There is considerable reason to say they are not.

One reason for doubt is rooted in their history. American school methods and facilities have evolved from what society deemed best at a given moment. They have been molded by other cultures, by custom, by regulation, and even by law. Today, acceptable ideas of school scheduling, size of classes, teacher load and responsibilities, instructional materials, and architecture have become hardened. These practices have not been changed basically for generations, and their inflexibility makes it difficult to alter them now.

Improvement in American education has been by refinement, not by redefinition. Each improvement has had its effect, but all have been limited by the existing framework of the schools.

A second reason for doubt arises from a limited interpretation of the concept of universal education. We have given it a single, flat dimension—that every boy and girl has an equal right to spend a certain number of years under a school roof. That concept today is ripe for re-examination. There are at least two other dimensions in the idea of universal education: (1) The *maximum* attainment of each student's talents, no matter how unequal that maximum be. (2) The development of each student's ability to go it alone, to understand education as a process that continues long after school years.

Changes are especially urgent because schools must provide

education for vastly increased numbers of persons, for longer spans of productive life, at far higher levels of understanding, competence, and skill—and always with the goal of strengthening our democratic way of life.

The task calls for a realignment of educational priorities and a re-examination of school functions and needs. We must see if what we are now doing is the best that can be done. That is precisely what committees of the National Association of Secondary-School Principals, hereafter referred to as NASSP, set out to do in 1956. Such re-examination includes in its scope all the component parts of a school: its students, its teachers, its curriculum, and its facilities.

The Students

Students need opportunities to develop individual responsibility and the skills of independent study. These two closely related qualities constitute the bench mark of good education in any individual.

Instead of providing for independent learning, school organization in most cases serves to chalk the student's steps clear across the educational stage. School bells begin and end the day and punctuate the beginning and ending of each class period. School scheduling as presently practiced usually locks library and laboratory for individual students except during brief periods of the school day. Instruction in each subject is cut and tailored until each unit fits a pattern designed for orderly administration.

Directed and supported at virtually every step of the way through high school, too many students find it difficult to travel on their own when they reach college or go to work on a job. Few high-school graduates have achieved adequately the skill of independent study, nor has much happened to make them feel that they should.

Students need opportunities to develop the inquiring mind. Today's instruction may even have the opposite effect. The pupil works his way through a school assignment, shuts the book, and moves on in the ordered regularity of his schedule. Any lingering wonder, any curiosity, is buried under the necessity to turn to other work.

This kind of instruction creates the idea that education has terminal points. Such an idea, especially in light of world conditions, is highly dangerous. Dean Francis S. Chase, of the University of Chicago, at the 1960 White House Conference on Children and Youth, warned: "It is not merely useless but actually harmful to transmit the findings of science without providing at the same time an understanding of the strategies of inquiry through which the findings were reached. Otherwise, advancing science may make obsolete all that one knows within a few years and leave no trail to new knowledge that can be followed by one who has learned as ultimate truth even the most advanced concepts held by scientists in one's youth."

We must develop the spirit of inquiry in young people. As they go through school, they should learn to react critically to what they read and hear and to approach problems with the curiosity, the will, and the techniques to solve them.

Students need to learn the skills of effective discussion. More opportunities are needed for them to examine together and exchange ideas on important issues of the day or issues within a subject area. Such examination and exchange leads to critical thinking and stimulate further inquiry. They are often the first steps in the process of acquiring knowledge and then doing something with that knowledge.

Discussion in today's schools is too often limited to a few remarks between the teacher and one pupil. Really effective discussion of important content develops best in the small group of no more than 15 persons, a setting logistically difficult to achieve in today's schools.

Tied to the need for effective discussion is need to acquire a far more complex talent, the talent for effectual human relations. We have heard and read a lot about it; we have developed sociometric techniques for measuring it. But based on human behavior around the world, development of this talent is barely discernible.

Effective human relations are an outgrowth of respect for the innate dignity of other humans and an understanding of the varieties of thought and behavior that cloak that dignity. Children are not born with this sense of respect and appreciation; they learn it as they go through life. These skills are augmented by the practice afforded in frequent participation in classroom affairs.

Speaking at a 1959 conference on secondary education, held annually at Syracuse University, Dr. William M. Alexander, of Peabody College for Teachers, described the dimensions of a balanced school program. An optimum condition of balance exists, he said, "when each youth is able to participate effectively in such learning experiences as will promote his maximum development as an individual. . . ."

Few schools are organized today so that each youth may participate effectively. In the customary classroom, the shy child remains mute, the less inhibited joins energetically in classroom affairs, the aggressive demands his share and more of the teacher's time and attention. Individual differences appear, but too little is done to cope with them.

Students need satisfaction in learning. Such satisfaction not only reinforces what has just been learned but also provides motivation for moving on to the next step. One way to derive satisfaction from learning is to know immediately what has been achieved in performance of a given task. No student enjoys waiting until the teacher can turn to him or has the time to grade his paper. Satisfaction in learning is developed when the student discovers immediately that he has learned something new or that he must do something else to reach a goal.

Education answers many purposes and satisfies many needs. This report has selected only a few, but the selection was made deliberately. The purposes and needs mentioned here are among the most highly important of the schools' responsibilities. They are also the most frequently neglected. The conventional classroom inhibits them; traditional scheduling largely ignores them.

The Teachers

Few statements on quality education deal with teachers' needs in day-to-day school operation. Teachers, apparently, are taken for granted as a part of the classroom scenery, like desks, chairs, and books.

Professional teachers need greater opportunity to use professional skills. Typically, they work an average 48-hour week. They meet five classes a day, five days a week, for a minimum total of 25 hours a week with students. In addition, they supervise study halls, grade papers, keep records, collect money, sponsor student activities, and perform a host of other tasks. Not enough time remains to do what professional teachers should do: keep up with developments in individual subject fields, plan and prepare lessons, develop imaginative instructional materials, and improve evaluation of student work. Lack of time for professional work damages professional pride. About a third of a teacher's day goes to clerical and subprofessional tasks, another third to work which could just as well be done by various kinds of automated devices. A situation that provides only a third of a day for performance of work he is trained to do—and finds satisfaction in doing—contributes little to the morale of a talented, conscientious teacher.

Teachers need an appropriate place to perform the professional work that underlies professional teaching. Space needs to be arranged for instructional conferences between teachers, and between teachers and administrators, for the pooling of ideas which focus on educational goals and measure educational achievement. Here, at their fingertips, teachers need instructional aids—tapes, transparencies, an array of teaching materials. Here, too, they should find clerical and other needed help.

A higher maximum on teachers' salaries is needed. Many educators and concerned laymen are sincere in their belief that salary problems can easily be solved if salaries are materially increased across the board. Advocates of merit salaries point to a flaw common to almost all salary scales: no special provision is made for an especially fine job of teaching. All teachers are paid alike, according to the extent of their training and the number of years of their experience. Apparently, all teachers are to perform all schoolroom tasks. But some teachers will perform them better than other teachers, and the better all-around performance can be exposed through some clever evaluative device. Then the superior teacher is paid a superior salary. There is validity in both contentions: higher salaries are needed generally and fine teachers should receive superior salaries.

But what is really wrong with teachers' salaries? Neither educators nor the public have analyzed thoroughly the various school and educational tasks, or the persons who should perform them. Actually, the setting in which teachers are required to work may inhibit the most competent, creative teaching. Schools must be organized so that individual teacher competencies are better utilized and personal satisfactions more fully realized. Different purposes in instruction require different class organizations, procedures, and skills. Those which require the highest teacher competency should offer the highest wage. The potential salary, under these circumstances, would be far higher than is usually envisioned today.

The Curriculum

The word, curriculum, can refer to an entire educational program, a single course, or any part of either. In this instance, we are referring to only a part of the curriculum, the content.

The two major needs in curriculum content are, logically enough: the most feasible way to acquire content (an urgent need in this day of advancing knowledge) and the soundest way to retain it. Techniques for the highest retention of content have been the object of decades of research. For example, student motivation toward accepted goals is important. The degree of retention is frequently the result of the nature of the acquisition, and that content is best retained which has been acquired through a combination of acts: hearing, seeing, discussing, writing, feeling, and doing. But in many schools there are only two ways to acquire content: by hearing the spoken words of the teacher or of other students and by reading the printed words of books or periodicals. Even the second of these is limited to brief periods of the school day. A school library frequently poses a two-part problem: when to get into it and how to get books and periodicals out of it.

The culprit responsible for the students' limited access to content is the kind of school organization that forces the curriculum into rigid units of the school day. The school week is subdivided into five look-alike days, and each day is further subdivided into units of 40 to 55 minutes each. Curriculum content is then arbitrarily fitted into the units, like mail into boxes in the post office. At the post office there is sometimes a slot for airmail. In schools there sometimes are accelerated classes in selected subjects for gifted children. There may be ability grouping or ability tracks. But in almost all schools time and curriculum content must fit into the same neat, presized "Carnegie" units. When a student completes a given number of these units, he then may graduate.

By itself, and without the rigidity of presized units, curriculum content divides into more natural, more logical arrangements. It is more natural, for instance, to divide it into two fundamental parts: *basic content* for *all* persons and *depth content* for persons with the *ability and interests that go beyond basic provisions*.

Required *basic education* should cover all subject areas—the humanities, social studies, languages, mathematics, science, fine arts, and practical arts. It should include information as up-to-date as this morning's paper. No longer, for example, should one unit of prepackaged science suffice for high-school graduation, with other learnings in science dependent upon student choice, faculty prodding, or what the school happens to offer.

Depth education is available in all subject areas. The amount of time spent in it and the nature of what is done is determined for each student on the basis of his interests and abilities. Professional decisions by teachers and counselors start, schedule, and terminate the program for each student. Groups are organized when there is a commonality of interest and need among several students.

So the curriculum needs to perform the dual functions: keep everyone up-to-date in order to cope with the personal and group problems of the age and culture and challenge the specialized talents of the individual. These goals require a complete break from the rigid organization of time and content in today's schools which so often is determined on the basis of the size and location of a school.

The Facilities

Re-examination of school functions and purposes starts from realization that vastly greater numbers of persons must learn far larger amounts of knowledge than ever before if the answer to world survival is to be found. The total problem includes better development of student talents and maximum use of professional skills, *plus* efficient use of school facilities: that is, modern instructional aids, school space, and school funds.

Three observations can readily be made about education and technology: (1) *Although technological advances are made by educated people, education makes relatively little use of the advances.* (1) *Where technology is used in schools, it usually is used to embellish established programs rather than as planned parts of those programs. (3) In using technological facilities, education has most often modified or adapted those designed for other occupations rather than created designs specifically for educational purposes.*

The operation of our schools is sometimes compared to the operation of big business, but the analogy fails in some ways. Fifty years ago, for instance, American industry invested about 75 per cent of its capital dollar in plant and about 25 per cent in tools. At that time American education was doing approximately the same thing. Today industry has almost reversed this allocation of capital, while education has continued its ratio with major emphasis on the building and minor on tools with little change except in unusual cases.

Technology can be used to do many things for education. It can begin in the administrative offices, working out flexible school programs. In classrooms and laboratories, it can help with the tasks of introducing concepts, communicating new ideas, and keeping instruction abreast of the times. It can aid in independent study and testing, and can take over routine tasks in guidance and counseling offices. Educational goals must be worked out in detail so that the best instructional facility in each case—television, radio, overhead projectors, recorders, films, slides, tapes—can be suited to the goal.

School buildings mirror our educational concepts. America has a predilection for straight lines, rectangles, squared-off blocks, and nowhere is this more true than in the usual schoolhouse. The average school is made up of a series of rectangular rooms, each the same size and each with space for about 30 students, strung along both sides of a tunnel-like corridor. If 150 students are to be given exactly the same presentation, five of these rooms must be used for five different classes. If 15 students are to be guided in the development of ideas on a given subject, one of these all-alike rooms must be used. After hours, shut against the echoing corridor, here is where the teachers must work, each one alone in his classroom.

The kinds of schoolrooms vary with the learning activities, with each schoolroom designed for the specific function it performs. Schools that make the best use of the time and talents of both students and teachers make greater use of modern instructional aids and offer flexible use of school space.

The subject of school facilities leads to consideration of school finance. How school funds are spent is a matter of very real public concern. Many worried schoolmen can testify that schools do not obtain enough money from local taxes and bond issues. In many communities, the taxpayer has braced himself against higher real-estate taxes. Efforts to appeal to his conscience and to make him change his mind by contrasting what he spends for cosmetics and liquor against what he spends on education have met only partial success. School-budget figures are examined today as never before.

If schools are to meet today's educational needs, not only must they seek new sources of financial support, but they must also make educational dollars go further. Today's schools are too costly in terms of the waste of human resources and the inadequate use of modern physical facilities. Adequate financial support for schools requires a shift in viewpoint by both educators and laymen. Tomorrow's school construction and school operation will not cost less; there is evidence that they may cost more. They will continue to need financial support to the maximum that our citizenry and our laws provide. But for the kind of education that insures survival, the schools will have to make more effective use, revolutionary use, of the school dollar.

Education in this country has steadily improved since the systematic study of the science of education was started about 1890. No doubt it will continue to improve at about the same speed, and schools in the year 2000 will be somewhat better than they are today. The question is, could they be better than that?

History shows that all improvements have had a common characteristic: they could fit into the existing framework of school arrangement. History reveals, also, a long list of other possible improvements—radio, films, slides, core curriculum, consumer education, aviation education, global geography, television—which were greeted with enthusiasm at the outset but never really put to fullest potential use. They could *not* fit into the rigid framework.

The NASSP experimental projects in staff utilization, the discussions of commission members, and the examination of many proposals suggested over the last five years have thrown into focus changed ideas for improving schools. These, too, have a common characteristic: they *demand flexibility* in *all* school arrangements, in scheduling, in facilities, in architecture, in staff use, and in the organization of instruction. They constitute a new plan for tomorrow's schools, but a concept of the most adaptable kind.

Some of the ideas drawn today into the guide to better schools may be invalidated by unforeseen events tomorrow. In that event, the plan can still fulfill its primary purpose—to stimulate research and developments in improved organization, learning, and staff use in schools.

The plan will not create a specific kind of school, either rural, urban, or suburban. It does not apply specifically to a very large school or to a small one. It applies, instead, to a hypothetically average school, with an average student body and staff. There is the possibility, however, that the increasing mobility of our population will contribute to just such an average school.

Here then is the school of the future.

Some Classes Will Be Smaller

The organization of instruction, as drawn up by the plan, will provide *at times classes with 15 or fewer pupils especially for small-group discussion.* In these classes, teachers will weigh pupils' reactions to lesson content and will assess pupils' knowledge. They will also observe pupils' ability to handle data and solve problems and, highly important, how they react to one another. Instructors will guide and stimulate students' thinking, directing discussion along useful, fruitful lines; they will serve as consultants and advisors.

Small-group classes will combine four purposes: (1) Provide opportunities for teachers to measure individual students' growth and development and to try a variety of teaching techniques which will be suited to the students' needs. (2) Offer the therapy of the group process, whereby students are induced to examine previously held concepts and ideas and to alter rigid, sometimes mistaken, approaches to issues and people. Students will learn, in other words, how to become better group members. (3) Permit all of the students to discover the significance of the subject matter involved and to discuss its potential uses, rather than just to receive it passively and return it in tests, as happens too often in today's classrooms. (4) Provide students with opportunities to know their teacher, on a personal, individual basis. . . .

Independent Study Will Be Emphasized

The organization of instruction in tomorrow's schools will provide many more opportunities for individual students' *independent study,* inside schools as well as outside, during school hours as well as after them.

In this way, it will provide for differences in individual interests and abilities. It will meet the test of practicality, from the student's viewpoint, of studying something important and useful to him. It will permit study in depth. Study in a subject area that makes sense to him will usually lead to interest and a search for information in related areas. It will help him develop the ability to go it alone, to learn by doing. It will produce in many students greater creativity and sense of inquiry.

In most schools today, work outside classes is called homework. Homework can be performed at home, after school hours, or it can be performed at one of a string of desks in a study hall, supervised by whatever teacher happens to be in charge during that period, regardless of his subject. Ordinarily, the homework consists of so many *assigned* pages to read in a school text, so many questions to answer, or so many words to write.

Schools that experiment with independent study find it difficult to stimulate even the most able students to do truly creative, independent work. They are accustomed to doing only what the teacher assigns and little more. Teachers' assignments have left little room in many cases for the exercise of initiative. Thus in some of the studies what was supposed to be independent study looked quite similar to the homework that usually occurs.

In the school of tomorrow, students will undertake special projects, which they have selected themselves, or which teachers have suggested. The projects will clarify, add to, or enrich subject matter presented in large classes and further explored by discussion in small classes. Teachers will learn to present materials in an open-ended manner. That means in such a way that students will be encouraged to question the information, rearrange the data, seek further answers, and try to surpass previous accomplishments.

Because there will be more opportunities for individual study during a school week, students will typically spend more hours on this work than they do now on homework. The length of time will depend on the nature of the project and the sophistication of the student. How much time will be determined by *professional decision*, based on the judgment of teachers and counselors, with consideration of parents' wishes. It will vary with the age of the student and with the stage of the program for changes in the high school. Less time for independent study will probably be scheduled for younger students and in the beginning stages of a high school's reorganization. Experimental studies show variation is needed among all ages and types of students. Generally speaking, however, independent study will average 40 per cent of the school's schedule for students.

Independent study will involve many types of activities: reading, viewing, listening, writing, working on automated learning devices, and doing a variety of things under supervision in different kinds of laboratories. Individual differences among students will be recognized in these activities in ways that are impossible in today's schools. Individual students, their teachers, and their counselors will determine the amount of time and the nature of the different activities. . . .

The reading, listening, and viewing rooms, the cubicles, and the laboratories will provide the setting for independent study. Both teachers and students will adopt new approaches to student studying in the school of tomorrow. Teachers will suggest and guide rather than merely assign. Students will gradually increase their responsibility for reaching individual goals. They will learn to select and carry through projects and to show initiative in seeking study materials and aids. They will experience satisfaction in an environment that stimulates creative efforts. Tomorrow's program will spotlight development of students' independent study skills, recognizing individual differences in their ability to think and solve problems on their own, but always striving to raise the standards of accomplishment for all of them. Teachers will become increasingly expert in getting students to use these facilities to the best degree.

Some Classes Will Be Larger

Tomorrow's schools will assemble *large classes* of from 100 to 150 students or more whenever the educational purpose calls for it. If a class is to hear a presentation by a teacher or some other speaker on a face-to-face basis, 150 students probably will be the maximum class size. If the purpose, however, is to view a film or a television program, the number may range up to 300 students or even more. Scheduling in most schools even today allows ready assembling of large classes. Tomorrow's schools, with more flexible scheduling, will be able to arrange as many large classes as curriculum plans require. Combined, these purposes suggest that about 40 per cent of a student's time in school will be spent in large classes. . . .

Large-group instruction offers no surprise to high-school students because by this time in their lives they have had many experiences in large groups. This instruction will be used to introduce units of work, to explain terms and concepts, to demonstrate, to summarize, and to give some tests. The material can be presented with more uniformity in the large classes and thus will serve as a safeguard against possible gaps in students' learning, the too frequent result of mobility of school population and turnover in school staffs.

In tomorrow's schools, more students will be exposed to skilled teaching in all subjects because the most capable and experienced teachers *in specific fields* will teach large classes. Every teacher, inevitably, is more experienced in one subject or one phase of a subject than in another. So the students can be better motivated by contact with the very best teacher available for that phase of the subject. The large class will avoid the duplication of effort required when teachers must teach the same subject matter to a number of classes, as in today's schools.

Usually, the large group will be taught by a member of a *teaching team,* an arrangement whereby two or more teachers with assistants plan, instruct, and evaluate co-operatively two or more class groups in order to take advantage of their respective special competencies as teachers. Other teachers of the team who ordinarily would be covering the same ground during that class period can thus find the time to prepare for their own, future large-class presentations or to perform other professional tasks that today's school arrangements seldom permit.

Tomorrow's schools will find a number of other advantages in large-class instruction. It makes technological equipment more economically feasible. Many schools which can't afford these aids for five or six customary-size classes will be able to equip a single large classroom.

Economy—in this case economy of time—will allow tomorrow's schools to schedule more presentations by outside specialists, by teachers from nearby universities who are experts in certain fields, and by community-resource persons. For example, in one of the experimental schools, a local physician came to the school and talked at one time to all of the biology students about the circulation of blood. His experiences as a surgeon gave him more background about the heart and blood system than any teacher in the school possessed. The crowded days of most of these people make it difficult for them to leave their own work for more than an hour or two at a time.

For students, large classes will offer another particularly important advantage: They will serve as transitional experiences for college classes and for many other occasions of adult life. Students can learn to take notes, hold back questions until an appropriate time, and develop more responsibility for planning their own learning.

Where the total number of students enrolled in a subject is fairly large, more than one large class will be organized, and students will be grouped according to their past achievement in the given subject. By narrowing the range of student ability within the large class in this way, teachers will be better able to choose the depth of material and to gauge the pace and delivery of presentation.

Usually, large-group classes will be scheduled for 40 minutes, less a few minutes for assembling and leaving. In already existing buildings, they will take place in the cafeteria, little theater, unused study hall, in two adjoining classrooms which can be converted into one, or in several rooms joined by television.

The school of the future will recognize the relationships among various aspects of learning: what happens to students when they take part in small classes of 15 or less for purposes of discussion; when they work in a relatively independent manner in laboratories, libraries, and cubicles; or when they listen to or view a demonstration or explanation in the setting of large-group instruction. Today's school attempts to provide the setting for these diverse functions of instruction in a self-contained classroom with one teacher in charge.

Tomorrow's school will multiply the setting and the number of specially competent teachers that function in the teaching-learning process. Discussions among teachers and counselors in the setting of the teaching team will provide co-ordination of learning experiences provided for students. Thus small-group discussion, large-group instruction, and independent study will be related to the needs of different students.

Teaching will be viewed as both a science and an art by teachers who have both the professional competence to make decisions and, equally important, the time to study, plan, and evaluate what they and the students do and accomplish. The goal for teachers will be more effective and efficient instruction. Students will learn better the necessary skills and knowledge in subject areas while they become more inquisitive, creative, independent, and competent in interpersonal relations.

Teacher Assistants Will Be Used

Through the use of teacher assistants and team teaching, tomorrow's schools will make possible the full *professionalization of teaching*. Staff members will be selected for particular competencies and for specific tasks. Together with professional teachers, the assistants will create a new staffing pattern for schools. The NASSP studies involved a variety of assistants and highlighted the importance of job specifications for each type. Staff specialists, community consultants, general aides, clerks, and instruction assistants, along with professional teachers, will comprise the staff. In relation to the total number of students, the school of the future will employ more adults to work with students but fewer adults will need to be professional teachers.

Teachers will turn to *staff specialists* to supplement their own professional work in such areas as guidance, research, health, reading, instruction of exceptional children, audio-visual materials, and curriculum development. The specialists will be full-time persons who might serve several schools as needed. How many are employed and the terms of their employment will depend on such local circumstances as size of school, special needs of students, and special talents of teachers.

Teachers will call upon *community consultants,* who are particularly competent in certain fields, to make special presentations or provide special information. They will keep a file of the names of such persons, to which the entire community—civic organizations, parent-teacher associations, newspapers, radio and television stations—will be invited to contribute. Typically, consultants will appear before large classes and their presentations will be recorded on tapes, records, or in kinescopes, slides, or films for use with future classes.

General aides will perform those clerical and routine duties which now take much of a teacher's day. Aides should be high-school graduates, with some college work desirable. For a high school of 400 students, or for each 400 students in a larger school, about 50 hours of services by general aides will be used. The aides will control and supervise students on school grounds, in cafeterias, corridors, and auditorium, and in some extraclass activities. Ordinarily, aides will be employed on a part-time basis, from 10 to 20 hours a week.

Clerks will type, duplicate materials, check materials and prepare reports, grade objective tests, keep records, check and distribute supplies, take attendance and perform other routine services and clerical duties. They will be high-school graduates with a business education. For every 400 students, schools will use about 100 hours of clerical services per week, usually employing each clerk on a 40-hour per week basis.

To perform those tasks which fall below the professional level of teaching but are above clerical chores, schools will employ *instruction assistants.* The instruction assistants will read and evaluate some parts of English themes, science reports, etc.; confer with students about their progress and provide teachers with reports; serve as laboratory assistants; supervise specific out-of-school projects; and assist with extraclass activities. Usually, they will be college graduates and always they will have had special training for their specific duties. For every 400 students, about 200 hours per week of such services will be performed, with each instruction assistant typically employed 10 to 20 hours per week.

. . . .

Schedules Will Be More Flexible

Every 50 to 55 minutes the comparative quiet of today's schools is shattered. A bell rings, students burst into corridors, tramp to other classrooms, doors shut, the bell rings again, and a new class period begins. *The bell is no respecter of students' interests or teachers' plans.* It cares little that equipment in some classes takes 10 minutes to store or that presentations in others must be interrupted midway. Its sole function is to punctuate the day into six or seven exactly equal periods of time.

Students today spend about six hours a week on each of five subjects. These six hours per subject usually involve attending a daily 40- to 55-minute class session, plus an average for each subject of about 20 minutes' work daily in study hall or at home. Students spend approximately 30 hours a week in school, not including time spent in extraclass activities and homework.

Tomorrow's schools will put flexibility of school arrangements ahead of the rigidity of the bell. The day will be divided into 15- or 20-minute modules of time, instead of equal periods, with no standard intermissions when the entire school crowds the halls and rest rooms at once. Following the recommendations of teachers and counselors, individual schedules will be worked out by electronic devices and will show where each student is at all times every day. Changes in schedules will be made whenever counselors and teachers feel it is wise. A student's schedule will not be the same for each day, and he will bear primary responsibility for keeping his appointments. Subjects in which he has an absorbing interest and in which he has undertaken special projects will be scheduled so that he will not have to interrupt them to march off to another class—perhaps one which is quite unrelated at that moment.

The school of the future will schedule students in class groups an average of only 18 hours a week. The average student at the level of today's tenth grade will spend about 12 of the 18 hours in *large-group instruction* and six in *small-group discussion.* In addition, students will spend, on an average, 12 hours each week in school in individual *independent study*. Thus, most students will continue to spend about 30 hours a week on their regular subjects, as they do now. But they will find it possible to spend more time because school facilities will be open to them.

The time spent in large-group instruction and small-group discussion will be divided among the various subject areas as seems appropriate. Experience and judgment will determine how many hours, per school year, are desirable in the various school subjects. . . . Experience will indicate the desirable length of time, the frequency, and the time of school day that these groups should be scheduled.

Students who do not have out-of-school jobs or heavy activity schedules often will spend as many as 20 or 24 hours weekly, instead of today's average of about 10, in individual study. For some students, a professional decision will reduce those hours. The number of hours and the locations of independent study will vary with the needs and the capacities of individual students. . . .

Faculty members also will find their day governed by the needs of the curriculum, rather than by the insistence of the bell. Individual teachers will be scheduled 10 to 20 hours per week for class instruction, the number of hours depending on class purposes and sizes. The 15- to 20-minute modular arrangement of the school day will allow the flexibility needed to schedule each day according to the nature of the instruction plans. In this way, teachers will also find the free hours necessary for professional tasks and for conferences with individual students who request help with problems, or who are referred by instruction assistants or counselors. . . .

Today's schedules lock both student and teacher activities into a rigid framework and keep them there for a semester or a year. Tomorrow's schedule can be changed at will when needs dictate variations. . . .

Students' Individual Differences Will Be Recognized

Today's schools find it increasingly difficult to cope with individual differences. Most of a student's school life is spent in self-contained classrooms with other students, all of them doing much the same things, in virtually the same way, for about the same length of time. School goals, too, have become increasingly uniform, with all students taking the same standardized or teacher-made tests and all graduating at about the same age. Some uniformity in education, of course, is inevitable. It is characteristic, for example, of basic skills: reading, writing, listening, viewing, and speaking. And society suggests that fundamental blocks of content should be acquired—rules of grammar, for instance, and simple mathematics, history, and the facts of science.

In the process of learning, it is at the level of *inquiry* that individual differences will be allowed greater freedom of action. When students reach this level, individuality shows in their various interests, concerns, and curiosities, and in the methods they choose to satisfy them. The amount of time and effort spent in basic skills and in acquiring fundamental content will be minimized through more effective teaching-learning procedures. Skills, knowledge, and inquiry merge into one in the learning process, and education without any one of them is incomplete. If teaching stops with skills and knowledge, it gives little more than lip service to recognizing differences among students. Inquiry in turn motivates and strengthens skills and knowledge.

Time allowed for individual study—that is, study in depth in particular subject fields—will vary according to the subject and student maturity. An increase with each additional school year should be expected.

In the school of the future, three important school arrangements will provide for individual differences: a greater proportion of school time and appropriate spaces for individual work, independent of group membership, with a minimum of faculty supervision; a combination of horizonal (more of the same subject or grade level) and vertical (advanced subjects) enrichment, with professional decisions determining the amount of each, according to the individual student's learning speed and maturity; flexibility in grouping and regrouping of students, for example, when the learning goals of a group of individual students are seen to coincide to a workable degree, small groups will be organized on the basis of which students need what kinds of teaching; and large groups will be organized by including those with some similarity in past achievement of skills or of content in the subject in question.

. . . Each student will have a program professionally drawn up for him as an individual. His interests, achievement, and ability will help him select personal and vocational goals. The organization and setting of the school will make possible such an individual program.

Teachers' Individual Differences Will Be Recognized

Teachers, like students, differ in physical, mental, and social characteristics. Some are extroverts, who find great satisfaction in presenting materials before large groups and who are particularly skillful in stimulating students through this kind of instruction. Others enjoy more personal relationships with students and possess the particular talents required for guiding small-group discussions or working with individual students.

Some history teachers are more interested—and better read—in certain phases of history than they are in others. Some English teachers like literature better than grammar, and some science teachers prefer one branch of science over another.

Some teachers are strict disciplinarians; others produce good results with more leeway. Some teachers are physically strong and can work long hours; others, who make a valuable contribution to teaching, can work only a shorter time.

But today's school treats them all alike. They have similar training programs. They are paid according to uniform salary policies. They work under standard teaching loads. Moreover, the self-contained classroom locks them in and denies their differences. It makes a farce out of the concept of equality of educational opportunities for all students because it refuses them access to the wide range of varied talents possessed by different teachers.

Tomorrow's schools will recognize the differences among teachers by: team teaching; differentiated assignments and work loads; salary differentials. The educational philosophy and the size of the school will determine the type of teaching team. Some schools will team teachers within a subject area, while others will cut across subject areas by organizing the curriculum on a related-learnings basis. Teams could number only two teachers but usually will be larger and will include instruction assistants and clerks. Co-operatively, they will plan, instruct a group of students, and evaluate results.

Variations in assignments and work loads will be based on the differences in what teachers do. The number of hours per week with groups of students will typically range from 10 to 20, with an average of 15. Team leaders and specialists who help other teachers with small-group discussion, large-group instruction, and independent study—those teachers, in other words, who must spend more time in daily preparation and contacts—will usually be assigned about 10 hours before students. Teachers who are scheduled for 20 hours will be those who need to spend less time in preparing materials, developing curriculum, and improving evaluation.

Salary scales will have their foundation in training and experience, as now. But the scales will also provide added salaries for different teacher assignments. The highest salaries will be paid team leaders and teacher-specialists, those who are most skilled in small-group discussion, large-group instruction, and in stimulating independent study.

One of the most highly important aspects of tomorrow's scales will be the openings cut in salary ceilings, so that opportunities for financial advancement by talented, career teachers will not run into a dead-end stop as they do today when they reach the top of salary schedules. Such persons must be allowed to reach very high salaries *as teachers*. Teachers in local schools should have opportunities to work toward salaries of $15,000 to $20,000, and possibly more.

Schools and Colleges Will Join in Teacher Education

Today's teacher education is left largely to higher education and, frequently, to higher education of a particular kind. This arrangement, in the past, led to a schism within higher education itself, to some isolation of teacher education institutions, and to a loss in understanding all around.

Tomorrow's recruiting, screening, and education of professional teachers will be the *shared purpose* of secondary schools, colleges, and universities in a program that will begin at least as early as junior high school. The staff of the school of the future will be more diverse in character, and training programs will be developed for various assistants as well as for teachers. Because job specifications will be explicit, with clerks hired for clerking and teachers hired for teaching, the selection of school personnel will be more discreet, governed by precise, research-based procedures.

High-school students will have the benefit of more comprehensive vocational data and self-appraisal inventories developed by colleges and universities. They will be able to visit and participate in university educational experiments. Counselors in secondary schools and consultants from higher institutions will plan teacher-assistant activities for junior and senior high-school students. As teachers and consultants develop a working partnership, they will attain a clearer understanding of varying points of view and of the criteria for selection of trainees. At the same time, the students will become more expert in their vocational choices.

In higher education, also, significant changes in teacher-education programs will result from closer co-operation between instructors in professional and in nonprofessional courses. The inseparable nature of content and methods of teaching will be recognized more than today. Instructors in arts and science courses will aid prospective teachers to understand course content so that they, in turn, can teach it. In professional courses, instructors will tie the techniques of teaching to the subject matter to be taught. Both kinds of college teachers will use methods they expect school teachers to use, so the trainees will be able to observe good teaching practices. College teachers not in the education field will learn more about secondary schools and professional education teachers will learn more about the requirements of subject-matter content. Together, they will plan and teach courses in teacher education, as teams.

In the first year of college work, teacher trainees will work in secondary schools, largely in observation and routine duties, for five hours a week. Introduced thus, in gradual stages, this "learning by doing" will be increased year by year, as the trainees are able to assume greater responsibilities. By the fifth year, trainees will be spending 15 hours a week in secondary schools, mainly as teachers on an internship basis, and will be paid for the time they teach.

Schools will employ beginning trainees as clerks, general aides, and instruction assistants, depending on their competence and maturity. In this instance, too, schoolteachers and college instructors in all fields will work together in planning what trainees will do and in evaluating results.

At periodic meetings selected secondary teachers and supervisors and college instructors will discuss trainees' experiences in secondary schools in relation to both education-theory courses and subject-matter courses. These meetings will also serve to bring about a better integration of the various areas of the trainees' college work and of the points of view of all the persons involved.

As they work in schools, the trainees will be able to appreciate better the various courses they take in college by observing teaching problems at first hand. Thus, they will develop a learning readiness for their professional courses in education and a better understanding of what they need to know in specific subject-matter fields in order to teach that subject matter.

Programs of internship and postgraduate professional courses will also be available for those teacher trainees who develop an interest in teaching after they have entered college or after they have completed undergraduate work. Secondary schoolteachers and supervisors will also work with college instructors in developing and carrying out programs to select and train teacher assistants and other educational personnel, all of whom will require training programs that differ from those of professional teachers and from each other.

Full-fledged teachers will continue their professional development and growth by several means. They will be kept up to date in content and in methods by the co-operative efforts of college teachers and principals and supervisors. Through timesaving assistance, both human and mechanical, they will find opportunities to share ideas with their colleagues and to learn from one another. Through audio- and video-recording devices, they will be able to see and hear themselves teach, as well as to observe students' reactions to their teaching. All these methods will provide improved opportunities for self-appraisal, essential to continued growth.

The all-important key to continued growth, however, will be the development of the experimental point of view—the constant seeking of better ways to teach. "Better products through research" might also be a useful slogan for education.

The education and development of professional teachers will be the shared responsibility of many more persons than are involved today. It will begin in junior high schools, develop naturally in college and university years, and continue as long as the teachers teach.

The image of the American teacher must be redrawn so that the professional status of teachers is unmistakable.

The public image of a teacher today is simply of a person in charge of a class of 25 to 40 students. But even this image is so blurred that sometimes it could be mistaken for that of someone else. One reason is that teachers gradually have inherited so many clerical and routine tasks that little evidence of the unique nature of teaching remains.

Teachers themselves have done little to change the public image and, apparently, many teachers regard teaching as a job rather than a profession. They have seldom asked for enough time, daily, to make better preparation for what they do in classrooms. Many do not belong to professional organizations or take part in professional activities, and as soon as they can, they leave teaching for other employment. Those who attempt to emotionalize loyalty to teaching find it a poor substitute for developing professional satisfactions.

Many persons outside schools, accordingly, have conceived the notion that "anyone can teach." Efforts to change this idea have included only the adoption of codes of ethics, the drawing up of requirements for certification (easily set aside in emergencies), the adherence to ideas about class size (not adequately supported by research), and the insistence on higher salaries for everyone (regardless of assignment or competence). None of these relates directly to the *functions* of teaching, which are the very essence of professionalization.

In tomorrow's schools, a combination of the approaches described in this report will sharpen the idea that there is more to teaching than simply being present in a classroom. Here are some concepts about tomorrow's teachers as professionals:

They will differentiate between what they must do and what subprofessional assistants and machines can do. They will have and use professionally designed workrooms and tools. They will recognize differences in teachers' abilities. They will be assigned responsibilities according to their individual skills and will be paid according to the level of those responsibilities. They will be carefully recruited and carefully taught. Above all, they will behave like professional persons, with knowledge, skill, and pride in what they do.

Before the public conceives an image of the professional teacher, that image must be created in the minds of teachers themselves. Teachers in the school of tomorrow will achieve true professionalism by trying imaginative approaches leading to more efficient use of teaching time and abilities and, consequently, to improved teaching. They will earn the respect of their students by keeping their own knowledge up-to-date and by preparing and using up-to-date teaching materials and tools. Tomorrow's teachers—and the public—will recognize the fact that those professional tasks performed outside the classroom are crucial in determining how well teachers teach.

Curriculum Will Be Reorganized

Modern comment on today's school arrangements is sprinkled with such descriptive terms as egg crate, lockstep, and, most recently, ice tray. Perhaps no area of school organization fits these epithets so readily as the curriculum. Today's curriculum is indeed iced into separate cells. There are, first of all, the grade compartments—second, fifth, and tenth. Then, there are the subject-matter compartments—third-grade arithmetic, sixth-grade English, eleventh-grade history.

School scheduling, with its orderly series of periods of equal length, has hardened the divisions between subjects, even those whose relationship is obvious. In many schools, for instance, science is rigidly compartmentalized. Students who "take" biology have little knowledge of chemistry; those who study chemistry are shielded, by the divisions, from physics. Literature is too seldom tied in with history, and geography is surrounded by a vacuum.

A student's progress is measured on a scale of years in the elementary school and by units of credit in the secondary. In both, there are a series of terminal points. Thus, a student *finishes* the first grade or the fourth grade. He *finishes* one year of world history, or of science, or of mathematics; and when he has finished enough units of credit, he can graduate. Having finished, he can, if he wishes, forget all about them. The student voted most likely to succeed is often the one who has accumulated the most knowledge and skill. He is like a good tape recorder—he can play it all back with high fidelity. He has had little time or motivation for inquiry or creativity.

In tomorrow's world, each individual must be able to attain the highest level of which he is capable in the basic skills: reading, writing, speaking, viewing, listening, and computing. Each individual must also, in a reasonable time, acquire as much knowledge as is possible for him. This knowledge must be in all fields: science, mathematics, history and other social sciences, languages, literature and the fine arts, and physical and mental fitness.

But each individual also must go beyond basic skills and present knowledge to develop the skills and practice of intellectual inquiry. These three—basic skills, present knowledge, and the skills and practice of intellectual inquiry—do not occur in isolation from each other. They are concurrent in the processes of learning. They are all present at all stages of education, although the emphases at different stages will be heavier on one than on the others.

In tomorrow's schools, the points of entry to and exit from elementary, secondary, and higher schools will be determined by each student's mental and emotional maturity—his readiness to move on—and by his capacity for organized instruction. This will require *professional decision.* Today's school settles entrance to and exit from school by *clerical decisions;* date of birth and number of credits are the determining factors.

The curriculum will be divided into stages or steps not identified as years or grades, and without any fixed number. The rate of progress through school will be determined by the student's previous achievements and by his capacity to take the next step. His readiness to move on, again, will be gauged by professional decision and not by a test, a grade, or a unit of credit. That professional decision will answer this question: Has the student assimilated as much skill, knowledge, and understanding in the present stage as can reasonably be expected of him?

Such individual progress will be at different rates of speed in different subject areas, or different skills, or even at different times in the student's life.

Wide variations will occur in how students spend their time, however. Professional decisions will give some students more hours of group work and others more hours of independent study. Some students will spend more time on the required content while others will have more time for study in areas of their personal interest and ability.

The number of hours required to keep students up-to-date in all fields of knowledge will be progressively less as they grow older, because they will have mastered to a reasonable degree the basic skills and content of the various subjects. Conversely, the amount of time for specialized pursuits will increase progressively with the maturity of the student.

. . . .

Tomorrow's school is already partly here in quite a number of places. The image of the school is seen in experimental studies sponsored by the NASSP Commission concerned with better staff utilization and in similar studies conducted by other groups. [These] . . . help to focus on change and provide guides to better schools.

The school of the future described here cannot be achieved immediately in most situations, but it will never become a reality unless vigorous steps are taken. The ideas have suggested projects to some schools. Experimental studies are needed in many others. The times rush by. A superior school today may be an inferior one tomorrow unless bold steps are taken to seek better ways of serving students.